Complete Guide
For Easy Car Care

D. A. LIEN

Dean, Occupational Education
Hartnell College

W. E. ENGLISH

Chairman, Engineering and Technology Division
Cuesta College

PRENTICE-HALL, INC., Englewood Cliffs, New Jersey

Library of Congress Cataloging in Publication Data
LIEN, DAVID A
    Complete guide for easy car care

    Includes index.
    1. Automobiles–Maintenance and repair. I. English,
W. E., joint author. II. Title.
TL152.L492   629.28'8   75-9637
ISBN 0-13-160226-8

© 1975 by PRENTICE-HALL, INC.
Englewood Cliffs, New Jersey

10 9 8 7 6 5 4 3 2 1

Printed in the United States of America

Prentice-Hall International, Inc., *London*
Prentice-Hall of Australia Pty, Ltd., *Sydney*
Prentice-Hall of Canada, Ltd., *Toronto*
Prentice-Hall of India Private Limited, *New Delhi*
Prentice-Hall of Japan, Inc., *Tokyo*
Prentice-Hall of Southeast Asia (Pte.) Ltd., *Singapore*

To our many students
whose encouragement
and persistent "why don't you ..."
made us realize how useful
such a book would be.

The authors wish to express particular appreciation to the following individuals and business firms whose cooperation in supplying illustrations and informative materials enabled us to complete this text.

American Chain
American Motors Corporation
Theodore Audel & Co., Division of Howard W. Sams Co., Inc.
Autopulse, Div. of Walbro Corp.
Bear Mfg. Corp.
Mrs. Bernard Becker
David Brown Features
Bussman Manufacturing Division of McGraw-Edison Company
Cartoon Features Syndicate
Channellock, Inc.
Chevrolet Motor Division, General Motors Corporation
Chicago Tribune-New York News Syndicate, Inc.
Chrysler Corporation
Delta Products Inc.
Dodge Division, Chrysler Corporation
Electric Fuel Propulsion Inc.
Herbert E. Ellinger, author of *Automechanics*
Federal-Mogul
Ford Marketing Corporation
Ford Motor Company
General Electric
General Motors Corporation
Ideal Corporation
Libbey-Owens-Ford
Lincoln-Mercury Division, Ford Motor Company
Los Angeles County Air Pollution Control District
Mazda Motors of America, Inc.
Meredith Publishing Inc.
Monroe Auto Equipment Company
Motor Vehicle Manufacturers Association, Inc.
NAPA/National Automotive Parts Association
Newspaper Enterprise Association
New York News
Oldsmobile Division, General Motors Corporation
Pontiac Division, General Motors Corporation
The Prestolite Company
Publishers-Hall Syndicate
The Register and Tribune Syndicate, Inc.
SAAB/SCANIA of America, Inc.
Sears-Roebuck Company
The Timken Company
TRW Replacement Division
Union Carbide Corporation
Volkswagen of America, Inc.

Contents

THE AUTOMOTIVE COOLING SYSTEM 63

THE CARBURETOR AND ENGINE FUEL SYSTEM 81

THE EXHAUST AND EMISSION CONTROL SYSTEMS 101

BUYING A NEW CAR　　　　　　　　　　　　　　　　**275**

BUYING A USED CAR　　　　　　　　　　　　　　　　**287**

ECONOMIC CONSIDERATIONS OF CAR OWNERSHIP　　　　**301**

ACCIDENTS AND INSURANCE　　　　　　　　　　　　**311**

TAKING A TRIP　　　　　　　　　　　　　　　　　　**321**

Preface

As cars become increasingly complex, they become increasingly expensive to repair. It has been conservatively estimated that one dollar of every three spent on repairs is wasted, either through incorrect diagnosis or outright fraud. Knowledge is the best weapon against this waste.

Good automobile *MAINTAINANCE* greatly prolongs the life of a car and keeps repair expenses to a minimum. One purpose of this book is to show the automobile owner how to perform virtually every needed maintainance task, thereby insuring that (1), the needed maintainance is performed, (2), it is performed properly, and (3), its cost is minimized.

In deciding what material to use in this book, the authors have called upon their experience as teachers of "Automotive Technology For Women," as well as the more traditional auto courses, and have established the general guideline "If the car owner can perform a given maintainance task at home, without special tools or skills, then it should be included." Every task discussed has been performed by hundreds of men and women students who had never previously attempted anything more complicated than starting the engine.

The second purpose of this book is to make the automobile owner a more sophisticated purchaser of the goods and services necessary to continued vehicle operation. The "gyp-artist" will have a much harder time taking advantage of the possessor of this knowledge.

No book can take the place of a good instructor, but it can allow the instructor to spend class time more efficiently by giving demonstrations, assisting students in learning how to care for their cars, and discussing consumer information that has special significance for a given geographic area. This book has served at every educational level, from high school through university, to meet the needs of the modern automotive consumer.

DAVID A. LIEN
W. E. ENGLISH

Basic automotive fastening devices and tools

The modern automobile is held together by a variety of fasteners, which are installed and removed by means of four or five kinds of tools. An efficient maintenance program requires an understanding of how these fasteners work and of the kinds of tools used to remove and replace them. Basic descriptions are provided in this chapter together with some hints on purchasing the fasteners, tools, and other supplies you will need for routine maintenance work on your own automobile. A few other specialized tools are discussed, as appropriate, in later chapters.

AUTOMOTIVE FASTENERS

The most common fastener in your car is the *bolt* and *nut* (Fig. 1-1a). The bolt has three important dimensions: diameter, number of threads per inch, and length. For example, 3/8 x 20 x 3 refers to a bolt of 3/8-in. diameter, with 20 threads per inch, and 3-in. length.

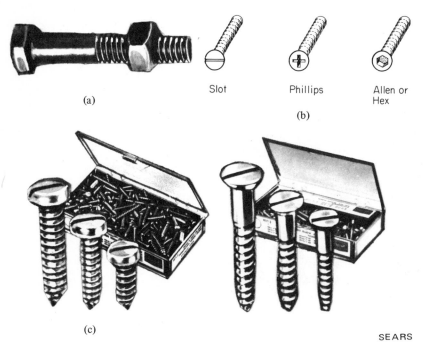

Slot   Phillips   Allen or Hex

(a)

(b)

(c)

Fig. 1-1 Common automotive fasteners: (a) bolt and nut, (b) slot, Phillips, Allen or hex screws, (c) sheet metal and wood screws

Bolts and nuts with *fine threads* have many threads per inch, in contrast to those with *coarse threads* that are used in less precise auto applications. The typical auto bolt has a hex head, meaning the head has six sides, as does its matching nut. Some bolts and nuts, usually those with coarse threads, have square heads.

Almost all bolts and nuts used on cars have *right-hand threads*. These are turned *clockwise* to tighten and *counterclockwise* to loosen. Certain special applications require the use of fasteners with left-hand threads, often imprinted with an *L* or other marking. On earlier Chrysler-made autos and some others, for example, the wheels on the left side of the car are fastened on with nuts or bolts that have left-hand threads, which must be turned clockwise to loosen.

Figure 1-1*b* shows three common screw heads. The *slotted* head is the most common and requires the use of the regular screwdriver. The *Phillips* head screw is often used to secure the trim inside the car, the window frames, door panels, and dash panel. It has an x-shaped slot on the head. It is considered more stylish and is often chrome plated. The *Allen* head or hex-head screw is less commonly used on cars than the slotted or Phillips head screw, but is the most scientifically designed. The *sheet metal* screw, used extensively on autos, differs from the household *wood* screw as shown in Fig. 1-1*c*. Note that the wood screw is tapered, while the sheet metal screw has the same diameter all down the shank. The sheet metal screw, which frequently has a Phillips head, is designed to tap its own threads in sheet metal, thus eliminating the need for a nut.

A special and very important type of fastener is the *castellated nut*, or "castle nut" (Fig. 1-2*a*). Slots cut in one side make it look rather like a castle turret. A safety pin or wire, called a *cotter pin* or *cotter key* (Fig. 1-2*b*), is inserted through these slots and through a hole in the bolt on which the castle nut is screwed. The cotter key prevents the nut from shaking loose or turning. It is used in such critical applications as holding the wheels on the car, holding the steering wheel on, and preventing the steering mechanism from coming apart. Figure 1-2*c* shows a castle type nut lock on a front wheel.

Five common types of *washers* that are used in autos with nuts and bolts are shown in Fig. 1-3. Each washer has a specific purpose and must be replaced, if removed for any reason, with another

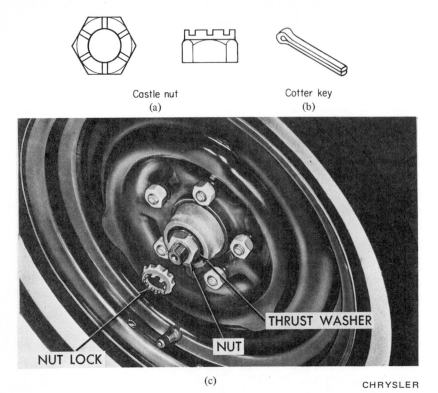

Castle nut
(a)

Cotter key
(b)

THRUST WASHER

NUT

NUT LOCK

(c)

Fig. 1-2 Special types of fasteners: (a) castellated nut, (b) the cotter key, (c) castellated nut lock as used on wheel with keyed thrust washer

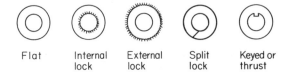

Flat   Internal   External   Split   Keyed or
        lock   lock   lock   thrust

Fig. 1-3 Common automotive washers: flat, internal lock, external lock, split lock, keyed

washer of the same type. The *flat* washer (Fig. 1-3*a*) is used to make the head of the bolt or nut appear larger so it will cover a larger area. Its smooth surface makes it easier to tighten down on the bolt or nut. *Internal*, *external*, and *split* lock-washers keep a nut or bolt from coming loose; their sharp edges which dig into the fastener as it is tightened, lock the nut or bolt in place (Fig. 1-3*b*, *c*, and *d*).

The *keyed* or *thrust* washer is used with a nut that is under constant pressure by a moving object (such as a wheel) (Fig. 1-3e). The "key" prevents the washer from turning and thereby safeguards the nut from the turning action of the wheel. A keyed washer is often used as an extra safety precaution along with the castle nut and cotter pin.

BASIC AUTOMOTIVE TOOLS

The most common of all hand tools is the *plier* (Fig. 1-4a), which is an extension of the hand and fingers. Often it is not considered a legitimate "tool" by mechanics since a more suitable tool is usually available for a given task. A *locking plier*, also called "vise grips," is shown in Fig. 1-4b. It is useful as a portable "vise" to squeeze and hold as needed. The "third handle" makes the release of the "vise" easier. Without this third handle, one's knuckles are easily skinned. Figure 1-4c shows the very versatile *arc-joint* plier (also referred to as a *water pump* or *slip joint* plier), which provides an extremely hard squeeze and has a wide range of adjustment.

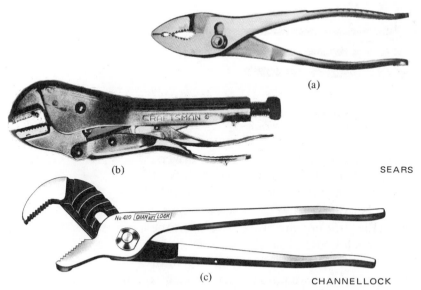

(a)

(b)

SEARS

(c)

CHANNELLOCK

Fig. 1-4 Automotive pliers: (a) basic plier, (b) locking plier, (c) arc joint plier

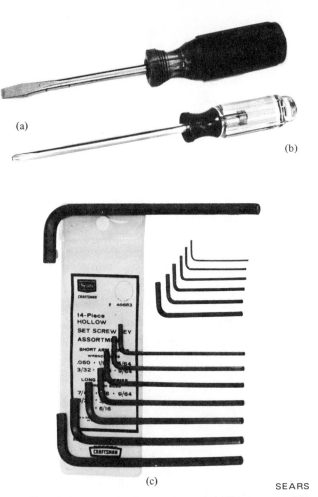

(a)

(b)

(c)

SEARS

Fig. 1-5 Screwdrivers and an Allen wrench: (a) slot screwdriver,
(b) Phillips screwdriver, (c) set of Allen wrenches

Figure 1-5 shows the two most common types of screwdrivers, the *slot* (Fig. 1-5*a*) and the *Phillips* (Fig. 1-5*b*). Several sizes of both types will be needed for car maintenance, depending on the size of the fasteners used. The Allen or hex-head screw requires the use of an *Allen wrench* (Fig. 1-5*c*) of the proper size to fit the hexagonal hole. An Allen wrench is used also in adjusting the ignition point dwell angle, which is part of a "tune-up" of most General Motors cars (Chapter 9). The required Allen wrench is sometimes furnished with the new "points." Allen wrenches can be purchased individually or in a set that includes a range of sizes.

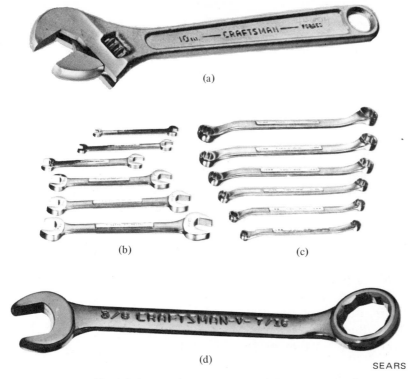

(a)

(b)   (c)

(d)

Fig. 1-6 Automotive wrenches: (a) adjustable wrench, (b) set of open end wrenches, (c) box end wrenches, (d) combination wrench

The most basic wrench is the *adjustable wrench* shown in Fig. 1-6*a*. This is called the "knuckle buster" by mechanics as it may not hold its adjustment well and often slips off the bolt or nut. For this reason, a set of regular fixed wrenches is more satisfactory. These fixed wrenches include the *open-end*, *box-end*, and *combination wrenches* shown in Fig. 1-6*b*, *c*, and *d*, respectively.

The open-end wrench grips the head of a bolt or nut at only two points, but it has the advantage that the nut can be approached from the side. The box-end wrench grips the nut on six sides and is safer to use, but it has the disadvantage that it must be lifted off the nut from the top each time the wrench position is shifted. Open-end and box-end wrenches usually have a different size opening at each end, while the box and open ends of a combination wrench are the same size. The ideal auto tool box contains complete sets of each type of wrench, but one set of six open-end wrenches with assorted box-end wrenches to meet special needs is probably the best compromise in terms of convenience, economy, and safety. A typical six-piece wrench set will fit the twelve most popular sized bolts from 3/8- to 1-in.

Socket wrenches have several handles and sockets that can be snapped on or off as needed. These are unmatched for handiness and are an absolute must for certain operations. Figure 1-7*a* shows a medium-size socket wrench set. Figure 1-7*b* shows a 12-point socket with its 12 notches. The 12-point socket shown is considered standard and can be used to turn nuts or bolts with four, six, or 12 sides. Four and six-point sockets are also available, with six-point sockets being the safest to use with standard six-sided nuts and bolts. The reverse side of the socket has a square hole. Several different handles can be plugged into this square hole.

Socket sets are available with square holes ranging in size from 1/4 in. to 2-1/2-in. square. (The larger sizes are used on trucks, farm machinery, and earth-moving equipment). Quarter-inch square hole "drive" tools are too small and weak for most auto maintenance, and 1/2 in. drive tools are a little too large, as well as more expensive. The 3/8 in. drive is the best overall choice, and adaptors are available (Fig. 1-7*c*) that permit different size drive hole sockets to be used with different drive handles.

The *ratchet* is the most useful of the handles. It is also the most expensive but is well worth the money considering the time it saves. Figure 1-7*d* shows a ratchet handle with a push button socket release—a handy feature when trying to remove a socket with oily fingers. The ratchet lets the handle turn the socket when the handle is moved clockwise toward the right, but when the handle is moved counterclockwise toward the left, the ratchet lets the handle slip or "ratchet," so the socket does not turn. A switch on the ratchet wrench allows one to tighten or loosen a nut quickly, depending on the switch setting, without having to take the socket off of the nut each time the handle is turned.

Socket *extensions* (Fig. 1-7*e*) that have a socket plugged on one end and a socket handle on the other enable one to reach otherwise inaccessible locations. A *universal joint* (Fig. 1-7*f*) between the handle and the socket permits operation in very difficult locations.

Other types of handles include the *breaker bar* (Fig. 1-7*g*) for "breaking loose" very stubborn nuts or bolts, the *crossbar* or

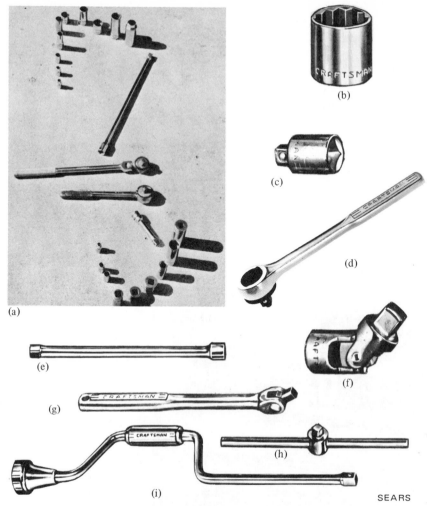

Fig. 1-7 Medium-sized socket wrench set: (a) medium sized socket wrench set, (b) 12-point socket (c) adaptor for 3/8-inch, (d) ratchet handle with push-button release, (e) socket extension, (f) universal joint, (g) breaker bar, (h) crossbar or T-handle, (i) the speed handle

T-handle (Fig. 1-7*h*), and the *speed handle* (Fig. 1-7*i*). The 1/2 in. drive breaker bar has a longer handle and provides greater leverage than the standard 3/8-in. breaker bars, and can be used with 3/8-in. sockets by means of an adapter (Fig. 1-7*c*). The weekend mechanic has little use for the T-handle or the speed wrench.

Other special sockets and accessories are available, but the basic 3/8-in. drive socket set with eight to ten sockets that range

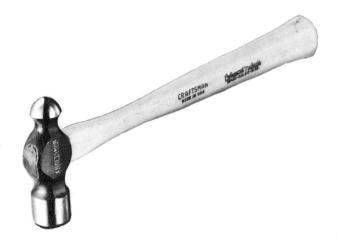

Fig. 1-8 Machinist's, or ball peen, hammer

Fig. 1-9 Typical tool box

in size from 3/8-in. to about 3/4-in. is adequate. One ratchet handle, several extensions, one universal joint, one special spark plug socket (covered in Chapter 9), and one 1/2-in. drive breaker bar (with 3/8-in. drive adaptor) are usually sufficient for routine maintenance and minor repairs.

Last on our list of basic hand tools is a hammer—preferably a machinist's or *ball peen* hammer (Fig. 1-8). This is quite different in design from an ordinary household hammer. It will not chip and throw dangerous steel splinters as readily as a carpenter's hammer does when striking hardened metal. Occasionally, a rubber, rawhide, or plastic-head hammer is useful.

A typical tool box is shown in Fig. 1-9. It is best to buy a tool box that one can carry easily with the basic tools in it, and large enough to hold additional tools that may be added later. Good tools need almost no care. Simply wipe them clean with an oily cloth after each use, keep them dry and out of the rain, and they will not rust or otherwise be damaged by time.

The nuts and bolts in foreign cars (and certain U.S. cars) are measured in the metric system (millimeteres), rather than the English system (inches). The sockets we have been discussing are all available in metric sizes and can be used interchangeably with the handles and other accessories of a standard socket set. Box end and open end wrenches in metric sizes are also readily available at most larger stores where auto tools are sold.

BUYING TOOLS AND PARTS

A modest investment in a quality set of tools will pay for itself during the first year of auto maintenance at home. These tools will last a lifetime, and several tool manufacturers guarantee their products essentially forever. Most auto supply stores carry good brands of tools, and many tool manufacturers authorize these stores to give on-the-spot replacements. Other manufacturers do not replace a defective tool so quickly, so ask about the tool replacement policy before you buy. Several of the national mail-order houses also carry premium lines of tools with unconditional guarantees. In addition, the mail-order houses frequently have tool sales that offer substantial savings. Many discount houses also carry tools,

"Simpkins couldn't find a half-inch wrench, so he got two quarter-inch wrenches."

but these are often of low quality and should be avoided generally. Do not purchase any tool unless its warranty provides for *on-the-spot replacement* if faulty or broken, at no charge to you.

Buying tools in sets, rather than singly, usually results in a significant dollar savings, however, be sure that the set you select has only the tools you really need. A little planning ahead, and the use of a checklist, will pay off in real dollar savings.

The percentage of price markup on auto parts and accessories varies from small to gigantic. The auto parts purchased at a service station pass through many hands, and each middleman takes his profit. For example, the typical air filter (Chapter 5), which must be replaced about once a year, costs the service station operator anywhere from one-half to one-fifth of what he sells it for, depending on how wisely he has purchased. A great dollar savings is possible simply by avoiding the last middleman, the person who sells to you at retail. In view of the number of auto parts that may be involved, as we shall see in later chapters, there clearly is a lot of money to be saved in the course of a year's maintenance. There is almost no way the average person can save money when buying tools, however, apart from watching for special sales.

The *wholesale auto parts house* sells parts and accessories to service stations and garages. The wholesaler wants your business, but frequently he doesn't dare take it because doing so might displease his regular customers to the point where they might take their account to another wholesaler. If a driver stops in to make a small purchase at a wholesale house and there are professional mechanics from garages buying there at the same time, the wholesaler will usually charge the driver the full retail price, rather than openly compete with the mechanics. However, if you can buy in the name of a legitimate business (the wholesaler may ask you for a state business tax number), there is usually no problem in buying wholesale. Some private discussion and prearrangement with the store manager or salesman may be necessary. He really wants all the business he can get; you just have to make it easy for him to sell to you.

Usually parts houses will sell to you at wholesale if you are an automotive technology student, and hence considered "in the business." For women, this may be more difficult, but if you are in an auto course designed for women, the instructor can usually arrange it, at least while you are a member of the class. Some parts houses give discounts to members of sports car clubs or similar auto organizations. Other parts houses find it more profitable to open their doors to the general public and sell in small quantities to a large number of customers rather than in large quantities to just a few major accounts. The prices at such parts houses are seldom truly "wholesale," but they are still substantially below list. (*List* means full retail price; *net* is the wholesale price.)

The next best place to find good prices on auto parts and supplies are the *large discount houses*. They may carry only a limited line of parts and accessories, but these are usually adequate for routine maintenance tasks. The prices at discount houses are often closer to list than to net, but the savings is still worthwhile. *Mail order auto suppliers* offer a large assortment of auto supplies generally at prices comparable to those of large discount houses, but the mail order buyer must pay postage and insurance. Another disadvantage is that getting adjustments on faulty merchandise may be a problem.

High-volume items like engine oil can be purchased at a savings in unlikely places. When you know exactly what you are looking for in lubricants (Chapter 3), you are safe in buying oil from a supermarket or drug store. Buying oil by the case (24 quarts) saves enough money in two oil changes to pay for three more changes.

Often rebuilt auto parts are less expensive than new ones, but for routine maintenance and service, such items as spark plugs and points, should be purchased new. Any part that is purchased for routine maintenance purposes should be brand new.

The reciprocating
internal combustion engine

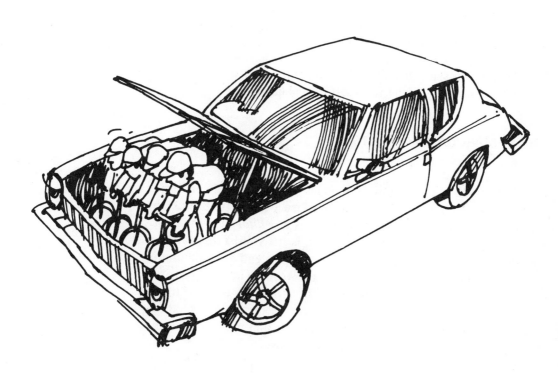

In the early days of the automobile, a wide choice of motive power was available. For a time, the dignified electric car was the unquestioned leader in the field, and a steam-powered passenger car was a real part of the competition. There was even a wind-up spring-powered car that was seriously intended for a personal transportation vehicle. Within a short time, however, all of these design concepts made way for that invincible machine, the *reciprocating internal combustion* engine.

Now nearly all modern automobiles, except those models that have rotary or "Wankel" engines (Chapter 19), are powered by reciprocating internal combustion engines that are based on a four-stroke cycle engine that was developed in 1878 by a German named Nikolaus August Otto. *Reciprocating* means back-and-forth or up-and-down motion. *Internal combustion* refers to the burning process inside the engine. A reciprocating internal combustion engine is driven by a fire inside, which provides the energy for an up-and-down or back-and-forth motion. Some information about the operation of this basic type of engine is helpful to an understanding of the external systems involved in car maintenance. Without delving too deeply into engineering details, we shall attempt to reason out the same problems that confronted Otto as he worked to invent a practical engine for a self-propelled vehicle.

THE RECIPROCATING PARTS

Consider an upright steel pipe 6-inches in length with an inside diameter of 4-inches. The inside surface of this pipe must be smooth and polished. This pipe serves as a *cylinder* for the reciprocating engine. A plug, called a *piston*, is fitted into this cylinder and slides back and forth freely inside it. One end of the cylinder is sealed at the top with a cap, called the *head*. Thus the piston is stopped at one end of the cylinder but is free to travel out the opening at the opposite end (Fig. 2-1). As the piston is pushed upward in the cylinder toward the head, the air that is trapped in the space above the piston is compressed and pressure builds up.

If we continue to force the piston, the trapped air will leak out of this *combustion chamber*. Since the compression of the air between the piston and the head of the cylinder is essential to engine operation, this air leakage must be reduced to a minimum. *Piston rings* were devised for this purpose to seal in the gases. A groove is cut inside of the piston about 1/2-in. down from the

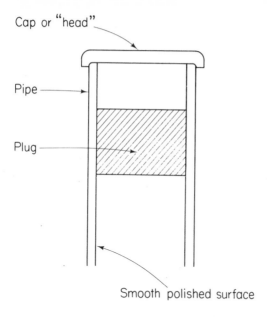

Cap or "head"

Pipe

Plug

Smooth polished surface

Fig. 2-1 The pipe, plug, and cap arranged to form the compression chamber in the cylinder

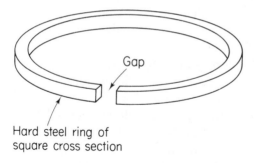

Gap

Hard steel ring of square cross section

Fig. 2-2 The piston ring. The gap in the ring allows it to be expanded to fit over the piston, then to be pressed into the groove to form a tight seal

top. This groove must have square sides and be of uniform depth around the circumference of the piston. This groove holds a hard steel ring that has an outside diameter slightly larger than the diameter of the piston. One small piece is cut out of this piston ring, as shown in Fig. 2-2, so that when the ring is squeezed this gap closes and the outside diameter of the ring becomes the same diameter as that of the piston.

With the ring held tightly in the groove so that the gap is closed, the piston is pushed up into the cylinder again, where the

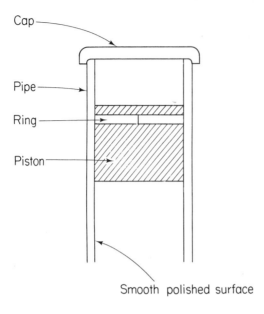

Cap

Pipe

Ring

Piston

Smooth polished surface

Fig. 2-3 The piston inside the cylinder with the ring fitted into the groove

ring then expands outward against the cylinder wall. Thus, an effective seal is formed between the piston and the cylinder, yet the piston is free to slide back and forth (Fig. 2-3). Such piston rings are used in modern engines, sometimes as many as four on one piston. Upper rings improve the air seal in the combustion chamber at the top of the cylinder to improve compression. Lower rings ensure even distribution of oil on the cylinder walls during the lubrication process and prevent lube oil in the cylinder from going up into the combustion chamber above the piston.

Now if we highly compress and then ignite some flammable fuel mixture in the combustion chamber at the top of the cylinder, the expanding gases from the burning fuel will push the piston down and force it out of the open end of the cylinder much as a projectile is fired from a cannon. It is this explosive force that must be harnessed if the power from the engine is to drive the automobile.

CONNECTING ROD, CRANK, AND FLYWHEEL

To harness this explosive power, one flange of a hinge is attached to the center bottom of the piston. A steel rod is attached to the free arm of the hinge and extends about 6 inches below the open end of the cylinder. The steel rod has a loop at its lower end that connects to a crank. This crank turns a heavy iron flywheel, as shown in Fig. 2-4. When fuel in the combustion chamber is ignited, expanding gases from the burning fuel push the piston downward. Now, however, the piston is hooked to the connecting rod and crank, so the power of the piston stroke forces the crank to turn the heavy flywheel. This action can be compared to a bicycle rider's leg pushing down on the pedal of a bicycle.

When the piston rod has pushed the crank down as far as it will go, a type of energy, called *inertia*, that is stored in the flywheel makes the wheel continue to turn, pushing the piston back up inside the cylinder.

In the single-cylinder just described, the hot spent gases in the combustion chamber continue to exert a downward pressure on the piston, in opposition to the force of the crank. If the cylinder or its head did not burst from the pressure, the piston would stop moving. If the gases in the combustion chamber cooled, the device

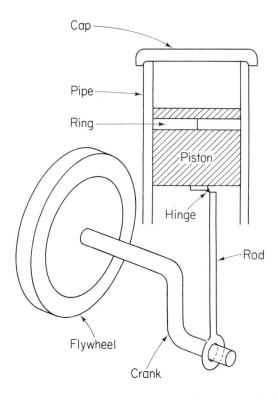

Fig. 2-4 The connecting rod, the crank, and the flywheel

would operate again when the charging with fuel, compression, and ignition process was repeated. Sustained operation would not be possible, therefore, unless an outlet was provided to permit the hot gases to leave the cylinder when the downward stroke of the piston has been completed. An inlet of some sort is also needed to supply fuel to the combustion chamber for ignition at the right moment in the engine cycle.

FUEL EXHAUST AND INTAKE SYSTEMS

Valves

To provide an outlet for the spent gases of the cylinder, a valve is provided. A valve operates much like a faucet in that it can be opened and closed at will. When closed, the valve in the cylinder head prevents new gas from escaping the compression chamber. When opened, it allows burned gas to flow out. The valve is inserted in the capped end of the cylinder and then connected to the flywheel by a second rod and crank. This is shown in Fig. 2-5. When the compression chamber is charged with fuel, and ignited,

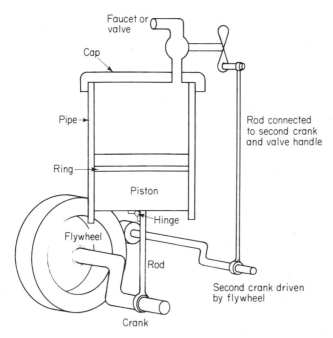

Fig. 2-5 A second crank, operated by the flywheel, controls the head valve and permits the release of spent gases.

the hot burning gases force the piston to the bottom as before, the crank turns, and energy is stored in the flywheel. During this part of the cycle, the valve is closed so the energy is contained and acts to force the piston down. At the limit of downward travel of the piston rod, the second crank rotates to open the valve. As the inertia of the flywheel pushes the piston back up into the cylinder, the spent gases in the compression chamber at the top of the cylinder escape through the open valve.

Such valves must be of special design to endure the pressures and temperatures experienced in this type of service. These special valves are called *mushroom* or *poppet* valves because of their appearance and manner of operation. Although these valves do not look like the common faucet, the work that they do is exactly the same. Figure 2-6 compares the automotive valve with the mechanical sink stopper found in many kitchen sinks or basins.

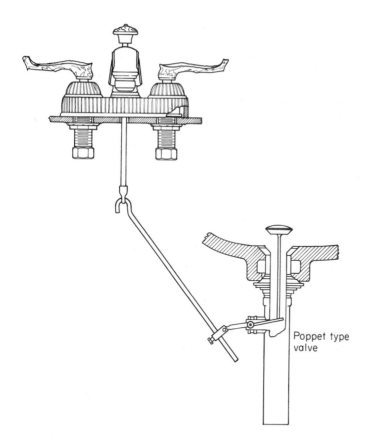

Poppet type valve

Fig. 2-6 The poppet or mushroom valve used in a sink stopper

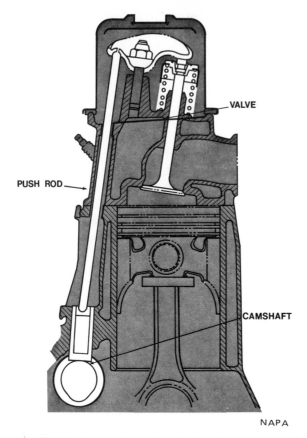

VALVE

PUSH ROD

CAMSHAFT

NAPA

Fig. 2-7 A cam-action push rod and rocker arm, arranged to
actuate a valve in a typical internal combustion engine

The flat top of a poppet valve has beveled edges that wedge
into place in the manner of a cork in a bottle. The pressure in the
chamber can push against the flat area thus causing the valve to
close more tightly. This characteristic makes poppet valves ideally
suited for use in the internal combustion engine. In Fig. 2-7 note
that the valve spring closes the valve initially; the strength or tension of this valve spring is very important, because if the valve does
not close tightly, the gases can leak out around the edges thus
reducing the pressure in the chamber and lowering the efficiency
of the engine.

Cams

The valve in the cylinder head is opened by overcoming the
valve spring tension with some mechanical force. In the typical internal combustion engine, this force is provided via a *cam*, either

directly or by means of a pivoted arm or a *push rod* (Fig. 2-7). Basically a cam is a wheel with a high spot, or lobe, on its rim that comes around once with each revolution of the cam wheel. As the cam wheel rotates, with the smooth surface of the cam just touching the bottom of the push rod, each time the lobe comes around it nudges the push rod up, applying tension to the valve spring and the valve is caused to open so the exhaust gases can escape. This is shown in Fig. 2-8. This cam action is almost universally used to operate valves in modern internal combustion engines.

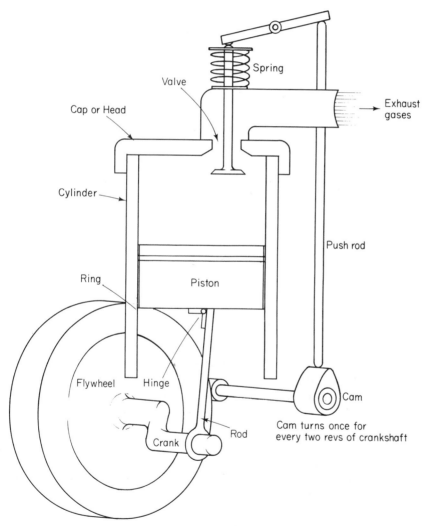

Fig. 2-8 Basic engine arrangement showing the "faucet" replaced by a poppet valve

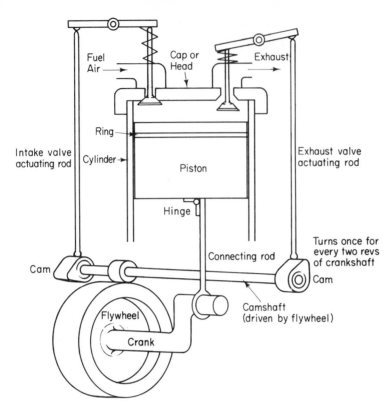

Fig. 2-9 Addition of a second valve permits the fuel-air mixture
to enter the chamber at the proper moment

To sustain the operation and keep it going, a second valve system is needed to admit fuel and new air into the combustion chamber. The new fuel charge must not enter the chamber while the compression and combustion of the previous charge is in process. If the fuel charge was admitted to the chamber when the exhaust valve was open, the new fuel would leave the chamber along with the spent gases. An intake valve that admits fuel by cam action at the correct time overcomes this obstacle. This second valve arrangement is shown at the top left in Fig. 2-9. These two valves, working in sequence solve the problems of fuel intake and exhaust escape from the compression chamber of the cylinder.

IGNITION

Most automobile engines that operate on the Otto principle ignite the fuel mixture inside the combustion chamber of each cylinder by means of an *electrical spark*. When two wires are connected to a source of high electrical voltage and are then brought close together, but not touching, a spark will jump between them. This is the fundamental concept behind the spark ignition system used in the internal combustion engine. The two wires are installed in a *spark plug* with a small space separating them. The spark plug is screwed into a hole in the cylinder head. When a high voltage is applied to the wires from outside the cylinder, a spark flashes inside the cylinder. Since the time that this spark is wanted is determined by the position of the piston in the cylinder, a switch can be used to time the spark. This switch is controlled by another cam that is operated, in turn, by the action of the piston and crankshaft.

Figure 2-10 shows the interaction of cam-controlled poppet valves for fuel intake and exhaust and the cam-controlled switch for ignition timing in the combustion chamber.

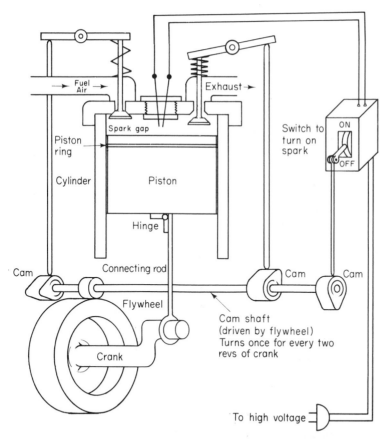

Fig. 2-10 A cam-operated switch passes high voltage electricity to spark gap at the proper moment

CARBURETION: MIXING FUEL AND AIR

The proper combustion of fuel in the cylinder requires oxygen in the combustion chamber. Exactly the right amount of fuel and air must be sprayed into the cylinder when the intake valve is open. This concept is shown by the atomizer spray pictured in Fig. 2-11. The atomizer is located at the port that serves the intake valve and is operated by a cam. Each time the intake valve opens, the atomizer sprays gasoline into the combustion chamber while the piston moves down. As the gas is sprayed in, a controlled amount of air is also drawn into the cylinder from the atmosphere so the air-

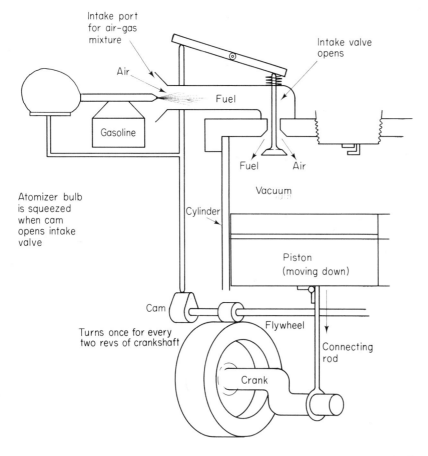

Fig. 2-11 A perfume atomizer is caused to spray fuel into the intake by means of the cam action

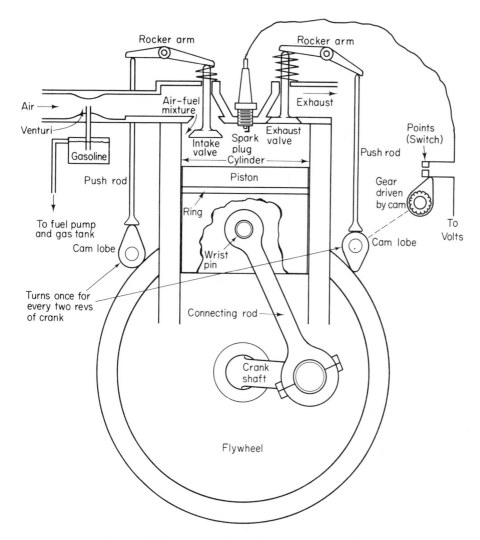

Fig. 2-12 Arrangement of the basic parts into a workable internal combustion engine. Note the improved switching arrangement for the spark (right) and the venturi type fuel feed (left).

fuel mixture in the chamber is kept in proper proportion. This mixing action is called *carburetion*, and it is a function of the carburetor, which is discussed in Chapter 5. The interaction of the carburetor and other parts is shown in Fig. 2-12. This figure shows all of the operations that are essential to the internal combustion reciprocating engine.

MULTIPLE-CYLINDER ENGINES

The important working parts of the reciprocating internal combustion engine are reviewed in Fig. 2-13. The four strokes of the Otto principle for a single cylinder (Fig. 2-14) may be described as follows:

1. On the intake stroke, the inlet valve opens and the fuel-air mixture is drawn into the cylinder.
2. On the compression stroke, both valves close, and the rising piston compresses the fuel-air mixture.
3. At the upper limit of piston movement, both valves are closed,

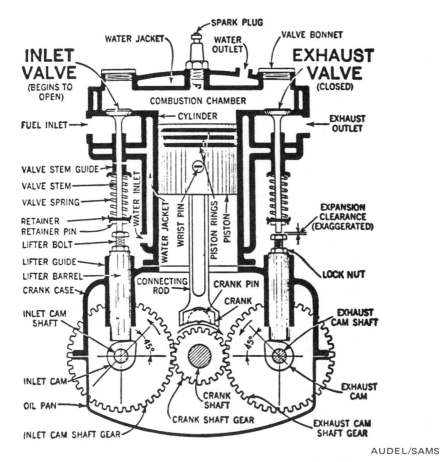

AUDEL/SAMS

Fig. 2-13 Cross section of an older type of gasoline engine, operating on the principles developed in this chapter

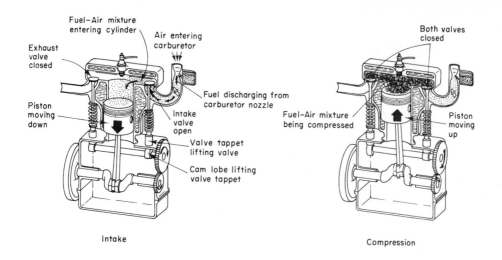

Intake

Compression

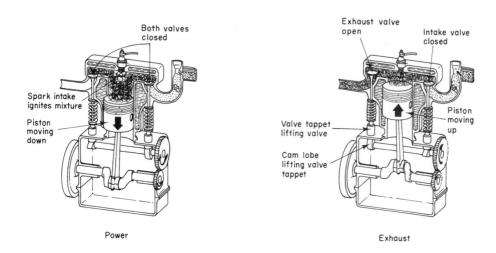

Power

Exhaust

Fig. 2-14 The separate strokes of the Otto four-strokes per cycle engine

the mixture is ignited, and combustion forces the piston downward on the power stroke.

4. On the exhaust stroke, the exhaust valve opens and the rising piston pushes spent gas from the combustion chamber.

Now we can apply these concepts to the operation of multiple-cylinder engines.

Although one-cylinder automobile engines were numerous

years ago, they are rare today and have all but disappeared. Today the most popular formats for passenger car engines include 4-, 6-, 8-, and sometimes 12-cylinder arrangements. A multi-cylinder engine has several cylinders like the one-cylinder device that has been described. The several cylinders are connected together to aid one another in their operation. Such arrangements require that the valves be operated from one common camshaft, which usually runs the full length of the engine and includes one lobe for each valve in the engine. With an intake valve and an exhaust valve for each cylinder, the camshaft for a four-cylinder engine would have eight cams or lobes. The camshaft for an eight-cylinder engine would have sixteen cams or lobes.

Figure 2-15 shows the camshaft as it is positioned in a 6-cylinder engine and shows how the push rods operate the valves.

In the manufacture of the auto engines, by far the most common practice is to bore all of the cylinders into one single casting that is called the *engine block*. In the background detail of Fig. 2-15, note the several pistons that are visible. They are closely spaced and operate inside of cylinders that are bored into one block. There is practically no limit to the way cylinders may be arranged in the block, but the most common forms are the in-line, V, and the flat or horizontal designs. Usually the engine cylinders are arranged in a symmetrical pattern to provide balance. The once common straight-8, or 8-cylinder in-line engines passed from the scene some years ago. Today, only two in-line formats remain in common use: the in-line four cylinder engine and the in-line six. Engine blocks of both types are shown in Fig. 2-16 *a* and *b*.

Probably the most popular block arrangement for passenger cars in the United States is the V-8, which has two in-line banks of four cylinders arranged in a V-shape (Fig. 2-16*c*). The piston rods for both banks of cylinders are connected to one common crankshaft. The result is an eight-cylinder engine that is much shorter than an in-line engine of equal power or displacement.

A few four- or six-cylinder engines are made up in the V format also, again to achieve a length advantage (Fig. 2-16*d* and *e*). There is also the so-called "slant-six" block (Fig. 2-15). Although this block resembles an in-line six in appearance and operation, the cylinders lean to one side a few degrees so that the engine block looks like half of the rather rare V-12 arrangement (Fig. 2-16*f*). The principal advantage of the slant-six block is a reduction of engine height.

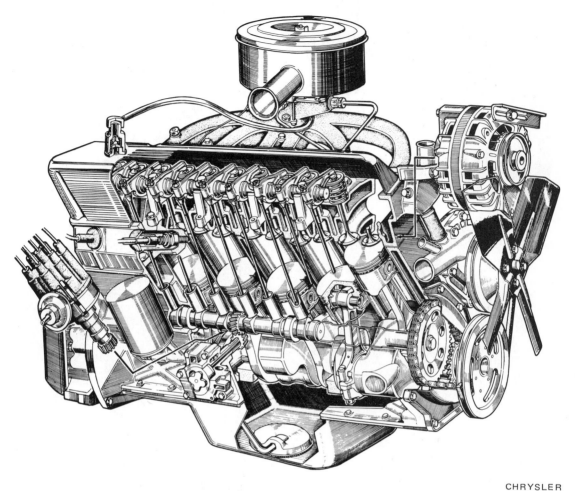

Fig. 2-15 A cutaway view of a modern engine made up of several cylinders connected together

These more compact engine designs allow for lower, shorter auto body styles and better distribution of engine weight. The relative merits of these engines are discussed later in this chapter.

THE CRANKSHAFT

The *crankshaft* is the primary means of taking the power out of an engine. This shaft is made up of several cranks put together and assembled end-to-end so that when one crank is up, the next crank

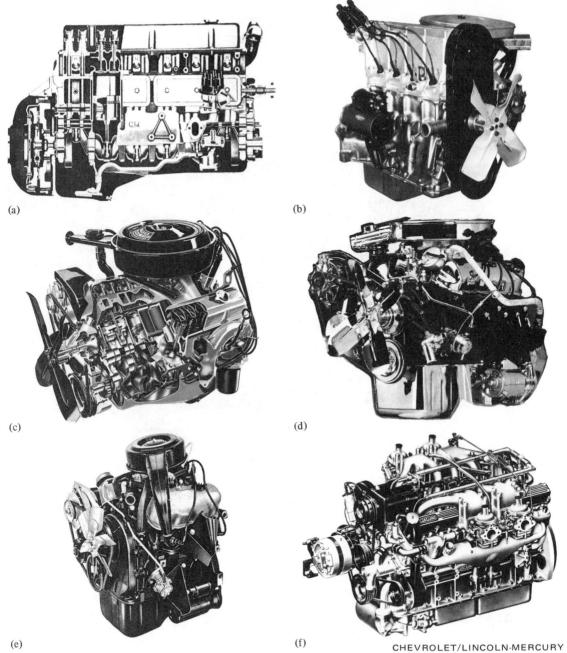

(a)

(b)

(c)

(d)

(e)

(f)

Fig. 2-16 Examples of various arrangements of multiple cylinders
used in modern automobile engines. (a) 6-cylinder in-line, overhead
valve; (b) 4-cylinder in-line, overhead valve; (c) V8 format,
8-cylinders; four on each side, (d) V6 format, 6-cylinders, three on
each side; (e) V4 format, 4-cylinders, two on each side; (f) V12
format, 12-cylinders, six on each side.

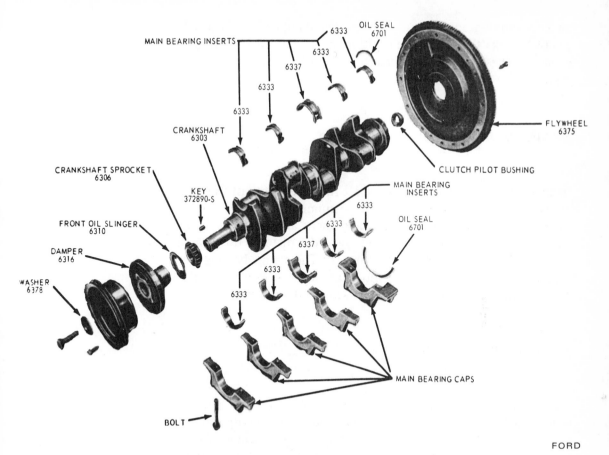

MAIN BEARING INSERTS

OIL SEAL
6701

6333

6333

6337

6333

6333

CRANKSHAFT
6303

CRANKSHAFT SPROCKET
6306

KEY
372890-S

FRONT OIL SLINGER
6310

DAMPER
6316

WASHER
6378

FLYWHEEL
6375

CLUTCH PILOT BUSHING

MAIN BEARING
INSERTS

6333

6333

OIL SEAL
6701

6337

6333

6333

MAIN BEARING CAPS

BOLT

FORD

Fig. 2-17 A multiple "throw" crankshaft, showing how individual cylinders work together to turn a common shaft

is down (Fig. 2-17). The crank "handle" to which the connecting rod is attached is called a *throw* or *rod journal*. In some engines, each cylinder has a separate throw to accommodate the connecting rod that serves each piston. In other engines two connecting rods are attached to each throw of the crankshaft. This arrangement is common in V-format engines.

The crankshaft shown in Fig. 2-17 has eight separate throws, a flywheel attached to one end, and a vibration damper attached to the other end. As its name implies, the *vibration damper* reduces the unwanted vibrations that develop while the engine is running at certain speeds. The vibration damper has two other important functions. First, it carries the pulleys that accept the fan belt and other belts used to operate accessories such as power steering and air conditioning equipment. Second, the damper has certain distinctive marks that show the position of the crankshaft within the engine. These marks are used to determine and adjust engine *timing*.

ENGINE BEARINGS

In an assembled engine, the crankshaft runs the length of the block along the center line at the bottom. Supporting bearings hold the crankshaft in the block in precise alignment and allow the crankshaft to rotate as it absorbs power from the pistons, through the connecting rods attached to the throws. The engine bearings that support the crankshaft in the block are known as *main bearings* (Fig. 2-17); *rod bearings* connect the rods to the throws.

THE OIL PUMP AND PAN

The *oil pump* is located below the engine block usually and adjacent to the crankshaft. The *oil pan* that shields the pump is bolted into place after the installation of the engine bearings and the pump. The pan is a reservoir for the engine oil and also serves as a protective barrier against foreign matter that might come up off the roadway and damage the moving parts of the engine. In short, it keeps the oil in while keeping the dirt out. The average driver is not likely to work on any of the parts concealed by the oil pan. A knowledge of these parts and their function is vital to understanding engine operation, diagnosing troubles when they occur, and making repair decisions that avoid unnecessary expense.

HEAD AND VALVE ARRANGEMENTS

Engine cylinders are commonly positioned so that the tops of the pistons, when all the way up, will be even with the top surface of the engine block. The cylinder combustion chambers are incorporated into one casting called the *head*, which closes off the top of each cylinder as shown earlier (Fig. 2-1). An in-line engine has one head with the several combustion chambers positioned so that when the head is set on top of the engine block and aligned, each combustion chamber caps the top end of its mating cylinder.

V format engines have two of these heads—one for the top of each arm of the V. Thus, each head in a V-6 engine has three combustion chambers. Each combustion chamber has a threaded hole into which the spark plug is inserted (Chapter 9).

In some cases, the valves described earlier are installed in the head (the I head); in other cars the valves are installed in the block (the L head). In the so-called "F" head engine, one valve is positioned in the block and the other in the head. Engines in which the valves are included in the head are called *valve-in-head* or *overhead valve* engines. Common valve arrangements are shown in Fig. 2-18.

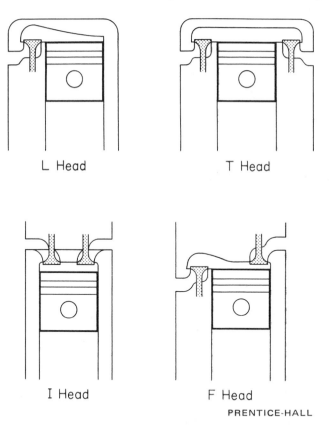

PRENTICE-HALL

Fig. 2-18 Some of the various ways of locating valves in modern engines: L head, T head, I head, F head

CAMSHAFT

In most automobile engines, the camshaft that supports the cams is in the block, parallel with the crankshaft and to one side of the line of cylinders. In an *over-head cam engine*, the camshaft is on top of the head; the most notable advantage of this arrangement over more conventional in-block assemblies is superior speed. Detailed comparison of various cam systems belongs in the realm of the engineer and the performance-minded mechanic.

After the head has been secured to the block, the internal engine functions are beyond the reach of the average driver. Again, however, some information about the mechanical systems and the locations and functions of the various parts helps in diagnosing trouble; for example, when adjusting valves or changing spark plugs, knowing what is under the head is indispensable.

GASKETS

A gasket serves the same function as the rubber ring in a jar lid. It is made of a compressible substance that fills in irregularities between metal surfaces to be mated thus providing a positive seal. Gaskets are used in several places on automobile engines — between the pan and the block to prevent oil leaks, between the head and the block to keep combustion gas pressure inside the cylinder and to keep the cooling water inside the water jacket, where the carburetor attaches to the intake manifold, etc.

MANIFOLDS

When the internal components have been assembled and the pan and heads are in place, the basic engine is virtually complete. In the configuration just described, however, each cylinder would require a separate carburetor, which is both unnecessary and uneconomical, and each cylinder would exhaust directly into the air through the exhaust valve, creating a deafening noise. To overcome this problem, the intake and exhaust systems are provided with *manifolds*. The *intake manifold* enables a single carburetor to serve all cylinders. The *exhaust manifold* directs the exhaust from all cylinders through a single exhaust pipe to a muffler, which reduces the noise to an acceptable level. These manifolds are near the combustion chambers and must be able to withstand the heat. For this reason, they usually are made of cast iron, the same material used in stoves, ovens, and furnaces.

The Intake Manifold

The fuel-air mixture created by the carburetor is directed to each individual cylinder by a plumbing arrangement consisting of a cast-iron pipe with one input and a series of outlets corresponding to the number of cylinders to be served. The carburetor is attached to the single inlet through matching flange and bolt arrangements. When the manifold assembly is bolted in place against the head or block, there is an outlet in line with the inlet port leading to the intake valve of each cylinder. Gaskets are placed between the manifold and the engine block or head and between the carburetor and the manifold to provide positive seals and prevent undesirable leaks.

On most in-line engines the intake manifolds attach to the side of the block or head; since the carburetor is mounted on the intake manifold, this arrangement usually puts the carburetor off to one side of the engine. On V engines, the intake manifold must provide equal length paths from the common carburetor to each of the cylinders set on opposite arms of the V. Thus, the cast-iron plumbing resembles a giant spider with a common inlet centered on top, where the carburetor is to mount, from which pipes lead out, octopus fashion, to the individual cylinder inlets (Fig. 2-19).

Special performance engines are equipped with multiple carburetors, sometimes as many as one for each cylinder. In such cases, special manifolds and custom linkage to throttle controls are required. The conventional production automobile, however, usually is limited to a single carburetor assembly with, perhaps, multiple *throats*, or air passages, through the fuel input system.

The Exhaust Manifold

The exhaust manifold connects all cylinder exhausts to one outlet (Fig. 2-20). V engines have an exhaust manifold on each side. Sometimes these manifolds are joined to a single exhaust pipe,

CARBURETOR MOUNTING FLANGE

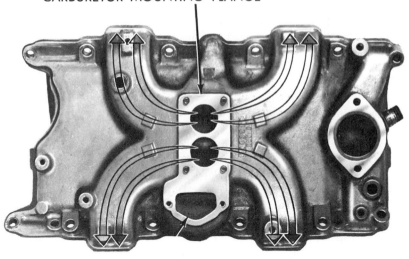

Fig. 2-19 Typical intake manifold that enables one carburetor to feed fuel to all eight cylinders of a V8 engine

and sometimes they deliver exhaust into separate exhaust pipes, one for each side of the engine. In either case, the plumbing system is the opposite of the system used for the intake manifold. The manifold has inlets equal to the number of cylinders it serves, and one outlet that connects with the vehicle exhaust system. It bolts directly onto the engine, and each inlet from the manifold must be aligned with its corresponding exhaust port in the head or block. The joint between the manifold and the engine sometimes is sealed with a gasket.

Like the intake manifold, exhaust manifolds operate in the hottest part of the engine; often they are red hot when the engine is operating at high speeds and under heavy loads. Touching the exhaust manifold of an operating engine or one that has just been turned off can result in severe burns.

Heat from the exhaust can be used to raise the temperature of the fuel-air mixture for more efficient combustion. The transfer of heat from the exhaust manifold to the intake manifold can take the form of mere physical contact between the two manifolds, or complex ducting that involves crossovers, which direct hot exhaust gases into the intake manifold or to the carburetor itself. Many systems use a heat-controlled valve, or *heat riser*, which may be

Fig. 2-20 A typical exhaust manifold for one side of a
V8 engine. Four exhaust valves feed into separate inlets,
and the collected gases combine to discharge through
the single, common outlet.

installed in the exhaust outlet to control and direct the heat for
faster engine warmup. The heat riser valve is opened or closed by
a heat-sensitive spring together with the flow of hot gases. This
system is comparable in operation to the automatic choke of the
carburetor (Chapter 5).

THE BASIC ENGINE ASSEMBLY

Figure 2-21 shows a typical engine assembly with details of the
common supporting systems. Some additional components must
be installed before the engine can be considered a working power
plant. These include the fuel, exhaust, cooling, and electrical systems, which—unlike the basic engine assembly—can be reached with
comparative ease. Many of these support systems can be adjusted
or serviced either partly or completely by the owner.

The choice of an engine becomes an increasingly important
decision as the availability of fuel decreases while costs increase.
The size of the engine and the weight of the car combine to establish fuel consumption. It does not always hold true that a smaller
engine is most economical. A small engine operating under constant heavy loads, such as pulling a trailer or station wagons with
heavy loads, will not only use more gas but will wear rapidly so
maintenance and repair costs will skyrocket. Similarly, a 6-cylinder
engine is not necessarily more economical in fuel consumption
when compared to an 8-cylinder engine.

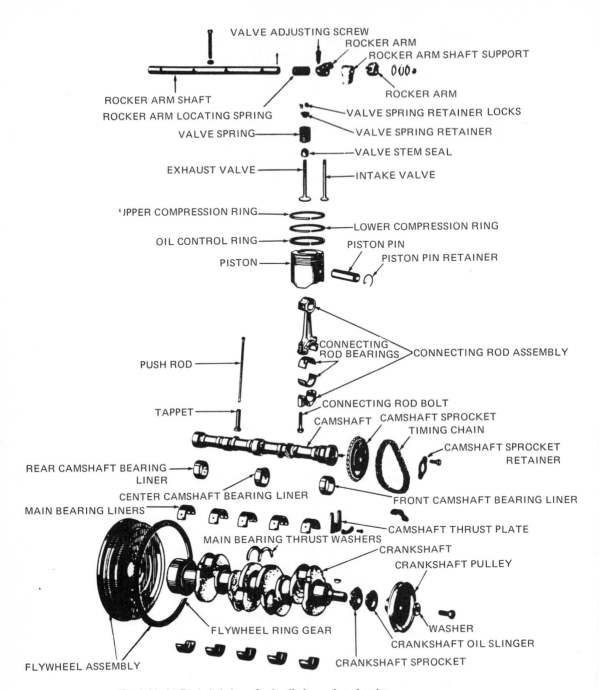

Fig. 2-21 (a) Exploded view of a 4-cylinder engine, showing parts and how they tie together; parts in (a) assemble within (b) on page 41.

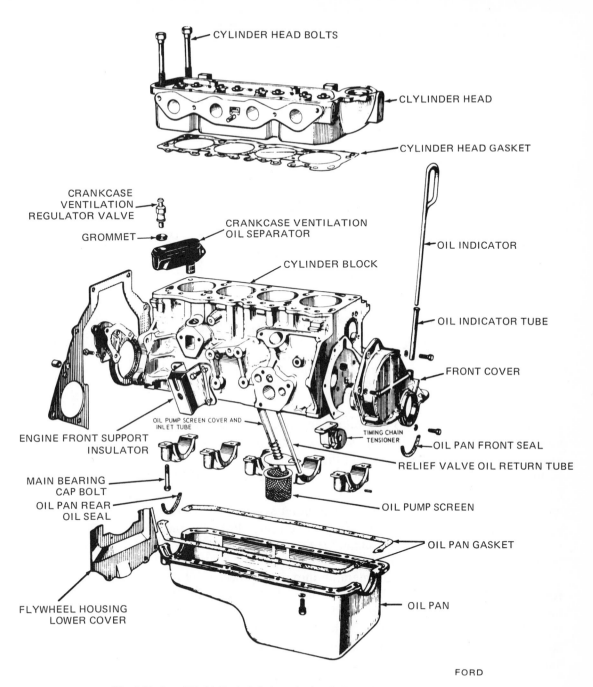

CYLINDER HEAD BOLTS

CLYLINDER HEAD

CYLINDER HEAD GASKET

CRANKCASE VENTILATION REGULATOR VALVE

GROMMET

CRANKCASE VENTILATION OIL SEPARATOR

CYLINDER BLOCK

OIL INDICATOR

OIL INDICATOR TUBE

FRONT COVER

OIL PUMP SCREEN COVER AND INLET TUBE

TIMING CHAIN TENSIONER

ENGINE FRONT SUPPORT INSULATOR

OIL PAN FRONT SEAL

RELIEF VALVE OIL RETURN TUBE

MAIN BEARING CAP BOLT

OIL PAN REAR OIL SEAL

OIL PUMP SCREEN

OIL PAN GASKET

FLYWHEEL HOUSING LOWER COVER

OIL PAN

FORD

Fig. 2-21 (cont'd.) (b) Exploded view of a 4-cylinder engine, showing parts and their assembly; parts in (a), shown on page 40, assemble within (b)

"All in all it's in pretty good shape. The only thing that needs replacing is the motor."

The problem of how to choose an engine can be resolved by understanding some basic factors which car manufacturers use in rating their engines. The practice in the industry is to rate engines in two categories; horsepower delivered at a given speed (RPM), and the total volume of the cylinders above the pistons in cubic inches, cubic centimeters, or liters. The latter system is preferred by most European and Japanese car manufacturers. For example, the British Jaguar's 6-cylinder engine is rated at 246 horsepower with a displacement of 258.4 cubic inches or 4.2 liters.

The displacement is of considerable importance because it determines the amount of gasoline drawn into the cylinders on the intake stroke. On average, the ratio of air to fuel is 14 to 1. Thus, for each intake stroke, 1/15 of the total volume taken into the engine will be gasoline. Obviously then, engine displacement has a definite bearing on gasoline mileage.

Because automotive engineers differ on the best ways to design engines, there is no standard ratio of displacement to horsepower.

There is one popular V-8 engine that develops 195 hp with a displacement of 283 cubic inches. A different manufacturer produces a similar engine that develops 185 hp with a displacement of 455 cubic inches.

When choosing an engine, one should consider the type of service the car is expected to give, plus such factors as the weight of the car and whether or not an automatic transmission is used. As a general rule, if an automatic transmission is used, a V-8 engine with the same horsepower rating is to be preferred over a 6-cylinder engine. The reason is that the 8-cylinder engine produces more torque (twisting power) and operates more efficiently with an automatic transmission.

If the car is to be used for slow driving and a considerable amount of up-hill pulling, an engine with good low-speed performance is desired. Most often this means a 6-cylinder engine with a long stroke because this configuration provides good low-speed torque.

In the final analysis the best engine for a particular application is the smallest engine that produces the horsepower needed from the least volume displacement and which has torque characteristics best suited to the most common driving conditions to be encountered.

One chapter covering each of the eight support systems external to the engine assembly follows. Both the operation of each system and routine techniques for servicing and adjustment by the owner are discussed.

The automotive lubrication system

PART I – HOW IT WORKS

The moving parts of an engine must be lubricated with a substance that will cling to the surfaces, make them slippery, and prevent the parts from sticking. Lubrication reduces the wear caused by friction, and liquid lubricants, such as oil, provide a measure of cooling as well. The fluid oils that are used in automobile engines are able to withstand the mechanical forces and operating temperatures that occur when the engine is running. Without lubrication, an engine would not last very long.

The modern automobile engine operates in a bath of oil, with the oil pan serving as a reservoir from which the oil is distributed throughout the engine. The pan on a typical automobile holds about a gallon of oil, which is many times the amount needed to cover the moving surfaces.

The Oil Pump and Pressure

The oil is kept moving by means of an oil pump, which causes the oil to flow over, around, through, and between all moving parts inside the engine (Fig. 3-1). The oil pump, inside the oil pan, might be compared to the heart of an animal. It constantly draws oil from the supply in the bottom of the pan (called the sump) and pumps it through a series of vein- and artery-like passages to the bearing surfaces where it does its work, then drains back into the pan for recirculation (Fig. 3-2).

The oil pump must develop enough pressure and maintain the flow of oil required to service the farthest parts of the engine. In overhead valve and overhead cam engines, oil must be transferred from the bottom of the engine to the top (Fig. 3-3). Furthermore, since the bearing surfaces are lubricated from within, the oil must be under enough pressure to force its way between the rubbing metal surfaces and keep them coated with a lubricating film (Fig. 3-3).

Oil pumps have evolved into one of the most reliable and long-lived parts of the internal combustion engine. Engine failure can rarely be attributed to oil *pump* failure. Oil *pressure* failure, on the other hand, is more common. As engine bearings wear, the space between the fixed and rotating elements increases, so the oil flows

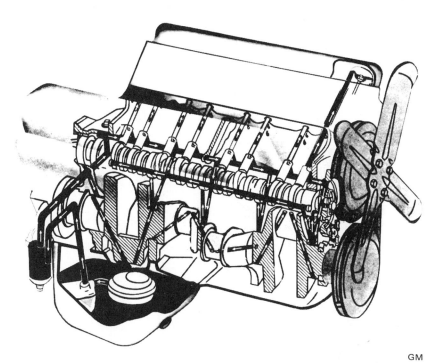

**Fig. 3-1 Pressure fed lubrication system, showing how oil is
distributed to the moving parts of the engine**

through the larger opening more readily, resulting in an oil pressure
drop throughout the entire system. In severe cases, the pressure
may be insufficient to force the oil to the extremes of the system,
or the amount of oil reaching the working surfaces of the rod and
main bearings may not be adequate. The amount of oil pressure
(in pounds per square inch) is shown on the instrument panel by a
lamp or a gauge. This oil pressure reading is one of the most
important indications that the driver has of the condition of the
engine. When the lubrication system is not maintaining the required
oil pressure, the engine must be stopped or serious damage will
occur.

Oil Filtering Devices

Oil picks up contaminants as it flows through an operating
engine. These include carbon that results from combustion in the
cylinders and fine particles of metal worn away during normal
operation. Foreign matter such as dirt from the spout of an oil can
or around the oil filler opening may get into the system from the

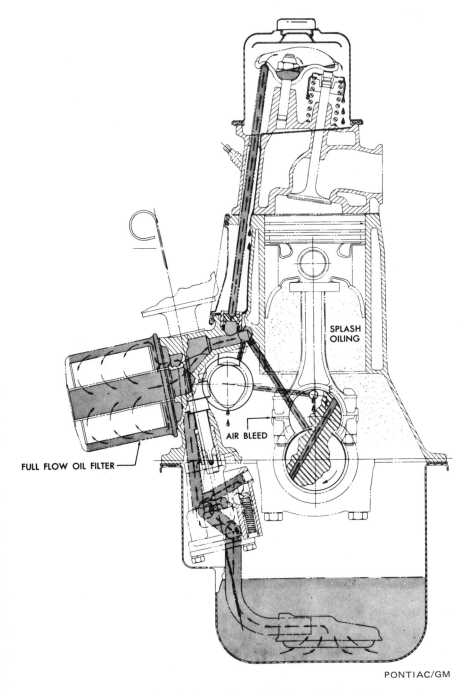

SPLASH
OILING

AIR BLEED

FULL FLOW OIL FILTER

PONTIAC/GM

Fig. 3-2 Showing how oil from the bottom of the engine is pumped
to the top to lubricate overhead valve parts

48

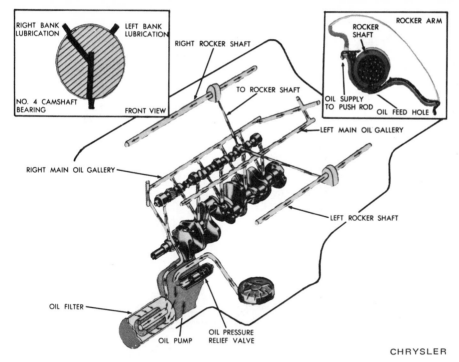

RIGHT BANK LUBRICATION
LEFT BANK LUBRICATION
NO. 4 CAMSHAFT BEARING
FRONT VIEW
RIGHT ROCKER SHAFT
TO ROCKER SHAFT
ROCKER ARM
ROCKER SHAFT
OIL SUPPLY TO PUSH ROD
OIL FEED HOLE
LEFT MAIN OIL GALLERY
RIGHT MAIN OIL GALLERY
LEFT ROCKER SHAFT
OIL FILTER
OIL PUMP
OIL PRESSURE RELIEF VALVE

CHRYSLER

Fig. 3-3 Complete oil circulation system, showing location of pump, filters, and screen. The inset shows how oil is circulated over the rocker bearing surfaces

outside, or fine dust particles may enter through the carburetor air inlet and work their way down to the pan.

The *oil screen* is the first barrier against the circulation of contaminants through the oil system. A circular screen-mesh filter of fairly large diameter is placed over the pump inlet so that all oil going to the pump must first pass through this filter screen. The usual location for this oil screen is at the lowest point in the sump, as may be seen from Figs. 3-1 and 3-2.

Although the oil screen has a fairly close weave, it cannot remove very fine particles. Even these very fine particles will wear away bearing surfaces just as effectively as sand paper or a file. This results in a drastic reduction in engine life. In addition, contaminants can gradually build up in the passages and ports through which the oil passes, eventually slowing down the flow of oil to the bearing surfaces. The usual result is a ruined bearing.

To trap the smaller particles that pass through the oil screen, a second barrier, called the oil filter, is used in the system. Oil

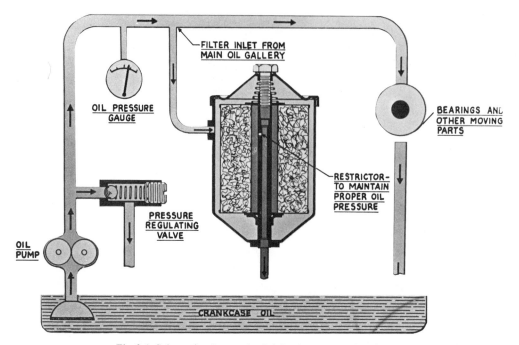

FILTER INLET FROM MAIN OIL GALLERY

OIL PRESSURE GAUGE

BEARINGS AND OTHER MOVING PARTS

RESTRICTOR- TO MAINTAIN PROPER OIL PRESSURE

PRESSURE REGULATING VALVE

OIL PUMP

CRANKCASE OIL

Fig. 3-4 Schematic of an engine lubricating system, showing a cross section of the oil filter

NAPA

filters are available in a variety of types and sizes suited to different engines. The car manufacturer will specify the appropriate filter that is to be used with the engine. If the oil pump is the heart of the lube system, the oil filter is the lung. In normal operation, the filter collects the fine particles and holds them until it is full; then it must be replaced. The effective life of an oil filter depends on the area and amount of operation, the amount of dust in the air, and the kinds of servicing that the car is given. Oil filters are usually accessible and easily removed. Figure 3-4 is a cross sectional view of a typical engine oil system including filter.

Oil Seals

The crankshaft of the engine extends in front of the block, where the vibration damper is attached, and to the rear of the block, where the flywheel is attached. At these two points, it is possible for lubricating oil, pumped under pressure to the front and rear main bearings, to leak out of the engine. *Oil seals* are installed at these critical points. These seals are seated so as to encircle the shaft at the edge of the oil pan and prevent the oil from leaking out and dirt from getting in. These seals are made of an impregnated rope-like material, leather, plastic, or specially formulated rubber, and they squeeze the shaft with enough pressure to prevent oil leaks while leaving the shaft free to rotate. Failure of these oil seals results usually after many thousands of miles of wear and shows up as oil dripping from the underside of the engine when the car is parked.

Oil Pressure Relief Valve

Conditions such as seal wear and worn bearings that may result in reduced oil pressure have been noted. It is possible, too, that at high engine speeds the oil pump may develop extremely high oil pressure, which could force oil seals out of their seats and cause severe oil leaks. To protect against this, the oil system is provided with a pressure-relief valve, which opens whenever oil pressure exceeds a pre-set level. When the relief valve is open, excess oil returns directly to the pan.

The oil pump is capable of bringing oil pressure up to the minimum required level even with the engine at idle. The pressure relief valve prevents oil pressure from going above the maximum safe level even at the highest speeds. The oil pressure is thereby held within a safe range at all times.

PART 2—MAINTENANCE

The automobile manufacturer designates the type of lubricants that should be used in the engine and other parts of the car. This information is usually provided in the owners' manual or it can be obtained from the appropriate dealer. By following the manufacturer's directions, the owner can receive maximum life from the engine at minimum cost. A major cause of premature engine failure is driver disregard of the manufacturers' instructions about the oil to be used and the time intervals between oil changes.

"There's still a lot we don't know about valve lifters."

Characteristics of Engine Oil

The quality of engine oil has improved markedly over the years, and along with these improvements have come new systems of rating the quality characteristics and viscosity of oil. These ratings are on each oil can. Figure 3-5 shows a typical one-quart can of oil and the technical data regarding its contents. The two characteristics the driver needs to look for and specify when selecting engine oil are the API quality rating and the SAE viscosity recommended by the auto manufacturer.

Fig. 3-5 Can of oil showing SAE and API ratings

Both new and old oil quality rating designations will appear on oil cans for many years. Table 3-1 describes and compares the old *M* ratings and the newer *S* ratings. *ML* oils (referring to motor light) are for use only under very mild operating conditions; *MM*-rated oil (motor medium) is suitable for use under moderate driving conditions at moderate speeds and pulling moderate loads in older

Table 3-1   American Petroleum Institute (API) Ratings

Old designation	New designation	Oil description
ML (Motor Light)	SA	Oil without additive, except that it may contain pour and/or foam depressant
MM (Motor Medium)	SB	Provides some antioxidant and antiscuff capabilities
1964 MS (Motor Severe)	SC	Oil meeting the 1964-67 requirements of the automobile manufacturer. Provides low-temperature antisludge and antirust performance
1968 MS (Motor Severe)	SD	Oil meeting the 1968-71 requirements of the automobile manufacturers. Provides greater low-temperature antisludge and antirust performance
1971-72 (none)	SE	Oil meeting the 1972 requirements of the automobile manufacturers. Provides high-temperature antioxidation, plus greater low-temperature antisludge and antirust performance

SA—for use under very mild operating conditions; basically straight mineral oil with no detergents or additives.

SB—for use under mild operating conditions; some antirust and antiscuff capability, but no detergent added.

SC—meets warranty requirements for 1964-1967 cars; controls high and low temperature deposits, wear, rust and corrosion. Mild detergent added.

SD—meets warranty requirements for 1967-1971 cars; provides more protection than SC, may be used in place of SC. Detergent added.

SE—meets warranty requirements for 1972 and later cars; additional high temperature protection, high detergent. May be used in place of SC or SD.

engines. This may include a mild detergent. The *MS*-rated oil (motor severe) is very high quality oil, the best available under the old rating system.

Due to different performance standards and definitions used in classifying *S* oils, which are intended for use in passenger cars and light trucks, it is not possible to directly compare them with the older *M*-rated oils. In general, however, we might compare the new *SA* oils with *ML*, *SB* oil with *MM*, and *SC*, *SD*, and *SE* oils with *MS*. All quality and performance tests an oil can meet are listed on the can. The automobile owner with normal engine needs is concerned only that the oil meets the requirements of his particular car; the other requirements it may meet are superfluous.

Frequently the oil can lists ratings in the *D* and the *C* series also. These ratings pertain to the engine oil's performance in a diesel engine. Owners of cars with diesel engines should look for the *D* or *C* rating specified in the owners' manual or check with the appropriate car dealer.

Some oil cans have the letters *HD* (high detergent) on them. The term *high detergent* has no precise definition, therefore its use in attempting to describe quality is essentially meaningless. The only time an owner should be aware of it is when considering *changing* from a lower-detergent oil (*SA* or *SB*) to a high-detergent oil (*SC*, *SD* or *SE*). Engines in which low-detergent oil has been used for a long time may be very dirty inside. They may be literally held together by carbon deposits and assorted gunk. The switch from a low-detergent (or no-detergent) to a high-detergent oil is said to have brought the remaining life of many an engine to an abrupt end.

viscosity rating

The second important oil characteristic is its viscosity (roughly its "thickness" or "weight"): Oil that is too thick cannot be pumped through the engine quickly enough to carry off the heat caused by combustion and friction. If the oil is too thin, it will not provide proper lubrication, and the engine may wear rapidly. Oil thickness changes with engine temperature. This may vary from sub-zero on a cold winter morning to 300°F in some parts when the engine is at operating temperature. An oil that has the proper viscosity at operating temperature might be thick as molasses on a cold morning and actually prevent the engine from turning over fast enough to start. In a climate where air temperature varies only slightly during the year, selecting a suitable oil viscosity from the owners' manual is simple. Table 3-2 shows one oil manufacturer's recommendations for selecting oil viscosity. Lubricants which do not have both an SAE grade number and the SE service classification shown on the container should not be used.

The typical new-car manufacturer will specify SAE30 as the best thickness to use in a new engine where air temperatures are generally above freezing. When winter comes, it may be necessary to change to a lighter weight oil in order to maintain easy engine starting. The letter *W* may be thought of as designating winter; SAE20W oil, for example, is slightly thinner when cold than regular SAE20.

Most petroleum refiners have developed multiviscosity oils (for example, SAE10W30). Special additives cause these multiviscosity lubricants to become more thin during cold weather and to thicken when it becomes warm—just the opposite of what usually happens. The advantage of such an oil is obvious. SAE10W30 weight oil

Table 3-2 Recommended Oil Grades

Multigrades	
SAE 10W-30 SAE 10W-40 SAE 10W-50 SAE 20W-40 SAE 20W-50	Where temperatures consistently are above +32°F.
SAE 5W-40 SAE 10W-30 SAE 10W-40 SAE 10W-50	Suitable for yearlong operation in many parts of the U.S.; may be used where temperatures occasionally drop as low as −10°F.
SAE 5W-20 SAE 5W-30 SAE 5W-40	Recommended where minimum temperatures consistently are below +10°F.
Single grades	
SAE 30	Where temperatures are consistently above +32°F.
SAE 10W	Where temperatures range between +32°F and −10°F.

CHRYSLER

may be used year-round. Although such high-quality multiviscosity oils meet the rigid requirements of the API/SE classification, many automotive engineers do not believe they afford as good protection for the engine as do single-viscosity oils. Some automotive manufacturers recommend the use of single-viscosity oils except in unusual circumstances. Single-viscosity oil is preferred in heavy-duty applications like truck engines and taxicabs where the engines are run steadily and are held at a constant operating temperature, with infrequent starts and stops.

Mixing Oils

There are two different types of crude petroleum used to manufacture engine oil: asphaltic base and paraffin base. Advertising notwithstanding, engine oil from either of these crude oils, if it meets the API rating, will give an engine good protection.

Years ago, when oil quality did vary widely, it was not advisable to mix different *brands* of oil. With rare exceptions, the mixing of modern brands of oils is not harmful, and it is safe to mix different weights of oil produced by the same manufacturer with the same API rating. Because of differences in chemical composition, however, it is good practice when changing brands to drain out all of the old oil and replace it with the new brand. This practice minimizes the risk of an undesirable chemical reaction between the oils.

Additives

Oil additives are vital to long oil life and proper engine protection. Typical additives in modern high-quality oils are detergents, foam inhibitors, oxidation inhibitors, corrosion inhibitors, viscosity improvers, pour-point depressant, and the like. Oil itself does not wear out. The vital additives do lose their effectiveness after a period of time, however, and the oil simply gets dirty. The only satisfactory remedy is periodic replacement of the oil.

Various other oil or gasoline additives are on the market, each promising great improvements in engine performance. Consumer studies of these additives have shown that many of them are about

95 percent kerosene and coloring and the other 5 percent "magic ingredients." In the trade, these additives are referred to as "tiger milk," among other things. Normally they are harmless and have been known to alleviate minor engine problems under certain selected conditions. However, cases have been reported of destructive chemical interaction with the standard oil additives, and professional opinion regarding their usefulness is far from unanimous.

In addition to the automobile manufacturer's recommendations, a good indication of the appropriate interval between oil changes is the color of the oil on the dipstick. If the engine oil is doing its job properly, it will pick up and carry with it small bits of carbon, by-products of combustion, and the small metal chips that result from wear. New engine oil turns dark brown within a short period of time as it picks up contaminants throughout the system. The oil turns black and gooey, however, when its additives have broken down, and it is saturated with impurities. Oil that has reached this stage should be changed. Whenever you check the oil for quantity, check its color as well. Some newer "high performance" oils turn black almost immediately and this test does not apply.

The oil capacity of you engine (in quarts) is given in the owner's manual. One extra quart must usually be added when a new filter is installed, since the filter itself holds about a quart of oil.

Generally, the oil filter should be changed every other time the oil is changed; again, the owner's manual gives clear guidance. If the car is operating in a dusty or sandy environment, more frequent oil and filter changes may be needed. The type and size of oil filter is specified by the auto manufacturer.

materials

The procedure for changing the engine oil and filter is outlined below. In addition to the right weight and type of lubricant and filter, you will need the materials shown in Fig. 3-6. A plastic

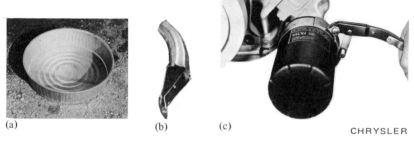

**Fig. 3-6 (a) drain pan, (b) oil pouring spout, (c) oil filter wrench
in place on filter**

dishpan or special receptacle (Fig. 3-6*a*) is needed to catch the
oil as it drains out of the engine pan. An oil can tapper and
pour-spout is shown in Fig. 3-6*b*. Such a spout is inexpensive and
is sometimes given away with the purchase of several cans of oil.
It is possible to punch holes in the top of an oil can with a screwdriver, but a pour-spout is far more convenient and less messy. Oil
filter wrenches (Fig. 3-6*c*) are inexpensive and are sometimes given
away with the purchase of a filter.

old oil removal

With most cars, draining out the old engine oil is a simple matter. One merely removes the drain plug (by means of an adjustable
wrench; Ch. 1), which is located at the lowest point on the pan,
and the oil drains into the receptacle provided. When the oil stops
draining, replace the drain plug and tighten it snugly. Do not overtighten the plug, however, for the threads are easily stripped.

Some cars are so low to the ground that to reach the drain
plug the car must be raised slightly by driving it up on a small
ramp (Fig. 3-7*a*) or by jacking it up several inches and supporting
it with an inexpensive jack stand (Fig. 3-7*b*).

filter installation

The oil filter unscrews in a counterclockwise direction; once
broken loose with the filter wrench (Fig. 3-6), it can be unscrewed
and removed by hand. Place the drainage receptacle under the filter

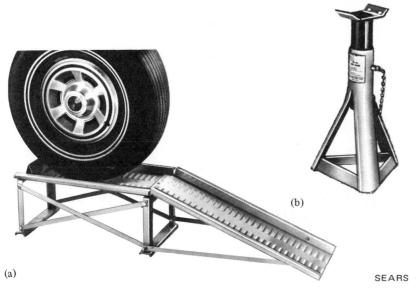

(b)

(a)

Fig. 3-7 A (a) portable ramp (b) jackstand

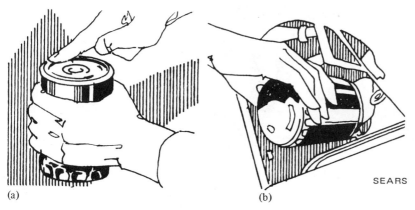

(a)   (b)

Fig. 3-8 (a) Coating filter gasket with oil to seal (b) Installing oil filter

during this process to catch any oil that may spill. Before installing a new oil filter, coat its gasket with a light film of oil or petroleum jelly to ensure a good seal (Fig. 3-8*a*). Screw the new filter into place by hand (Fig. 3-8*b*) and tighten it by hand. Do *not* use the filter wrench to tighten the new filter, or it may be extremely difficult to remove later.

The prescribed amount of oil is added as shown in Fig. 3-9. Next, pull out and check the oil level on the dipstick (Fig. 3-10) to make sure that there is enough oil in the engine, and that it has

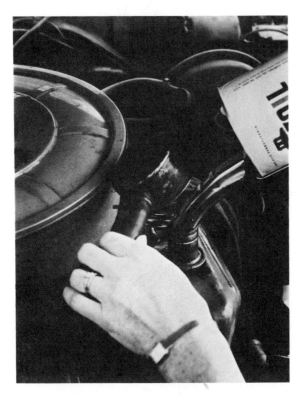

Fig. 3-9 Pouring oil in engine

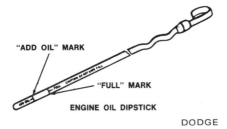

DODGE

Fig. 3-10 Checking oil with dipstick

not leaked out due to improper tightening of the drain plug or the new filter. Replace the dipstick and start the engine. Watch the oil pressure gauge or warning light carefully. The indicator should read "normal" after several seconds of engine operation. If not, stop the engine and recheck the oil level to see that the oil has not leaked out.

With the engine running, look under the car to see if any oil is leaking. Shut the engine off and check the oil level again with the dipstick. The oil level should be slightly above or below the "FULL" mark on the dipstick. This completes the oil and filter change operation.

General Hints

Some cars, such as the popular Volkswagen, have oil screens instead of replaceable oil filters. The procedure for changing the oil in such cars is the same as that outlined above, however, the entire oil screen assembly must be removed, cleaned in a solvent such as kerosene, then replaced.

Always change the gaskets when replacing a filter screen. Inexpensive gasket kits are available from the VW dealer. Tighten all bolts or nuts enough to prevent oil leaks but not so tight as to risk stripping the threads.

When the engine is running, oil is being sprayed all around the inside of it, and there are many places where leaks can occur. Besides the drain plug and oil filter, the other places that leaks commonly occur are where the oil pan attaches to the block at the bottom of the engine, and where the valve covers bolt onto the block atop the engine. About once a year it's a good idea to tighten all bolts or screws that fasten the oil pan and valve covers. If oil leaks persist, the pan or valve cover gaskets may need to be replaced.

Disposing of old engine oil is a problem sometimes. Service stations and garages put their waste oil in large oil drums and sell it, or pay to have it hauled away. The quantity of waste oil involved in a single oil change, however, is very small. Some people fill empty plastic milk or bleach bottles with the waste oil, write "waste oil" on the container, and put it out with the garbage for removal to the city dump. Many public dumps maintain barrels where waste oil is collected and sold. *Pouring oil down the drain to the sewer is against the law* in most places. Such wastes kill the algae in the filtration ponds where sewage is broken down before discharge into the ground water system.

The automotive cooling system

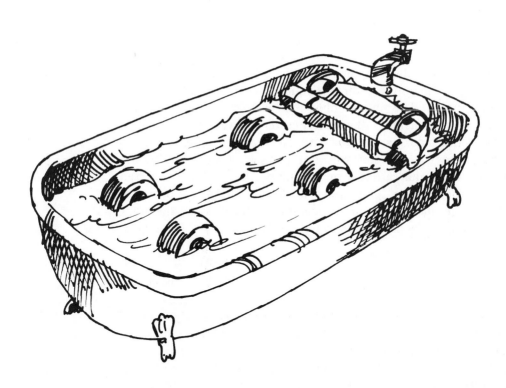

PART I — HOW IT WORKS

In Chapter 2, we covered the combustion process that takes place in the conventional automobile engine. This burning of fuel in the combustion chamber releases the heat energy that is needed to drive the pistons and make the car go. Not all engine heat is converted into useful power, however, so the extra heat must be carried away or the engine will overheat and be destroyed. Two common ways to cool the engine are air cooling and water cooling. Air-cooled engines are common in automobiles that are made in Europe. In the United States, the last significant air-cooled automobile engine was used in the Chevrolet Corvair, which is no longer in production.

Water-Cooled Systems

The water-cooled automobile engine is the most popular in the world, and is the only type now produced by American automobile manufacturers. The water-cooling loop in this type of engine has three main elements: the *water jacket*—a system of channels through the block—a *radiator*, and the *heater*. Water circulates through the water jacket where it picks up heat from the hot cylinder walls and carries it out of the block where it is released through the radiator. A thermostat controls the engine operating temperature, and continuous circulation of water through the block is maintained by a belt-driven water pump.

the radiator

The radiator resembles a honeycomb and is usually made of copper, which has excellent heat-transfer characteristics. The hot water flows through several small tubes, which are interconnected by the honeycomb of thin copper sheets (Fig. 4-1). The honeycomb structure of the radiator exposes the circulating hot water to a far larger volume of cool outside air than that afforded by the surfaces of the small tubes. Once cooled by its journey through the radiator, and its heat transferred to the outside, the water

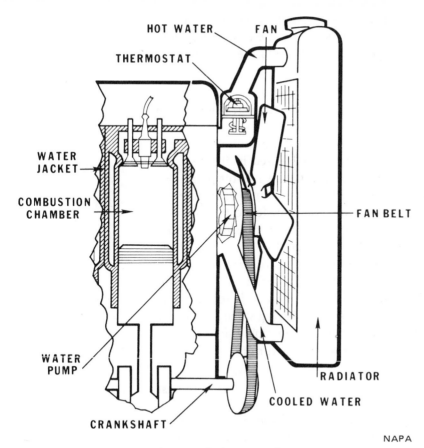

HOT WATER

FAN

THERMOSTAT

WATER JACKET

COMBUSTION CHAMBER

FAN BELT

WATER PUMP

RADIATOR

COOLED WATER

CRANKSHAFT

NAPA

Fig. 4-1 Major parts of the water cooling system

returns to the engine block, extracts more heat, and returns again to the radiator for recooling.

The radiator is attached firmly to the frame of the car, while rubber engine mounts allow the operating engine to twist and vibrate without transferring these motions to the car. For this reason, the radiator is connected to the engine by flexible hoses which permit the transfer of cooling water between the engine block and the radiator but prevent the transfer of mechanical vibrations. Hot water from the engine block enters the radiator through a hose at the top, and cooled water returns to the engine through a second hose which is connected to a fitting at the bottom of the engine on the water pump (Fig. 4-1). Both hoses are quite large, about two inches in diameter. Smaller hoses are used to carry part of the water to the *heater*, a small radiator inside the passenger compartment. Radiator hoses resemble common garden hoses; however, garden hoses could not withstand the high temperatures involved.

the water pump and fan

Continuous circulation of water through the cooling system is maintained by the *water pump*, which is located in front of the engine. The fan is positioned at the front of the water pump but behind the radiator. Its function is to pull air through the honeycomb of the radiator to improve the heat transfer to the air. The fan and the water pump are usually on the same shaft and are driven by the same belt (Fig. 4-1). If the fan belt breaks, the pump will stop and the engine will overheat. Most fans are solidly attached to the water pump shaft. In a number of cars, however, the fan is automatically controlled by a clutch so it rotates only when the extra cooling is needed, as when driving slowly on a very hot day, or when pulling a trailer. This is an economy measure, because the fan does use engine power when it is turning.

the thermostat

The need for cooling varies with engine speed. A properly designed water-cooling system will maintain an engine at the proper operating temperature during hot desert driving as well as in conditions of ice and snow. In a very cold climate, an unrestricted flow of water through the cooling system would increase engine warm-up time greatly. In fact, during below zero weather, the radiator could take out more heat than the engine could generate and hence prevent its ever reaching proper operating temperature. The engine operates best at some temperature near the boiling point of water. A "cool" engine might be at a temperature near 200°F.

The amount of water circulating through the engine, which affects the rate of cooling, is regulated by a thermostat (Fig. 4-2). This device operates somewhat like the poppet valve used in the engine. The thermostat is inserted in the path of the water flowing from the engine to the radiator. If the thermostat is closed, water cannot flow, no heat will be transferred to the outside via the radiator, and the engine will heat up rapidly. As soon as

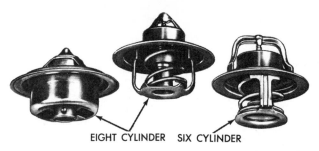

EIGHT CYLINDER SIX CYLINDER

CHRYSLER

Fig. 4-2 Thermostat

engine temperature has reached the proper operating level, a heat-sensitive spring in the thermostat causes the valve to open; the water flows, and normal cooling begins.

In most cars, the thermostat is inside of a housing that is attached to the top of the block or head near the front of the engine. The hose from the top of the radiator is usually connected to a short length of pipe that protrudes from the top of the thermostat housing (Fig. 4-3). Thermostats are available in several different temperature ranges to suit a wide variety of engines. Normally, one should use the thermostat prescribed for the engine by the manufacturer.

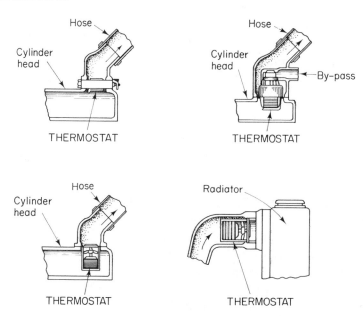

Fig. 4-3 Thermostat housing with pipe

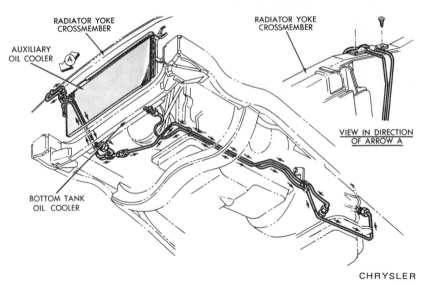

RADIATOR YOKE
CROSSMEMBER

RADIATOR YOKE
CROSSMEMBER

AUXILIARY
OIL COOLER Ⓐ

VIEW IN DIRECTION
OF ARROW A

BOTTOM TANK
OIL COOLER

CHRYSLER

Fig. 4-4 Transmission cooling system

automatic transmission cooling

In cars equipped with automatic transmissions, the radiator is constructed to provide cooling for the transmission as well as for the engine. Water does not circulate through the transmission, however, when the transmission fluid—actually a special type of oil—flows through tubes in a separate area of the radiator, the fluid is cooled for recirculation through the transmission. Small metal tubes that carry the automatic transmisison fluid are connected to a small radiator beneath the main radiator, and lead under the engine to the transmission (Fig. 4-4).

operating pressure

A certain amount of water is lost to evaporation during engine operation and may need to be added weekly. Water is introduced into the cooling system through the opening at the top of the radiator when the cap is removed (Fig. 4-5). The radiator cap, securely tightened, excludes all air and prevents leakage, thus ensuring a certain amount of pressure in the system. This pressure is desirable because it raises the boiling point of the water and permits engine operation at a higher temperature, which increases engine efficiency.

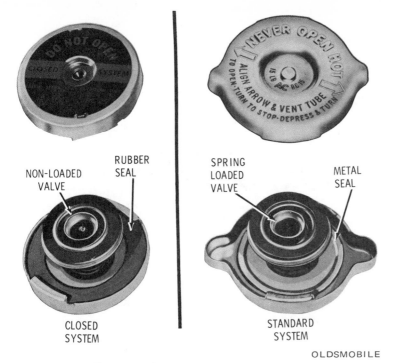

NON-LOADED VALVE   RUBBER SEAL   SPRING LOADED VALVE   METAL SEAL

CLOSED SYSTEM   STANDARD SYSTEM

OLDSMOBILE

Fig. 4-5 Radiator pressure caps

The radiator cap usually has a pressure-sensitive valve that releases excess pressure from around the bottom edge of the cap into a tube at the neck of the radiator filler. If pressure within the cooling system reaches an unsafe level, steam is blown out through this tube and emptied near the bottom of the radiator.

air conditioning condenser

An automobile with an air conditioner usually requires a second radiator. Sometimes this radiator is incorporated into the existing engine cooling system. More often, however, air cooling for the passenger section is provided by a completely separate unit called a *condenser*, which is similar to the engine radiator. The condenser carries heat from the passenger compartment and transfers it to the outside air. When servicing your car, it is important to distinguish between the air conditioning condenser and the engine radiator, because opening the lines to the condenser can be dangerous, and will result in loss of refrigerant, which is expensive to replace. The condenser is usually located in *front* of the engine radiator.

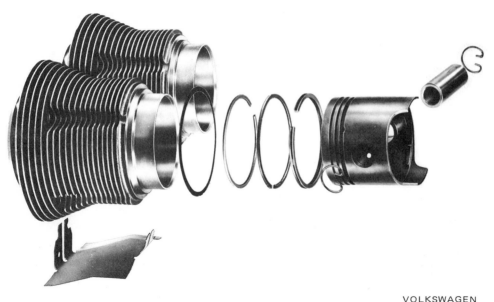

Fig. 4-6 Cylinder fins on an air cooled engine

Air-Cooled Systems

The Volkswagen and some other cars of European manufacture have air-cooled rather than water-cooled engines. The air-cooling system is based on the principle that air traveling over a large area carries away heat and transfers it to the atmosphere. The air must blow over a surface that is larger than the average cylinder if it is to transfer internal engine heat to the outside air. For this reason, the outside surface of the cylinders in a air-cooled engine is increased by means of fins or discs which are placed at close intervals along the cylinder's length (Fig. 4-6). Heat generated within the cylinder is transferred out to the surface of the fins where it can be swept away by the air flowing over the surface. The fins of the air-cooled engine serve the same function as the honeycomb structure of the radiator in a water-cooled system.

The natural flow of air past the fins is adequate for cooling small engines, as in motorcycles, light two-wheeled vehicles, lawn mower engines and other motorized portable equipment. Most automobile engines however, require a greater flow of air past the fins and the familiar engine-driven fan serves this purpose. The complete Volkswagen cooling system is shown in Fig. 4-7.

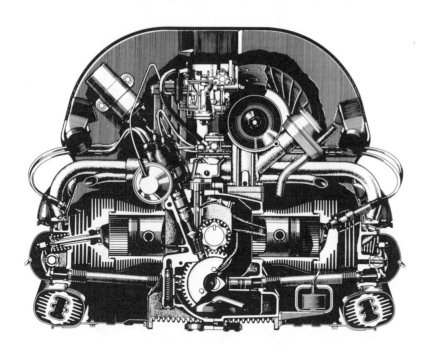

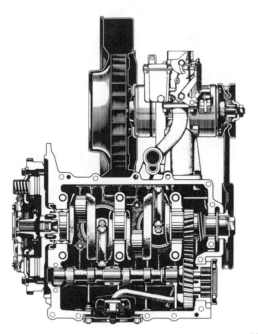

VOLKSWAGEN

Fig. 4-7 VW cooling system

The complete automobile cooling system is shown in Fig. 4-8, except for the passenger heater and automatic transmission loops. Connections between various parts of the system are sources of leaks and need to be checked periodically to avoid the serious trouble that can result from insufficient coolant.

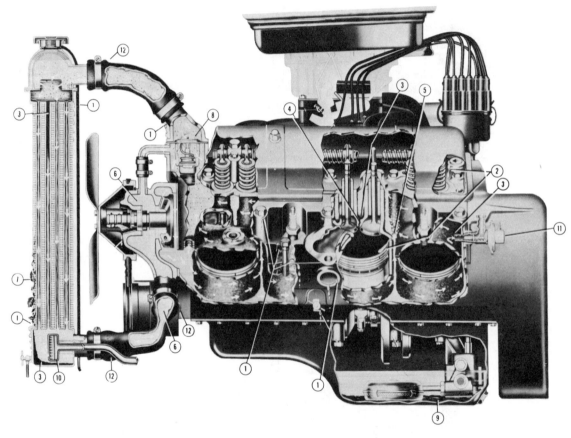

① EXTERNAL LEAKAGE	⑥ AIR SUCTION	⑪ HEATER CONTROL VALVE
② INTERNAL LEAKAGE	⑦ AIR FLOW RESTRICTIONS	⑫ HOSE DETERIORATION
③ RUST DEPOSITS	⑧ STUCK THERMOSTAT	⑬ FAN BELT DETERIORATION
④ HEAT CRACKS	⑨ SLUDGE FORMATION IN OIL	
⑤ EXHAUST GAS LEAKAGE	⑩ TRANSMISSION OIL COOLER	UNION CARBIDE

Fig. 4-8 Complete auto cooling system (water)

Other common causes of overheating are poor circulation of coolant because of a plugged system, or a malfunctioning thermostat, slipping fan belt, or broken water pump. Most of these can be avoided by proper maintenance and inspection. Overheating can also result from pulling too heavy a load or pulling up a long hill in too high a gear, improper engine timing, or from very low tire pressure. If you follow good preventive maintenance practice and drive within the capabilities of the engine, the cooling system should give little trouble.

An overheated engine can be destroyed if it is operated for any length of time at an unusually high temperature.

The Coolant

Water alone is a fairly effective coolant. It has the obvious disadvantage, however, that in cold weather it freezes and expands, causing damage to the engine block, radiator, water pump, hoses, thermostat, and so on. For this reason, the water is mixed with *antifreeze,* a fluid that will not freeze except at temperatures lower than those normally encountered. Alcohol is an inexpensive antifreeze that has been used for many years. It is a poor coolant, however, because it boils away, reducing the antifreeze characteristics of the remaining coolant. Cooling systems filled with a water-alcohol mixture tend to overheat when the air temperature rises much above freezing.

The antifreeze used commonly is ethylene glycol, which is sold under a variety of brand names, each mixed with various additives. This mixture has a dual advantage—not only does it freeze at a lower temperature than pure water, it also boils at a higher temperature, thus permitting a far wider operating range than can be achieved with water alone.

As noted earlier, modern high-temperature engines operate above the boiling point of water, thus need pressurization of the cooling system. As an additional precaution to prevent overheating, ethylene glycol (or "permanent") antifreeze should be used even during warm weather. It is a *must* for cars that are pulling a heavy load or have the extra burden of an air conditioning system.

The best cooling mixture is about 50 percent water and 50 percent ethylene glycol. This mixture boils at a temperature of about 226°F and freezes at about —34°F. Claims as to the ability of various other additives to improve cooling have not been sufficiently proven in testing. None showed a significant improvement over the 50-50 mixture cited.

The engine coolant mixture should be changed every two years, or whenever the radiator water becomes rusty. The rusty look indicates that the mixture has lost its rust-preventive properties, as well as the lubricating qualities it must have to keep the water pump from wearing out. When changing the radiator coolant, it is a good idea to "flush" the entire cooling system to remove old coolant, sludge, and rust particles.

The Cooling System Flush

Service stations have special equipment that permits a quick flush of the cooling system without dismantling it to the extent described here. By following the procedure outlined here, however, you will be able to inspect each of the vital cooling system parts and perform the radiator flush with the aid of a garden hose in about 20 minutes.

First, bring the engine up to operating temperature, turn the car heater on to its hottest position, then turn the engine off. Inspect the radiator cap for rust; if it is encrusted with rust, replace it with a new one when the flush is completed.

"At least it's nothing irreparable, like a flat tire."

Some cars have two valves, called *petcocks*, located on the bottom of the radiator near the lowest part of the engine block near the back. When the radiator cap is removed and both valves are opened, the entire cooling system can be drained. Opening just the radiator valve will drain the radiator and about half of the block.

On cars without petcocks, the lower radiator hose must be disconnected to drain the system.

Open the radiator and engine block petcocks, and drain out as much coolant as possible. Put the radiator cap back on. Disconnect both the top and bottom radiator hoses from the radiator only. Hose clamps like those in Fig. 4-9a can be loosened with a screwdriver, while the wire hose clamps (Fig. 4-9b) can be very difficult to remove without special pliers (Fig. 4-9b). These pliers are not expensive and save frustration and skinned knuckles.

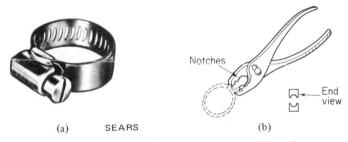

(a) SEARS (b)

Fig. 4-9 (a) Hose clamp, (b) wire hose clamp and hose clamp pliers (Note notches in the jaws to secure wire)

Inspect the radiator hoses. If they are cracked or bulging, replace them. If the new ones are hard to push in place, use clear petroleum jelly as a lubricant. (Do *not* use chassis or wheel-bearing grease as its additives attack rubber.)

flushing the radiator and block

Insert a garden hose in the bottom radiator hose hole, stuffing a dishrag or hand towel around it to create a seal. Turn on the water full force and let it run through the radiator and out of the hose-fitting at the top until the water flows clear and clean. The radiator is now flushed, actually "backflushed" since water was forced to flow "backwards" through it. This does a better job of cleaning and breaking loose chips of rust than a "forward" flush from the top down would have done.

Remove the thermostat from the engine block. Replace the thermostat *housing* (without the thermostat) on the block. Stuff the garden hose and rag in the top hose that is attached to the engine, turn on the water full blast and continue running water through the engine block until the water coming from the bottom hose runs clear.

radiator cleaner

If large chips of rust come out of the block or the radiator, the system is exceptionally rusty or dirty. In this case, buy a can of chemical radiator cleaner, hook the hoses back up, and use the cleaner according to the directions on the container. Then disconnect and flush the system a second time. A properly maintained system seldom needs this double flushings.

interior heater

Inspect the small hoses from the water pump to the car's interior heater. If the hoses are cracked, they should be replaced. Even if the heater is not being used, coolant can be lost through a leak in one of these hoses, and the engine will overheat. Remove both hoses from the water pump (or other convenient point) and force water through the small heater radiator in the car, as was done with the main radiator and the block. When the water running out of the heater is clear, re-attach the heater hoses.

thermostat

If the thermostat is rusty, buy a new one. This is an inexpensive way to avoid trouble later. Install the thermostat, using a new gasket if needed. (Be sure to have a replacement gasket handy, or another car available in case you need to purchase a new gasket.) Observe the markings on the thermostat to ensure that it is installed right side up.

Reassemble the cooling system with such new parts as are necessary, close the petcocks, and fill with a 50-50 mixture of water and ethylene glycol. If you choose to refill the system with 100 percent water instead, be sure to add a can of rust inhibitor and water-pump lubricant. Failure to do this will find you servicing the cooling system again in a very short time.

Common Causes of Overheating

The procedure outlined above will reveal many of the conditions that can lead to overheating. Periodic checks of the various components of the cooling system and the interconnections between them will help avoid problems on the road. Other potential sources of overheating that are often overlooked include the radiator cap, belt slippage, and faulty "freeze plugs" (or "soft plugs") which can act as "escape valves" for expanding coolant in freezing conditions.

the radiator cap

The radiator cap in the modern pressurized system is designed to hold the system at a certain pressure, typically about 15 pounds per square inch. (Fig. 4-5) If the spring in the cap weakens, the superheated coolant can escape through the overflow hose and the engine will overheat. The easiest way to spot this problem is to check the overflow hose a few minutes after the engine is turned off. If any coolant is dripping from this hose, replace the radiator cap with a new one with the proper pressure range. Since the cap on the car may not have been the proper one, have someone at the parts house or service station look up the correct pressure range for your engine. Always buy a radiator cap with the pressure release lever as shown in Fig. 4-5. This lever enables you to release pressure from the system before removing the cap, thereby reducing the chance of being scalded.

The fan belt must be quite tight. A simple test is to grab the fan (with the engine shut off, of course) and see if you can twist it to make the pump pulley slip without moving the belt. If the pulley does slip, the belt is too loose. Once a belt is properly tightened, it will not loosen significantly until it is worn badly or cracked, perhaps to the point of breaking. Of course, a cracked belt should be replaced.

The common "vee" belts drive a variety of pumps on the car, including the water pump, the alternator (Chapter 8) the power steering pump, the smog pump, and the air conditioning pump. If one belt is in need of replacement, it is likely that the others are nearly worn out too. Some auto owners change all hoses and belts every two or three years to prevent the common road breakdowns caused by broken hoses and belts. This practice is not as extravagant as it might sound, since the labor involved in replacing four belts on a car "loaded" with accessories is little more than that required to replace just one.

There are many sizes of belts and hoses, and it is important to know exactly which ones are required for your particular engine and accessories. On a typical "one belt" auto engine, a main pulley on the engine crankshaft drives both the alternator and the water pump.

The alternator is held in place by two bolts; when they are both loosened slightly, the alternator will move enough to permit removal of the old belt. A new belt is put in its place, is pulled tight by pulling on the alternator, and the two bolts retightened. This process often requires two persons, one to pull the belt tight, and another to tighten the bolts. Belts for other pumps are installed in a similar fashion. In some cases, the only way to get the bolts tight enough is to use a pry bar such as the jack handle (or a broom handle). The movable pulley brackets on some cars have 1/2-in. square holes into which a breaker bar or torque wrench can be plugged.

Service stations have guides that give the proper amount for each belt. Your neighborhood station attendant will probably provide this information. In general, however, just pull the new belt as tight as you can without breaking it (or the alternator case), and it will stretch slightly to the proper tension as it "breaks in."

Core Hole Plugs (Coolant)

Front

Block Drain Plug Location (Coolant)

AMERICAN MOTORS

Fig. 4-10 Holes in engine block for freeze plugs

Belt slippage can be caused by oil also. It is easy to get oil on a belt when checking the level of engine oil or some other fluid. The slipping belt then allows some pump to run below its necessary speed.

freeze plugs (soft plugs)

Leaks can occur around the so-called "freeze plugs." These small round plugs, which resemble paint-can lids, are pressed into holes in the block (Fig. 4-10) and provide access to the water jacket if major cleaning is required. They also provide a measure of protection in extremely cold weather. If the water in the engine-cooling system should freeze, the freeze plugs will push out, thus relieving the pressure and reducing the possibility that the block will crack. The wise motorist will occasionally check the freeze plugs and replace any that show signs of leaking. It is much less expensive to install new freeze plugs than to replace the block.

The carburetor
and engine fuel system

PART I – HOW IT WORKS

The carburetor was earlier explained as being similar to a perfume atomizer which sprayed gasoline into the engine intake. Following that, modification was made and the atomizer nozzle was placed in a venturi so that passing air would draw gasoline mist with it on its way into the engine. This idea is not as farfetched as it might seem, for Frank Duryea, who is credited with making and selling the first commercially successful gasoline automobile in America in 1893, fashioned the carburetor for his first car from a perfume atomizer and an alcohol lamp.

The basic function of the carburetor is to provide a mixture of fuel and air in the proper proportion for efficient combustion. In view of the wide range of engine speeds and climatic conditions in which the internal combustion engine must operate, the solution to the carburetion problem is not an easy one. The temperature of the intake air can vary from below zero to well above 100°F; air flow can increase up to one hundred times from idle to high speed; engine load conditions vary from near zero to extremely high (as in climbing hills or high speed passing); and air pressure ranges widely from sea level to high mountain roads. The carburetor must be a flexible apparatus indeed to provide efficient vaporization of the fuel and the proper mixture of fuel and air for the engine under such diverse conditions.

Basic Carburetor Components

All carburetors in common use in passenger cars are based on the principle of the *venturi*, which usually is positioned as shown in the simplified carburetor of Fig. 5-1.

The fuel supply for the carburetor comes from a chamber attached to the side of the venturi. Fuel is pumped into this "float bowl," as it is called, to an established level controlled by a float valve similar to that in the tank of a flush toilet. As the liquid is drawn out, a float on the surface of the liquid lowers and opens a valve, which allows fuel from the main supply to flow into the bowl. As fuel is introduced into the bowl through the open valve, the fuel level rises; when it has reached the pre-set level, the valve closes again and the flow of fuel into the chamber is stopped. Through this arrangement the carburetor float bowl is kept filled with fuel but is not allowed to overflow.

The fuel flows from the bottom of the float bowl to a spray nozzle positioned at the low-pressure section of the venturi. A valve called the *metering jet* is set in the path of the fuel on its way to the venturi. The metering jet controls the amount of fuel that can flow through the passage and, ultimately, to the engine.

As fuel is withdrawn, air enters the float chamber through a port, called the *bowl vent*, in the top of the chamber above the normal fuel level. Without this provision, a vacuum would be created above the fuel after a small quantity had been taken from the chamber, and this vacuum would prevent the removal of any more fuel.

A basic carburetor incorporating these features is shown in Fig. 5-2. Note that the nozzle is positioned in the venturi above the level of fuel in the float bowl. This arrangement is necessary to prevent fuel from flowing out of the carburetor and into the engine when it is not running.

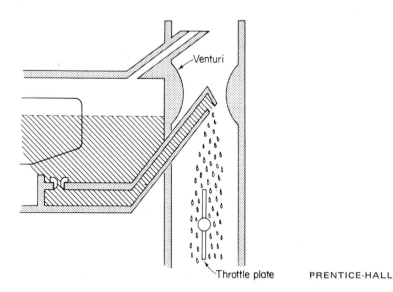

Venturi

Throttle plate   PRENTICE-HALL

Fig. 5-1 Simple carburetor showing fuel chamber, venturi, and nozzle

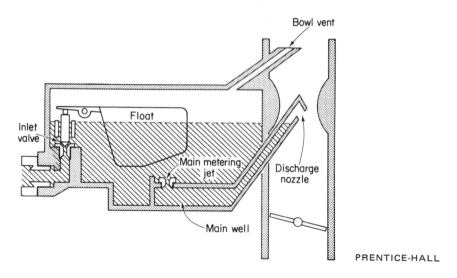

Bowl vent

Float

Inlet valve

Main metering jet

Discharge nozzle

Main well

PRENTICE-HALL

Fig. 5-2 Basic carburetor showing float valve fuel control system

the throttle valve

The throttle valve is a disc in the carburetor throat, well below the venturi section. The disc is pivoted at its center. When positioned horizontally, it completely blocks the tube; in a vertical position, it leaves the tube nearly totally open. The throttle valve is controlled by the accelerator pedal inside the car. When the pedal is all the way up, the throttle valve is in the closed (horizontal) position. As the pedal is pushed down, the throttle valve disc rotates until at full power the throttle valve is wide open. The flow of air-fuel mixture into the intake manifold, and hence the speed of the engine, is controlled in this manner.

idle and slow speed system

With the accelerator pedal all the way up and the throttle valve completely closed, fuel cannot be fed by means of the venturi and nozzle system. To allow engine operation at idle speed, a path is provided for fuel to enter the carburetor throat below the throttle valve. This fuel supply is controlled by a metering valve, the *idle mixture screw*. While the engine is idling, a substantial vacuum exists below the throttle valve, and the fuel can be sucked out of

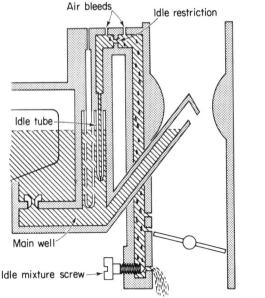

Fig. 5-3 Illustrating how an idle feed system can be included in the simple carburetor

the float chamber upwards through the *idle tube* to very nearly the top of the float chamber and through the idle screw valve. This system is illustrated in Fig. 5-3. The speed of the engine idle can be adjusted by adjusting the idle mixture screw or by adjusting the "at rest" position of the throttle valve.

choke and fast idle

When the engine is cold or has not been operated for a long time, evaporation, drainage, or leakage may lower the level of fuel in the float bowl. In this situation, the fuel supplied by the venturi and idle system alone might not be sufficient to start the engine.

The *choke valve* is designed to facilitate engine starts and warmup. This valve, which is similar to the throttle valve, is located at the top of the carburetor throat. The choke controls the flow of air into the carburetor. Because the choke is positioned at the *air horn*, the main air entrance for the fuel system, the whole engine operates as a vacuum pump when the choke is closed. Since little air can come in past the closed choke valve when the engine is cranked, each downstroke of the pistons will create a vacuum inside the carburetor below the choke valve. This vacuum draws fuel out of the carburetor ports leading into the float bowl just as one would drink soda through a straw.

By the time the engine starts, the vacuum will have increased greatly, and if the choke valve remains fully closed, the engine will draw in too much fuel and flood itself, run exceedingly rough, or stall. It is, necessary, therefore, to at least partially open the choke as soon as the engine starts. On cars with manual chokes this is a relatively simple matter, since the choke control is brought up to the dash as a pull handle. When preparing to start, the operator pulls the handle all the way out to close the choke valve. When the engine starts, the operator pushes the choke control in part way and, as the engine warms up to proper operating temperature, the choke control is pushed farther in until the choke valve is completely open. If the choke control is left out even slightly, however, fuel consumption will increase greatly, the engine will run poorly, and engine wear will increase. For this reason and for the sake of convenience, modern automobiles are nearly all equipped with automatic choke systems.

the anti-stall dash pot

In some cars, notably those with automatic transmissions, the engine has a tendency to stall if the throttle is released quickly. To overcome this problem, a *dash pot* is introduced into the throttle linkage (Fig. 5-4). A dash pot is similar to the devices used on some doors to slow the rate of closing just enough that the door will not slam.

the accelerator pump

When an engine is operating at a steady speed and the throttle is suddenly opened, the engine will not immediately respond. To eliminate this problem, the carburetor is equipped with an *accelerator pump*, which squirts an extra supply of fuel into the air stream going to the manifold when the accelerator is depressed. This provides fuel for the initial acceleration until the fuel feed system has had time to respond to the increased demands.

(a)

(b)

Fig. 5-4 Anti-stall dash pots (a) or return checks (b) installed on the carburetor

Air Cleaners

Clean air is essential to good operation of both the carburetor and the engine, since the air ingested by the carburetor will come in contact with valves and pistons in the engine. If the air coming into the system is not free of dust, dirt, and grit, engine wear will increase markedly. Small particles of dust can collect on valves and ports in the carburetor and reduce the efficiency of carburetion. In severe cases such contamination can stop fuel flow altogether.

For these reasons, all the air entering the carburetor must first pass through an air filter, or air cleaner, which is positioned over the carburetor air horn. There are several types of air cleaners, most of which fall into two categories: so-called "wet" air cleaners and "dry" air cleaners.

wet air cleaners

Two wet systems are in common use on modern automobiles. The *oil wetted* air cleaner is a doughnut-shaped, loosely packed, copper mesh. This mesh is similar to the copper pot cleaners often used in kitchens. The copper mesh is soaked in heavy oil before it is installed on the carburetor. Air passing through this environment will come in contact with the oily surface and a large proportion of the dirt and dust carried along with the air will be deposited on the oily surface.

The *oil bath* type of air cleaner combines an oil wetted filter with a second-stage cleaner consisting of a large, flat, round pan, the bottom of which is covered with oil to a depth of about one inch. The air entering the system first passes through the oil wetted mesh; a system of barriers or baffles then reverses the air flow inside the filter and directs it over the surface of the oil in the pan. This air motion causes particles still suspended in the air after the first filtering to fall into the oil bath. As the air sweeps over the oil, fine dust particles are deposited on the surface. Dust collected in this manner sinks to the bottom of the oil bath and only cleaned air is allowed to reach the carburetor.

dry air cleaners

Dry air cleaners are by far the most common in modern automobiles, primarily because they are very efficient and are easily serviced (Fig. 5-5). There are two general types of dry air cleaner: paper element and polyurethane element. The paper element air cleaner is made of a special paper, similar to that used in coffee pot filters, formed into a long corrugated strip and then wound spiral

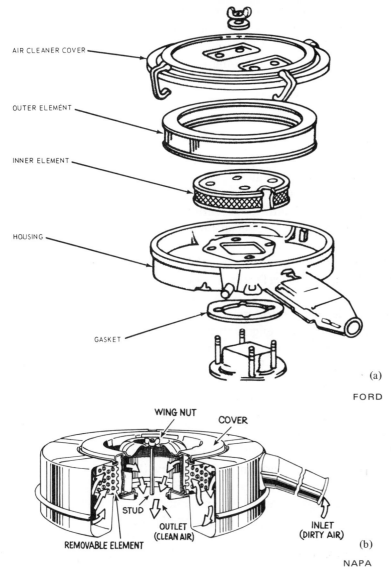

AIR CLEANER COVER

OUTER ELEMENT

INNER ELEMENT

HOUSING

GASKET

(a)

FORD

WING NUT

COVER

STUD

OUTLET
(CLEAN AIR)

INLET
(DIRTY AIR)

REMOVABLE ELEMENT

(b)

NAPA

Fig. 5-5 (a) Exploded view of a dry-type air cleaner of filter
(b). The filter of figure (a) assembled and ready for installation on the carburetor and cutaway view

fashion into a doughnut-like configuration. Air flows from the outside to the center, passing through several thicknesses of filter
paper before it reaches the carburetor inlet. Particles of dirt and
dust cannot pass through the tiny pores of the filter paper and
therefore do not find their way into the carburetor.

Polyurethane element filters are made of a soft plastic foam, similar in appearance to the plastic sponges sold for household cleaning chores or car washing. This type of filter is positioned in a metal support in such a way that all the air going into the carburetor must pass through the maze of polyurethane bubbles. Removal of dust particles by this means is very efficient.

Carburetor Modifications

The principles discussed above apply to all basic types of carburetors. In practice, the carburetors of modern automobiles can become quite complex. They may have additional features such as transfer ports, multiple venturi systems, or special high-speed jet arrangements. An individual carburetor may have several "barrels," resulting in a system that is equivalent to several separate carburetors. Such systems are what the mechanic refers to as "two-barrel" or "four-barrel" carburetors.

In *fuel injection* systems, the carburetor merely takes in air while the fuel is sprayed or injected into the engine directly through each intake valve. The main advantage of fuel injection in gasoline engines is better control of fuel quantity and improved combustion efficiency. An engine provided with fuel injection will burn more of the fuel taken into the combustion chamber, and the engine exhaust will contain fewer pollutants than that of the same engine equipped with conventional carburetion.

The early pioneers of fuel injection on modern gasoline engines were Mercedes-Benz and Volkswagen of Germany. Early Corvette engines were provided with fuel injection systems. The Corvette fuel injection system was discontinued in the 1950s, but Chevrolet has returned to it in recent years as a part of the continuing battle against air pollution. Current interest in fuel injection stems from its effective reduction of smog-producing pollutants.

The Fuel Supply System

In most of today's automobiles, the fuel tank is located at the back of the car and the carburetor is mounted on the engine near the front. Exceptions are cars with rear mounted engines. The conventional configuration is shown in Fig. 5-6. The fuel travels

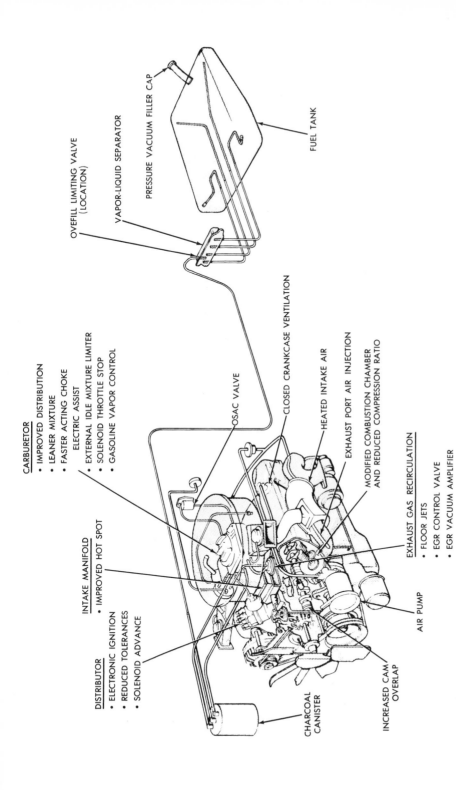

CHRYSLER

CARBURETOR
- IMPROVED DISTRIBUTION
- LEANER MIXTURE
- FASTER ACTING CHOKE
- ELECTRIC ASSIST
- EXTERNAL IDLE MIXTURE LIMITER
- SOLENOID THROTTLE STOP
- GASOLINE VAPOR CONTROL

OVEFILL LIMITING VALVE
(LOCATION)

VAPOR-LIQUID SEPARATOR

PRESSURE VACUUM FILLER CAP

FUEL TANK

OSAC VALVE

CLOSED CRANKCASE VENTILATION

HEATED INTAKE AIR

EXHAUST PORT AIR INJECTION

MODIFIED COMBUSTION CHAMBER
AND REDUCED COMPRESSION RATIO

EXHAUST GAS RECIRCULATION
- FLOOR JETS
- EGR CONTROL VALVE
- EGR VACUUM AMPLIFIER

AIR PUMP

INTAKE MANIFOLD
- IMPROVED HOT SPOT

DISTRIBUTOR
- ELECTRONIC IGNITION
- REDUCED TOLERANCES
- SOLENOID ADVANCE

INCREASED CAM
OVERLAP

CHARCOAL
CANISTER

Fig. 5-6 Showing all of the essential parts of the fuel system
from the tank to the carburetor

91

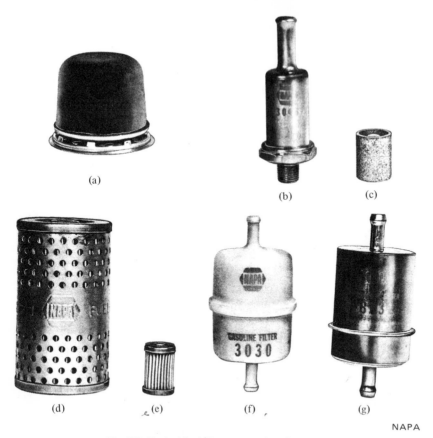

(a)

(b)   (c)

(d)   ₑ(e)   (f)   (g)

NAPA

Fig. 5-7 Typical fuel filters: a, c, d, and e are replaceable inserts, while b, f, and g are complete filter units

from the tank to the carburetor through a pipe system. Impetus for the fuel movement is provided by a *pump* installed in the pipe. A filter (Fig. 5-7) is placed in the fuel line, usually close to the carburetor, to remove any contaminants just before the fuel enters the carburetor so that recontamination cannot occur. In some instances, the fuel filter is built into the carburetor itself. Fuel filters should be replaced every year or two.

the fuel pump

Most American cars use a diaphragm-type fuel pump driven by an arm that extends into the engine and rides on a lobe on the engine cam shaft. A lobe on the cam shaft imparts a reciprocating motion to the arm which, in turn, works the diaphragm and causes the pump to operate. A common location for this pump is low down on one side of the engine. Other locations are possible, depending on engine design.

Some fuel pumps are electrically operated and can be placed at almost any point in the fuel line. It is customary to place it under the hood in the engine compartment, but in some cars it is located under the car in the fuel line or even inside the fuel tank.

the fuel tank

In most passenger vehicles, the gasoline tank is under the trunk floor. In some station wagons the tank is on one side above a rear wheel. In some cases, the gasoline tank is formed in the trunk floor panel and a cover, held in place by screws and sealed by means of a gasket, serves as the top of the tank and the floor of the trunk. For many years, air was allowed to enter the tank through a small hole in the cap as gasoline was withdrawn. This practice has given way to a sealed gasoline tank system in which the gasoline tank cap forms a tight seal and a slight pressure is allowed to develop in the tank to permit fuel flow. The sealed system prevents fuel evaporation, which was a significant source of air pollution.

In the past, most gasoline tanks were lined with lead, which resists the chemical reactions caused by gasoline. This practice has also been stopped in an effort to reduce lead contaminants in the air.

Most fuel tanks have a pipe plug or similar fitting in the bottom to facilitate draining. Emptying the tank is required when the car is transported by ship or air or to remove contaminants.

PART 2—MAINTENANCE

The engine converts chemical energy into mechanical energy to power the vehicle. The chemical most commonly used in autos is gasoline, which is a derivative of petroleum. Special additives control the performance characteristics of the fuel, such as its vaporization temperature, burning rate, and combustion by-products.

The fuel must remain in a liquid state until vaporized by the carburetor. If the fuel is allowed to vaporize in the line, since the fuel pump cannot pump vapor the engine will stop. This phenomenon is called *vapor lock*.

Fuels are blended differently for warm and cold weather. In cold weather, fast vaporization is desired for easy starting, and the vaporizing temperature of the appropriate fuel will be low. If such a fuel is used in a warmer region, vapor lock may occur, even though the day may not be really hot. To avoid it, buy local gas to dilute the "cold country" fuel with fuel mixed for warmer temperature operation.

Vapor lock is most common in the spring, when the fuel being sold may still be blended for fast starting in cold weather. It also can occur under some conditions even when the appropriate fuel is used. The temperature in the engine compartment may rise well above the vaporizing temperature of the fuel, particularly in slow or stop-and-go driving when the normal flow of cooling air is not present. The engine will stall and not restart, as it does not receive fuel.

Several things can be done. The simplest is just to open the hood and wait 15 minutes or more until the engine compartment cools down below the vaporizing temperature and the gas in the fuel line and fuel pump returns to a liquid state. This process can be speeded up by pouring cold water on the fuel line and fuel pump, or saturating towels with water and placing them on the line and pump.

octane rating

Octane Rating refers to the burning rate of a particular fuel. What is needed is a controlled burning and expansion. Without certain additives, gasoline burns much too fast, literally exploding in the combustion chamber. If the fuel burns too fast, the engine will "ping" and the internal parts such as pistons, rods, and bearings will be subjected to extreme stress. A "ping" is a "tinny rattling sound," which may sound like gravel hitting the underside of the car. It only occurs when the accelerator is depressed and the engine

WALL STREET JOURNAL

"You're out of gas."

is working hard. An engine stressed so badly that it pings may suffer major damage in a short time.

Tetraethyl lead or a newer substitute additive is used to slow a fuel's burning rate, as indicated by its octane rating, and reduce pinging. The higher the octane rating, the greater the reduction in burning rate. So-called "regular" gas has an octane rating of about 92, and so-called "premium" gas has an octane rating of about 100. Some newer "Wankel" or "rotary" engines can operate well on fuel with octane ratings as low as 70.

An engine's compression ratio (Chapter 2) is a major factor in determining the maximum allowable burning rate of the fuel it may use. Fuel under higher pressure burns faster, necessitating a higher octane rating to slow the burning rate back down to optimum. For this reason, powerful, high-compression engines need "premium" fuel, while lower compression engines can run on "regular." Some engines with still lower compression ratios can run on fuels with octane ratings of 80 or below.

Air pollution problems related to the burning of fuels with lead additives have stimulated efforts by refiners to solve the octane problem with different additives. One interesting result of these efforts is the discovery that lead does more in the burning process than just control the burning rate. When the lead was completely removed and other additives used, engines were found to suffer burned valves to an alarming extent. Unless a car's engine was designed *specifically* to run on "low lead" or "no lead" gasoline by the incorporation of especially designed valves and other parts, you should NOT use these fuels. The price paid in engine damage by so doing is excessive. Generally speaking, no-lead fuels should never be used in cars manufactured before 1970. For newer models, they should be used only if permitted by the manufacturer and specifically indicated in the operating manual.

Keeping the Fuel System Clean

Fuels also vary in amount of by-products they release during combustion. Fuels that burn "dirty" foul the spark plugs quickly and cause the engine to "miss"—that is, combustion may not occur in every cylinder when its turn comes.

the carburetor

During the life of a car, from 5,000 to 10,000 gallons of gas may be pumped through the fuel system. This gas will leave a residue, which in time may "gum up" the fuel system. The carburetor is particularly susceptible to this problem because of the very small holes through which the fuel and fuel/air mixture must pass. About every 30,000 to 50,000 miles the carburetor must be "boiled out" or "overhauled," that is, taken completely apart and cleaned in a powerful solvent. Sometimes it is possible to merely pour a carburetor cleaner through it and postpone the "boilout" for a time. Overhaul of a complicated modern carburetor can be quite expensive, and if you don't plan on keeping the car for a long time, the use of a "pour through" cleaner may be preferable. (Follow the directions on the can carefully.) Regardless of the fuel, unless the engine is driven at full operating temperature and speed from time to time, the plugs will foul and the combustion chamber will become encrusted with carbon. For this reason, a car will give much better service and life if it is taken out on the highway and "exercised" for at least 15 minutes every several weeks.

The air cleaner removes the impurities in the air before it is mixed with the fuel. All air entering the carburetor must pass through the air cleaner, which collects dirt and dust particles (not to mention bugs, leaves, etc.).

Dry Filters. Remove the air cleaner as shown in Fig. 5-8, and hold it up to the light. If you can see light through it, it does not need replacement; if it is opaque, however, it is clogged with contaminants, which will restrict the flow of air. With an insufficient air supply, the fuel mixture is too "rich," resulting in wasted gas and degraded engine performance. The expected life of a dry filter ranges from one day to five years, depending on the cleanliness of the air it must filter.

Polyurethane filters are highly efficient but require more servicing than the paper filter discussed above. About once a year, a filter of this type should be carefully cleaned in kerosene, dipped in engine oil, and put back on the engine. For reasons of convenience, some owners prefer to replace polyurethane filters with paper elements.

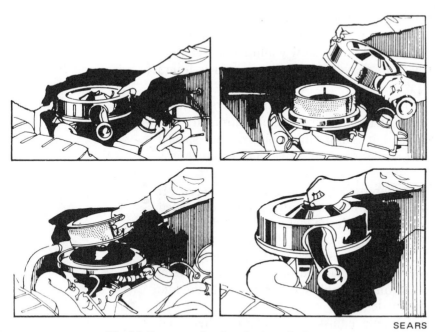

SEARS

Fig. 5-8 Remove and replace dry-type air cleaner

Wet Filters. The wet filter uses an oil trap to catch dust and bugs as described earlier. To service the wet filter, one must remove the entire assembly from atop the carburetor, pour out the dirty oil, wipe out the oil trap, and refill it with clean oil. Any heavy oil will do (30 weight or more), just so it's sticky. The regular engine oil usually will serve the purpose. Be careful not to exceed the specified amount of oil or it will splatter all over the inside of the engine compartment. The condition of the oil and depth of entrapped dirt should be checked each time the engine oil filter is changed.

Carburetor Adjustment

Adjustment of this fairly complicated device is best left to a qualified mechanic. There are two minor adjustments, however, that can be accomplished at home.

Some carburetors have an "idle *mixture* screw," which can be adjusted to achieve the proper mixture of fuel for your altitude under idle conditions. You will need a tachometer which indicates the engine speed in revolutions per minute. (Some sports cars have tachometers mounted on the dash along with the other instruments.) Unless a portable tachometer is available, one person makes the adjustments while another reads the tachometer on the dash. With the engine warm and idling, slowly adjust the idle mixture screw in and out with a screwdriver until the point is found where the engine idles fastest.

Because of the danger of misadjusting the carburetor so that it does not meet the smog regulations, some manufacturers are factory-setting the mixture and it is not adjustable without special tools and parts. On most modern cars, there is no *high speed mixture adjustment.*

The other common carburetor adjustment is for *idle speed.* It is just an adjustment of how far the accelerator pedal is depressed when your foot is not on it. Watch the tachometer while making this simple adjustment to obtain the specified engine idling speed.

If the car has an automatic transmission or air conditioning, you must find out whether the car should be in neutral or drive, and whether the air conditioner should be on or off while the idle speed adjustment is being made.

Aside from the two simple adjustments described here and servicing the air filter, the carburetor is best left alone unless you wish to move from the realm of maintenance into that of repair.

All gasoline comes from a refinery, perhaps through a pipeline to a distributing point, where it is sold to dealers and distributors in the region as the ordinary *pipeline product* (PLP). At this point, certain additives are mixed, ranging from simple coloring to more significant (and patented) additives. As far as the auto owner is concerned the selection of a fuel is based on the engine performance it delivers. A fuel's vaporization characteristics (octane and volatility) are the main factors in determining its suitability for a given engine. There is little to be gained by buying expensive "premium" fuel if an engine was designed to run on regular fuel. There is, in fact, real danger in this practice. For one thing, fuel burning too slowly for a particular engine can also burn the valves. Aircraft engine manufacturers have been known to void the engine warranty if fuels were used with a higher octane rating than specified.

The major "brand" differences between fuels are in the advertising. The gasoline offered at a "cut rate" gas station is often the same as the product sold by a major dealer down the street. It may even have been delivered in the same gasoline tanker truck. The only difference is the price and the broader range of services offered by the major brand dealer.

The reliability of gasoline stations often varies with the nature of their clientele. One that caters to a neighborhood clientele and does not depend on tourists may be a good place to buy your gas. The station operator must supply quality gas that satisfies his customers or they will not return. Tourist-oriented stations, on the other hand, whether cut rate or major brands, do not rely on repeat business; at such stations, price may have little to do with quality.

Some tank truck owners, called "wild catters," buy inferior gas from a refinery for a low price, and sell it for less than the usual wholesale price. The only stations that usually dare buy "wildcat gas" are those with a continually changing set of customers.

If you should get a tank of very bad gas, you can either drive until it is about half gone and then refill the tank with very high octane gas to bring the octane rating up; in extreme cases it may be necessary to siphon out the bad fuel with a hose, or drain the tank.

The exhaust and emission control systems

PART I—HOW IT WORKS

We have seen that the operation of the internal combustion engine depends on the burning of fuel in each of the combustion chambers in sequence. If the engine exhaust ports were simply left open to the atmosphere, the engine and passenger compartments would soon fill with exhaust gas, which would impair engine performance and subject passengers to the deadly fumes. To prevent this, the exhaust system receives waste gases from the exhaust manifold and carries them to the rear of the car where they can be more safely discharged and dissipated in the atmosphere. Single and dual exhaust systems are shown in Fig. 6-1. Differences between these two arrangements are discussed later in this chapter.

system components

The exhaust system has three main components: exhaust piping, muffler and resonator, and tail pipe, all fabricated from heat-resistant steel (Fig. 6-1). In addition to providing a passage

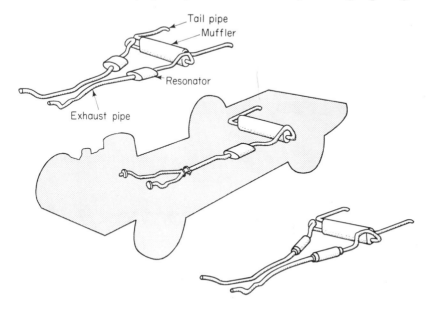

Fig. 6-1 Single and dual exhaust systems

for burned gases, the exhaust system, specifically the muffler section, quiets the exhaust noise generated by the operating engine. Each discharge of exhaust from a cylinder creates a noise like the blast from a gun. Each blast is the result of a "pulse" of hot gas being released through an exhaust valve. The noise level can be significantly reduced by routing these exhaust pulses through a muffler. The action of the muffler might be compared to a person blowing into a balloon with a small leak: The air may be blown into the balloon in short puffs, but it will leak out through the hole in a steady stream.

When a single muffler does not adequately deaden engine noise, a secondary muffler known as a *resonator* is used. The resonator usually is positioned in front of the main muffler and joined to it with a short length of exhaust tubing called an *interconnecting pipe*. The resonator resembles the muffler but is much smaller. Some mufflers have a built-in resonator section, as described below.

After passing through the muffler, the exhaust gases are directed through the tail pipe to the extreme rear of the vehicle where they are discharged.

mufflers and resonators

Automobile mufflers fall into two general types: the straight-through type and the reverse-flow type. Figure 6-2 shows a cutaway or a typical muffler. Regardless of the internal configuration, the muffler must allow for both the expansion of the gases and a certain amount of cooling. In accomplishing these two functions, however, the muffler must not impede the flow of gases sufficiently to cause significant "back pressure," which in turn will restrict the

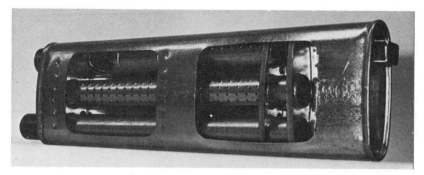

PRENTICE-HALL

Fig. 6-2 Cutaway view showing the interior of a muffler

flow of exhaust gases through the valves and out of the combustion chamber. High back pressure will reduce engine efficiency, hurt gasoline mileage, and in extreme cases, result in engine damage.

Muffler life depends on the operating environment and the driving habits of the owner. It is difficult to predict muffler life with any degree of certainty. Like the rest of the exhaust system, mufflers wear from the inside out. The metal is slowly eaten away from the inside by the corrosive action of acids condensed out of the exhaust gas as it cools. Less condensation occurs in the hotter sections of the system, and therefore they are less vulnerable to corrosion than the cooler sections. For this reason, the tail pipe is first to go, however, because of the large amount of condensation there and the great number of places where acids can collect. Some mufflers are lined with a lead, aluminum, or zinc coating to retard corrosive action and prolong muffler life. Others, known as *glass-packed mufflers* are packed with an acid-resistant fiber such as glass wool or rock wool, which helps deaden noises but does little to reduce corrosion.

A *unitized muffler* contains both baffles and resonator in a single housing. The resonator section of a unitized muffler smoothes out any uneven flow of gases that may persist after the main muffling job has been done. In a straight-through, unitized muffler, the resonator section is usually an open space followed by a short length of muffler pipe similar to the main section. In a reverse-flow, unitized muffler, the resonator function is performed by the open areas between the separate sections of the muffler pipe within the housing (Fig. 6-2). A separate resonator is used when a unitized muffler cannot be accommodated in the space available under the car. This often is true of long, low cars with high performance engines.

single and dual exhaust systems

Most four-and six-cylinder cars are equipped with a single exhaust system, which is connected to a single exhaust manifold. In this arrangement, the gases collected by the exhaust manifold are discharged into the exhaust pipe and directed downward, through the pipe, to a position below the floor of the car and then rearward to the muffler. The muffler may be mounted in line with or across the car frame. Again, the position and the orientation of the muffler is determined largely by the amount of space available under the car.

In V engines equipped with two exhaust manifolds, one on either side of the engine, a *Y* pipe connects the two manifold outlets to a common junction leading to a single muffler (Fig. 6-1*b*).

Many cars equipped with V-8 and larger engines have dual exhaust systems. Some dual installations consist of two complete systems, one connected to each exhaust manifold on either side of the engine. A very common dual system uses a short interconnecting pipe, the *H* pipe, between the two engine banks, thus allowing each bank to share two smaller mufflers, one on each side. Some systems consist of two exhaust pipes and resonators followed by a dual muffler mounted across the frame of the car (Fig. 6-1*a* and *c*).

system interconnections and support elements

Exhaust system components must be tightly attached to one another to prevent leaks between the engine and the exhaust outlet at the rear of the car. This purpose usually is served by sturdy clamps at each joint in the system. In some cases, the joints are welded at the time of manufacture and no clamps are required. Welded joints make replacement nearly impossible for the average car owner.

The entire exhaust system must be suspended securely under the frame so that it does not interfere with other systems such as brake cables and hoses, transmission linkage, drive shaft, rear axles, and fuel lines. For this reason, the exhaust system tubing is bent to conform to the space available under the car. Once installed, the tubing is held in place by means of clamps, brackets, and hangers (Fig. 6-3). In most supports of this type, a fabric, plastic, or rubber element prevents the transmission of vibrations from the exhaust system into the passenger compartment.

Emission Control Systems

The particular form of air pollution which we call smog is not new. The discharge of smoke and fumes into the air and sunlight causes smog, whether the discharge originates in the internal combustion engine or in a volcanic eruption. Smog really began to develop as a major problem with the rapid proliferation of auto-

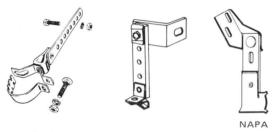

NAPA

Fig. 6-3 Types of hangers used to attach exhaust system parts to the underside of a car

mobiles in the late 1930s and early 1940s. After World War II, the number of automobiles on the highways of the world reached huge proportions, and smog began to plague the large cities.

The city of Los Angeles fell an early victim to smog because of its unusual combination of climate and topography. The city is situated in a bowl, or depression, facing the Pacific Ocean. There is cool air aloft, and great quantities of hot gases from factory chimneys and automobile exhausts rise from the city. When there is a wind, these gases are harmlessly dissipated. In the absence of wind, they remain trapped over the city in what weather observers call an *inversion*. Figure 6-4 shows an example of severe smog conditions.

sources of automobile pollution

In automobiles, most of the chemicals that cause smog come from evaporation of gasoline from the tank, the carburetor, or other leaks around the fuel system; vapors released through breather access to the crankcase; and the exhaust.

Gasoline is technically classified as a *hydrocarbon*. Unburned hydrocarbons that evaporate from the raw fuel or come out of the exhaust pipe as a result of incomplete combustion, contribute heavily to the formation of smog-producing air pollutants. If combustion in the engine was complete, the exhaust would contain only carbon dioxide and water, plus whatever air was not involved in the combustion process. Because combustion is not perfect and some of the unused air reacts with the by-products of the combustion process to form pollutants other than those originating in the cylinder, the exhaust is a witches' brew far removed from the innocuous carbon dioxide, water, and air.

LOS ANGELES COUNTY

Fig. 6-4 Two views of the same scene in Los Angeles, California, with and without smog. This shows what an extreme problem air pollution can be. It has been shown that most of the air pollution that causes this smog came from internal combustion engines.

An automobile engine running at normal speeds and in good adjustment will emit three basic pollutants: hydrocarbons (HC) from unburned gasoline, carbon monoxide (CO), and oxides of nitrogen (NO_x). Perhaps the best known of these pollutants is *carbon monoxide*. This deadly poison comes from combustion of a mixture of oxygen in the air and carbon from the burning hydrocarbon in the cylinder. A concentration of just 0.2 percent of carbon monoxide can be fatal, and this amount can accumulate in an enclosed one-car garage with an engine running for only three to four minutes.

Some of the unburned gasoline does not combine with air to form carbon monoxide; instead, it is emitted as a *hydrocarbon vapor*. *Oxides of nitrogen*, formed at high temperatures, are combinations of nitrogen, a harmless gas that makes up 80 percent of our atmosphere, and various amounts of oxygen.

One day's average driving for the typical engine without smog-suppressing devices will produce about 1.25 pounds of pollutant material. If the engine is out of adjustment or in need of repair, pollutants may run as high as four to five pounds. A few million cars operating in a heavily populated area can produce tremendous quantities of pollutants. The estimate for Los Angeles is 2,000 tons a day from automobiles alone. Even when a car is parked, gasoline evaporating from the fuel tank and the carburetor contributes to the smog problem in the form of hydrocarbon vapor.

Measures to control auto-caused pollution have been directed toward the sources outside the combustion chamber as well as those inherent in the combustion process itself. The first group of measures includes evaporation control systems, the PCV valve, unleaded fuels, and catalytic converters. Improved combustion has been sought through air injection systems, vacuum advance defeat, and combustion chamber modifications.

Carburetor and Fuel Tank Evaporation. To reduce hydrocarbon vapor escaping from the fuel system, engineers have developed the *fuel vapor recovery system*, which collects vapors from the carburetor and fuel tank and directs them to the engine intake to be

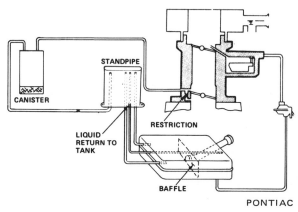

STANDPIPE

CANISTER

RESTRICTION

LIQUID
RETURN TO
TANK

BAFFLE

PONTIAC

Fig. 6-5 A system to prevent evaporation of hydrocarbon fuel (gasoline) from the fuel tank and fuel feed system

burned. Sometimes these vapors are condensed back into a liquid and returned to the tank for later use. Nearly all systems provide for (1) reduced heat transfer to the carburetor to minimize fuel vaporization; (2) closing off both the fuel tank and the carburetor float chamber so that they do not vent to the atmosphere; and (3) the use of charcoal cannisters similar to those in gas masks to *adsorb* (trap) the vapors. The charcoal in the cannisters acts as a magnet, attracting the vapors when they come near it. A typical system to control direct evaporation is illustrated in Fig. 6-5. Fuel from the tank is drawn by the fuel pump and delivered to the carburetor in the normal manner (Chapter 5). When the engine is running, all vapors are drawn into the engine with the normal fuel supply and burned. When the engine is turned off, the fuel remaining in the float chamber evaporates, and the vapors are directed through the *restriction* to the charcoal cannister where they are adsorbed.

Vapors forming in the fuel tank travel out of the fuel tank vent pipes to the *stand pipe* chamber where they cool and condense. The resulting liquid fuel then travels through the liquid return line back to the tank where it either recycles as vapor or is drawn off and fed to the carburetor as fuel. Evaporative cycling is at its greatest when the temperature is high.

Any vapor that does not condense in the stand pipe chamber may find its way through a restricted line to the charcoal canister. The restriction allows vapor to pass, but not liquid; thus, the canister cannot be flooded. A *check valve*, which allows fluid to flow

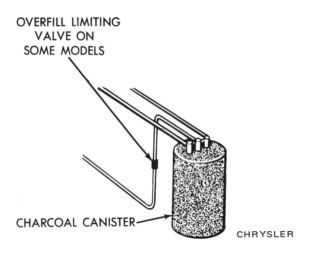

OVERFILL LIMITING
VALVE ON
SOME MODELS

CHARCOAL CANISTER

CHRYSLER

Fig. 6-6 A standpipe or liquid vapor separator returns condensed
fuel vapors to the fuel system

in only one direction, sometimes is used to protect the charcoal
canister. Fig. 6-6 shows a typical stand pipe and charcoal canister.

When the fuel tank is sealed off to control evaporation, there
is no way to relieve pressure if high temperatures cause expansion
of the fuel when the tank is full. Some vehicles incorporate a fuel
expansion tank inside the main fuel tank (Fig. 6-7); as the fuel
expands and pressure builds up in the main tank, some of the fuel
can go into the expansion tank, thus preventing excessive pressure
from developing. When the main tank is no longer full, fuel from
the expansion tank is released back into the main tank. A typical
complete evaporation control system is shown in Fig. 6-7.

The PCV Valve. In some systems, condensed fuel from vapor
in the carburetor is stored in the crankcase to be drawn off through
the PCV (*positive crankcase ventilation*) valve when the engine is
started. The PCV valve is perhaps the first smog-control device.

When the engine is running, some of the combustion products
will leak past the piston rings and find their way into the crankcase.
Some liquid fuel can enter the crankcase in the same way. The
lubricating oil, when heated, also gives off some polluting vapors.
Clearly, the crankcase must breathe to free itself of these fumes,
but if they are vented to the air, air pollution results. The PCV
system overcomes this problem.

Fumes from the crankcase are drawn up through a tube connected to the intake manifold so that they are routed back into the

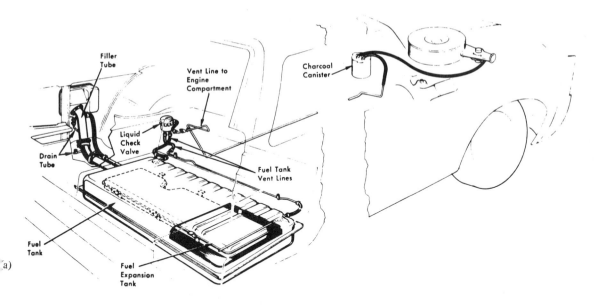

(a)

Fig. 6-7 Typical evaporation control system

combustion chamber to be burned. The PCV valve holds back the flow of air when the engine is idling so that a proper air-fuel mixture can be maintained. The valve opens during normal operation of the engine to allow free circulation and positive crankcase ventilation. Figure 6-8 shows the typical PCV systems of six-cylinder and V-8 engines. The PCV valve must be kept clean and freely operating to ensure proper engine operation and control of crankcase emissions.

Leaded Gasoline (*ETHYL*). Another effort to reduce combustion-caused air pollution is directed at the fuel itself. One of the problems that faced engineers in the early days of automobile development was the elimination of "ping" (Chapter 5). A significant breakthrough in solving that problem was the addition of tetraethyl lead, hence the term "Ethyl," which altered the combustion characteristics and stopped the pinging. It turns out, however, that the lead in gasoline is emitted in the engine exhaust as a form of gaseous compound, which if breathed can accumulate in the body and cause a variety of illnesses. Unleaded fuels have been developed in an effort to eliminate this source of pollution, but they are not suitable for all automobiles currently in use.

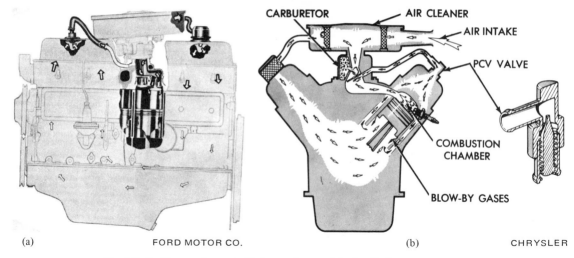

AIR INTAKE

PCV VALVE

COMBUSTION
CHAMBER

BLOW-BY GASES

(a)   FORD MOTOR CO.   (b)   CHRYSLER

Fig. 6-8 Positive crankcase ventilation system on (a) a 6-cylinder engine and (b) an 8-cylinder engine.

Catalytic Converters. Some of the other polluting gases in the exhaust can be reduced by the action of a *catalytic converter.* This device eliminates the most objectionable pollutants from the exhaust through catalytic action. Certain chemical changes will occur in the presence of a *catalyst* without affecting the catalytic agent itself. In effect, the exhaust gases are transformed, through contact with the catalyst, into less harmful substances. An effective catalyst for pollution control is platinum, which is expensive.

With leaded gasoline the lead soon forms a coating over the catalyst and makes it ineffective. The lead must be omitted from the fuel therefore if the catalytic converter is to work.

With the PCV valve, evaporation control systems, catalytic converters, and unleaded fuel, it appears that the limits have been reached in terms of reducing pollutants from sources *external* to the combustion chamber. Much of the pollution coming from the engine stems from inefficient combustion in the cylinders. It is to this second area that the engineers have directed their efforts to further improve the internal combustion engine in terms of minimizing air pollution.

Air Injection. Air injection is one approach to improved combustion. Fresh air is blown into the exhaust stream coming out of the exhaust valve, providing a fresh supply of oxygen that tends to continue to complete combustion of the burning gases as they leave the engine. In this *thermacter system,* an air pump forces air through a manifold system, which directs the air to the proper places in the exhaust system. A check valve prevents the exhaust from backing up into the air pump, and a bypass valve diverts the air to the atmosphere when it is not needed in the engine as, for example, during deceleration.

Vacuum Advance Defeat. Another approach to improved combustion is the *defeat of vacuum advance.* The vacuum developed in the intake manifold is evidence of engine speed and loading and has been used as a means of automatically adjusting the time when a spark occurs in the cylinder to ignite the fuel-air mixture. Such adjustment results in optimum engine performance, but in altering the burning time of the fuel it ultimately causes excessive emission of harmful exhaust products at times. The vacuum advance defeat system is designed to avoid advancing the timing when a harmful level of pollution might result.

The *combination emission control system* purports to overcome both the problems of high heat and dieseling (engine continues to run after the ignition switch is turned off) that accompany systems based on defeat of the vacuum advance. CEC system combines a series of actions on various components to defeat the vacuum advance system when necessary as when the car is driven in reverse, during a short period when the car is first started, or as on other systems, when the engine temperature rises too high. In cars with air conditioners, the CEC system employs a device to engage the air conditioning compressor clutch when the ignition is turned off. The resulting additional load on the engine helps to prevent dieseling.

Some smog control systems involve direct ignition timing alterations. One system employs a dual diaphragm vacuum advance mechanism that operates to adjust ignition timing to the optimum position for minimum pollution. As with many other systems, this system incorporates heat-sensing devices to override the smog control when the engine temperature exceeds safe limits.

When high engine temperatures require overriding the smog control system, as above, the natural result is that smog is produced. One approach to overcoming this obvious deficiency is the *thermostatically controlled air cleaner.* This device feeds warm air to the engine air intake during cold operation, as in cold climates or at inital startup time. By this means, cold engine performance is improved without requiring override of the smog prevention adjustment to timing.

Improvements in Combustion Chambers. Several internal improvements have been introduced in an effort to combat pollution.

Among these are longer stroke engines, which allow longer burning times in the cylinders and, thus, more complete combustion of the fuel; improved piston rings, which reduce the amount of blow-by and fuel leakage into the crankcase; and the redesign of combustion chambers to reduce the area-to-volume ratio. This last concept is based on the fact that the greater the surface area in the cylinder, the greater cooling that can take place; the result is less efficient combustion. The best configuration for this purpose would be a sphere, which is impossible to achieve in an operating engine. The hemispherical chamber yields the most efficient combustion. Wedge type chambers, those with sloping tops on the pistons usually found in L head engines, are the worst from the standpoint of smog.

Combined Systems. All the major auto manufacturers have incorporated most, if not all, of the above systems in their cars. One major company calls their overall system the "Improved Combustion System" (IMCO). Another manufacturer describes the all-inclusive smog control system as the "Controlled Combustion System" (CCS). The remaining member of the "Big Three" calls its system the "Cleaner Air System" (CAS). The last company also attacked the problem from the ignition standpoint, in effect making the ingition timing more precise and allowing for better control during "defeat." These measures tend to keep engine performance as high as possible while reducing pollutants to a minimum. The all-electric iginition system (Fig. 6-9) eliminates the mechanical breaker points, substituting a magnetic pulse generator (the reluctor and pickup coil) and usually also calls for an electronic ignition system.

effectiveness of smog-prevention measures

Efforts to reduce pollution caused by automobile engines have been so successful that some experts state that if all the cars now licensed in New York were late models equipped with the newer anti-smog apparatus, New York City's smog would be reduced to the pre-1939 level. Other authorities claim that 75 percent of the nation's automobile caused smog is generated by 25 percent of the licensed passenger cars—those manufactured prior to 1965. In a recent move to correct this situation, some states, cities and counties have enacted legislation requiring older cars be equipped with more modern emission control devices.

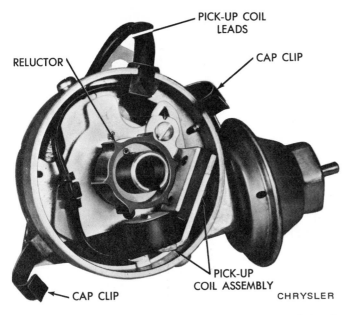

PICK-UP COIL
LEADS

RELUCTOR

CAP CLIP

PICK-UP
COIL ASSEMBLY

CHRYSLER

CAP CLIP

Fig. 6-9 Magnetic pulse generator system for the all-electric
ignition system

PART 2—MAINTENANCE

The Exhaust System

With the exception of exhaust systems that incorporate emission
control devices, the simple automobile exhaust system requires
almost no maintenance. The importance of the exhaust system
has already been stressed. Only after it has quietly done its job
for many tens of thousands of miles is it necessary to replace major
parts. Most exhaust system parts can be replaced at home with a
few special tools; however, the nature of that work is closer to
repair than maintenance, and beyond the scope of this book.

The only moving part of the exhaust system is the heat-riser
(Chapter 2), which is installed in the exhaust system near the
engine to hold back the heat from the manifold for faster engine
warmup (Fig. 6-12). If the heat-riser should become stuck in the
closed position, the engine will run very poorly, therefore, it should
be checked from time to time. If its operation is sluggish, application of a little penetrating oil should make it move more freely. If lubrication does not solve the problem, the heat-riser must be replaced.

Will you check the left front tire?

About once a year, you should go through the entire exhaust system and check every bolt and nut to be sure they are tight. The bolts and nuts that hold the exhaust manifold(s) to the engine block have a special tendency to work loose since their temperature varies so widely. Work from the engine back through the rest of the exhaust system, tightening everything in sight. Any broken clamps or hangers should be replaced. While inspecting the system, be sure that no hot exhaust system parts have moved near other critical systems such as brake fluid lines, fuel lines, electric wiring, etc.

The exhaust gases from an engine in good condition are nearly invisible but nevertheless very poisonous. For this reason, it is important to check the exhaust system for leaks from time to time. To do this, it is necessary to cause the engine to produce visible smoke. An easy way to generate smoke is to remove the air cleaner from the carburetor; with the engine running at a fast idle speed, slowly pour some ordinary carburetor cleaner into the carburetor's air intake. The engine will sputter and run poorly, but it will produce a great deal of temporary smoke, all of which should be expelled only from the end of the tail pipe. Any smoke coming from an exhaust manifold, muffler, or interconnecting pipe indicates a leak, which should be corrected as soon as possible. Blocking the output of the tailpipe with a rag while the engine is running will help reveal any leaks.

Some mufflers have a small pinhole at the lowest point to allow drainage of moisture that may have condensed inside. A small amount of exhaust leakage from this hole is normal. A good exhaust system can be expected to last from 30,000 to 60,000 miles, with the exhaust manifolds lasting the life of the engine. However, when any one part of the exhaust system has rusted out, failure of the other parts is usually not far behind. When any repair is made, therefore, it usually is less expensive in the long run (and certainly much easier, since everything is rusted solidly together) to replace everything back of the exhaust manifold, including the clamps, brackets, and hangers. When a muffler fails it should be replaced with one specifically designed for the engine on which it will be used.

Sometimes when a car is driven over rough or very rocky roads, a bracket or hanger will become bent, resulting in some part of the system banging noisily against the frame of the car. If the car is backed into a snowbank or mudbank the tailpipe may become plugged and the engine will run poorly. A simple inspection will determine if any of these problems has arisen, and the solution is simply to restore things as they were. A severe dent in the tail pipe can restrict the flow of exhaust gas. If the dent is near the end of the tail pipe it may be corrected by pushing a long screwdriver or wrench into the tail pipe and bending it open again.

engine tune-ups

The addition of more and more smog control equipment makes it mandatory that the car be kept in good condition. The single most important factor in meeting smog control laws for automobiles is a properly tuned engine. Older cars could be operated even if poorly tuned or badly in need of a new tune-up; owners of post-1970 cars equipped with smog control devices, however, must pay additional attention to engine tune-ups (Chapter 9). Carburetors or fuel injection systems of newer cars cannot simply be adjusted with a screwdriver (as was the case with earlier cars). Maintenance adjustments to the smog control devices themselves require expensive test equipment. The owner of only one or two cars could probably not justify the cost of such equipment.

Beyond the normal tune up there are a number of routine maintenance tasks that fall within an owner's tools, time and ability.

The belts, hoses and clamps related to smog equipment must be checked frequently for signs of cracking or leaks. Additional attention will have to be given to the vehicle's filters, particularly the carburetor air filter. The PCV valve and gas tank vent cap should be checked from time to time to see that they are functioning properly. Most PCV valves can be checked by simply removing and shaking them to see if they rattle. If they don't rattle, they should be replaced. Good maintenance procedure would indicate the routine replacement of the PCV valve about once a year.

If the exhaust system of your car contains a catalytic converter, it will be important to check the system periodically to be sure there are no leaks. All exhaust gases should be routed through the special exhaust purifying system. Do not overlook the owners manual as a guide to specific maintenance action required on smog-reduction equipment.

inspections

As progressively stronger smog control laws are passed in the various states, provision is being made for inspecting vehicles to ensure their conformity with the law. Numerous states are licensing private service stations as Official Smog Inspection Stations. As in many areas of endeavor, official licensure can become a license to steal. The electronic smog analyzers used to check smog emissions can be temporarily adjusted to indicate that your car's emissions exceed the legal level. Some shady operators resort to this practice as a means of selling engine tune-ups, overhauls, smog pump replacements, and other repairs or maintenance items. Since the average auto owner will not own testing equipment to check the emissions himself, the best insurance against such fraud is to be sure that the car is properly maintained and to have it inspected elsewhere if trickery is suspected. High-mileage cars, of course, may indeed need major engine repairs, such as new piston rings and valves, in order to meet current smog laws.

The drive train

The drive train delivers the power from the engine to the drive wheels. In most cases, the engine is mounted at the front and the drive wheels are at the rear.

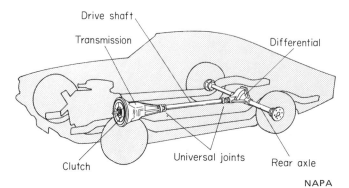

Drive shaft

Transmission

Differential

Clutch

Universal joints

Rear axle

NAPA

Fig. 7-1 The principal parts of the drive train with typical locations on the car

There are three basic elements in the drive train: the *clutch*, the *transmission*, and the *differential* (Fig. 7-1). The drive shaft connects the output of the transmission to the input of the differential. To accommodate variations in the position of the differendial resulting from movement of the car, flexible joints or *universal* joints, are used to connect the drive shaft.

The Clutch

A typical automobile engine, when operating at its slowest speed, will turn the flywheel at about 400 revolutions per minute. At that speed the engine is just barely able to keep itself running and cannot deliver any significant power to move the car. Once running, even at normal idle speed, the car would move forward at a fairly rapid rate, if the engine and drive shaft were connected.

To overcome this problem, a *clutch* is introduced between the engine and the transmission. When the clutch is "engaged," it connects the engine to the transmission by pressing a disc against the face of the engine flywheel. The disc, or clutch plate, is connected by means of a shaft affixed to its center to the transmission input.

The operation of the clutch may be compared to a record on a turntable. The turntable corresponds to the flywheel on the engine, and when power is applied the turntable will spin. If a record is placed on the turntable and held tightly by its edge, the turntable will continue to turn, slipping under the record, and the record can be held still. If downward pressure is applied to the record, friction between the record and the turntable will increase, and it will become more difficult to hold the record until eventually the record must turn with the turntable or the drive motor will stall.

When the automotive clutch is engaged, pressure is applied by means of strong springs that push the clutch plate tightly against the face of the flywheel. The clutch is "disengaged" by pressing a foot pedal that works against the springs to release pressure and allow the flywheel to rotate while the clutch plate remains stationary (Fig. 7-2). Figure 7-3 is a labeled cutaway photo of an actual clutch. The spline in the illustration is an elongated gear that allows the clutch plate to remain attached to the transmission shaft even when the clutch plate moves back and forth as it is bought into contact with, and moved away from, the flywheel.

The clutch is disengaged when the engine is started, when the transmission is shifted to another gear, and when the brakes are

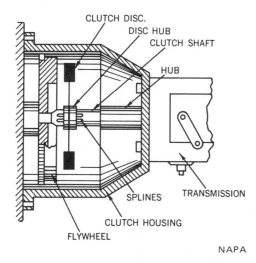

Fig. 7-2 Schematic arrangement of clutch parts showing how the clutch operates between the flywheel and the transmission

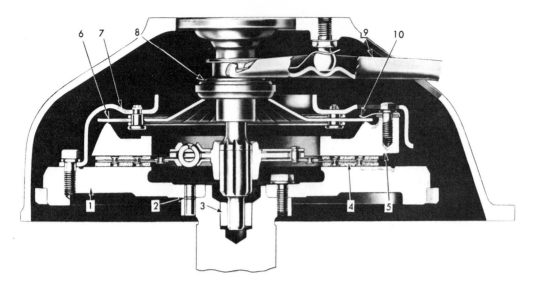

1.	Flywheel	3.	Pilot Bushing	5.	Pressure Plate	7.	Cover	9. Fork
2.	Dowel-hole	4.	Driven Disc	6.	Diaphragm Spring	8.	Throwout Bearing	10. Retracting Spring

CHEVROLET

Fig. 7-3 A cutaway view of a modern automobile clutch

applied. If the brakes are applied while the clutch is engaged, the motor will try to move the car while the brakes are trying to stop it. This action usually results in stalling the engine and can result in damage.

If an attempt is made to shift gears in the transmission while the clutch is engaged, it is difficult to move the shift lever if the gears are also engaged. If the rotating gears are disengaged, when they are brought into contact a loud, grinding noise results and the gears may be severely damaged.

The Transmission

The transmission derives its name from its function, which is to "transmit" power from the engine to the drive shaft. It does this in two ways. First, it provides a direct mechanical connection from its input to its output so that the output shaft will rotate at the same speed as the engine flywheel. This is the condition when the transmission is in *high* gear. At other settings of the transmission shift mechanism, the speed of the output shaft will not be the same as the engine speed. In the case of reverse, the output shaft will rotate at a much lower speed than the engine and in the opposite direction.

gears and gear ratio

A gear is a wheel with notches cut into its edge. The notches on one wheel are made to match those on another so that when they are in contact the two sets of notches, or "teeth" as they are known, are "engaged" or "meshed." With this arrangement there is little likelihood of slippage because the meshed teeth are locked together during rotation. The only way that slippage can occur is if the teeth break off. This can happen but it is a rare occurrence today.

An excellent example of this type of gearing is the common, hand-operated egg beater. As the large wheel on the crank is turned slowly the beaters, attached to much smaller gears that mesh with the large gear, turn at high speed. As long as the gears remain meshed there is no slippage (Fig. 7-4).

Fig. 7-4 A hand drill or egg beater can be used to show gear ratio and action of rear end gears

If two gears are the same size, the second one will turn at the same speed as the first, but in the reverse direction. If the second gear is smaller, say one-half the size of the first, it will turn at twice the speed; if the second gear is larger, it will turn more slowly. The difference in speed between two wheels is termed *ratio*; the former case is a *gear down* ratio and the latter a *gear up* ratio. These changes of speed are not achieved without cost, however, as power delivered to the wheels is traded for speed. If a shaft of one horse-power output turns a wheel at 1000 rpm and this shaft turns a second shaft through a gear so that the second shaft rotates at 2000 rpm, the second shaft will only deliver half of the power but the wheels will turn twice as fast. If the second shaft was geared so that it turned at 500 rpm, it could deliver twice the power but it would take twice as long to do it.

gear ratios and engine power and speed

In the automobile transmission, several gear ratios are provided between the engine speed and the speed of the output shaft. A transmission is described by the number of choices available. Thus, a "three-speed" transmission would have three possible gear ratios to drive the car forward. The reverse gear is not usually included in the numbering of "speeds." A "four-speed" transmission has four forward ratios; in some transmissions, a variation called "overdrive" provides an additional forward speed in which the output shaft of the transmission is actually rotating at a higher speed than the engine, hence its name. Overdrive is only effective at normal road speeds and is usually shifted in or out automatically at the proper speed. Overdrive is useful in increasing gasoline mileage, but pulling power and acceleration are lost when the car is in overdrive.

Gear arrangements in automobile drive systems allow the selection of the suitable gear ratio for prevailing driving conditions. Low gear causes the drive shaft to turn at slow speed so that a lot of power is available to start the car moving or to push it up a steep hill. Second gear provides a little more speed than low gear but still gives an increase in power over high gear for pulling up long grades or for bringing the car up to speed after low gear gets it rolling. High gear, third gear in a three-speed transmission or fourth gear in a four-speed transmission, connects the shaft straight through so that the drive shaft is turning at the same speed as the engine flywheel.

With the manually operated transmission, each time the gear ratio is changed the operator must depress the clutch pedal, change gears, and then release the clutch pedal at just the right rate and at the proper time. This requires a lot of practice and some skill and can become very demanding, particularly in heavy traffic. Whenever the car is brought to a halt it is necessary to press the clutch pedal so that the engine will not stall. Then, as the traffic begins to move, it is necessary to "run through the gears," with the attendant shifting and clutch operation until the speed of the car is up to the flow of traffic. A power flow diagram showing how power is transferred through a typical transmission is shown in appendix A.

For these reasons, it is not surprising that the development of automatic shifting devices began early in the automotive age. The Ford Model T came close to having an automatic transmission. Though it had a clutch, it had no shift lever. A third pedal on the floor served to select the gear from a choice of two forward and one reverse. This bit of magic was accomplished by a special arrangement of *planetary gears* which is used in nearly all automatic transmissions today.

An actual automatic transmission did not come into existance as standard equipment until just before World War II. Chrysler had offered "fluid drive" on their 1938 models, and Oldsmobile the "hydra-matic" drive in 1939. As early as 1935, the Terraplane came equipped with an "electromatic shift." So close was this last development to a true automatic transmission that Hudson began using the Terraplane type transmission, with modification, on their cars with automatic shift in the 1950s. These early attempts were fraught with problems and only after several years of development were reliable automatic transmissions made available to the motoring public. Most passenger cars sold in the United States today are equipped with automatic transmissions that are reliable and almost as economical as the manual shift variety.

the fluid clutch

In the automatic system, the pressure plate type of clutch is replaced by a *fluid clutch*. The operation of this device can be compared to two fans facing one another. One is turned on and rotates by means of power from the motor; the other, facing it, rotates

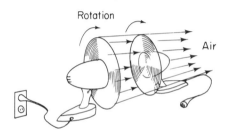

Fig. 7-5 Two cooling fans facing one another illustrate the principle of the fluid coupler which replaces the clutch in automatic transmissions. Air moved by the fan that is turned on flows through the blades of the fan that is turned off, so that both fans turn.

windmill-fashion in the breeze created by its powered mate (Fig. 7-5). Mechanical innovations in an actual transmission increase the efficiency and reliability of this concept, which in its modern form is known as a *torque converter* and resembles a huge metal doughnut with a shaft protruding from its center. Inside the device are carefully designed blades, known as turbine and impeller blades, which may be compared to the fans in the basic analogy. Instead of relying on air to transmit the motion, the torque converter is filled with oil, which serves as the working fluid. Through the operation of a one-way clutch, the oil is allowed to circulate freely and cause only slight pressure against the output turbine blades. This condition compares to the clutch plate slipping against the face of the flywheel. When the one-way clutch is locked up, the oil forced by the blades of the impeller against the blades of the turbine causes the output shaft to turn and thus transmit power through the device. Operation of the torque converter in this mode compares to the condition when the clutch pedal is up and the clutch plate is pressed tightly against the face of the flywheel. The fluid clutch then allows for control of the power from the engine to drive shaft. Operation of the fluid clutch in no way affects the ratio of power available or changes speed. Some form of geared transmission is still needed to bring about the desired gear ratios.

the planetary transmission

Falling back upon the planetary gear system of Model T fame, the modern automobile designer came up with a suitable transmission to follow the torque converter in the automatic transmission. Grandma used to select the gear for the "Tin Lizzie" by pushing that third pedal downward "just so far." In the automatic transmission, the job is done by pistons pushed by hydraulic pressure. A veritable mechanical computer inside the transmission operates automatically to select the proper gear ratio.

The major components of the planetary gear arrangement are shown in Fig. 7-6. The elements of the planetary gear system derive their names, "Sun gear," "planet carriers," and the like, from their resemblance to the solar system. The secret of this system lies in the fact that the ratio of drive between the input and output shafts may be altered without actually meshing or unmeshing the

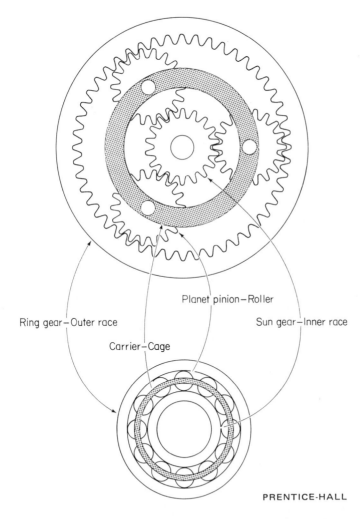

Ring gear–Outer race

Planet pinion–Roller

Sun gear–Inner race

Carrier–Cage

PRENTICE-HALL

Fig. 7-6 The arrangement of "planetary gears", commonly used in automatic transmissions

gears. The gear teeth of the planetary system remain engaged at all times. If one member of the planetary system is held fast the output shaft will rotate at a specific speed. If another member of the planetary is held and the first one released, the output shaft will rotate at a different speed, so there is a capability to "shift" gears simply by preventing selected parts of the gear case from rotating. These parts are held stationary by bands or clutches installed in the transmission in such a way that they can be operated by hydraulic pressure systems. When allowed to run freely, the entire planetary system rotates and no power passes through the system.

The various ranges available are selected either by automatic operation of the valves in the transmission "computers" or by setting the shift selector inside the car in the proper position. The car equipped with an automatic transmission, unlike one with a standard transmission, can be started while the transmission is "in gear," so the starter system is made inoperable whenever the selector is in a position other than "neutral" or "park." Without this precaution, the car could begin to move as soon as the engine was started. Figure 7-7 is a cutaway view of a complete automatic transmission and torque converter.

The Differential

The output of the transmission, automatic or manual, is connected through the drive shaft to the differential, a gear arrangement that drives the rear wheels. In this gear housing, usually situated between the rear wheels, the rotary motion of the drive shaft is made to turn at right angles to drive the rear axles. To accomplish this, a gear arrangement known as the *ring gear* and *pinion* is used (Fig. 7-8). The differential must change the direction of the shaft to cause both wheels to rotate in the same direction and it must allow one wheel to turn faster than the other so that the car can go around a corner without dragging the outermost tire along the pavement. The effect of the differential is similar to that of a common, hand-operated egg beater, in which the beaters rotate along an axis perpendicular to that of the handle being turned to operate them. If the handle was made to turn a wheel, it is easy to visualize how it could propel the system forward or reverse depending on the direction of rotation of the "shaft."

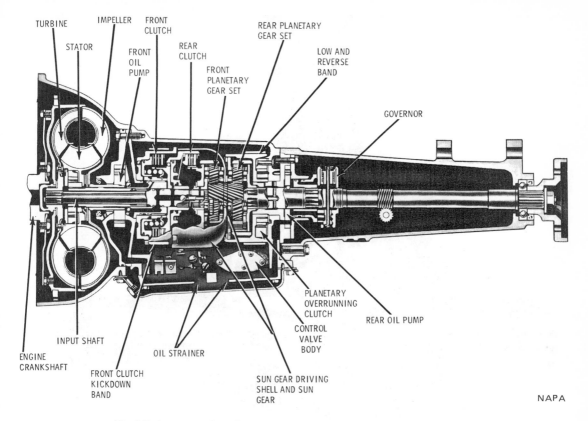

TURBINE
IMPELLER
FRONT CLUTCH
STATOR
FRONT OIL PUMP
REAR CLUTCH
REAR PLANETARY GEAR SET
FRONT PLANETARY GEAR SET
LOW AND REVERSE BAND
GOVERNOR
PLANETARY OVERRUNNING CLUTCH
REAR OIL PUMP
CONTROL VALVE BODY
INPUT SHAFT
OIL STRAINER
ENGINE CRANKSHAFT
FRONT CLUTCH KICKDOWN BAND
SUN GEAR DRIVING SHELL AND SUN GEAR

NAPA

Fig. 7-7 A cutaway view of a complete automatic transmission

A typical automotive differential system is shown in Fig. 7-8. Differentials of this type have one drawback. When one wheel is allowed to slip, as on ice or in loose sand, no power will be delivered to the other wheel. To overcome this problem a *limited-slip* differential is available. By means of a fairly complex arrangement of clutch plates, the differential is caused to deliver power to both wheels even though one of them may be slipping. This option is worthwhile when snow and ice are encountered in daily driving.

the drive shaft and universal joints

The drive shaft between the transmission and differential must be free to move up and down. The transmission is attached to the car frame and therefore is quite rigid, while the differential is mounted between the two axles, which are attached to the car

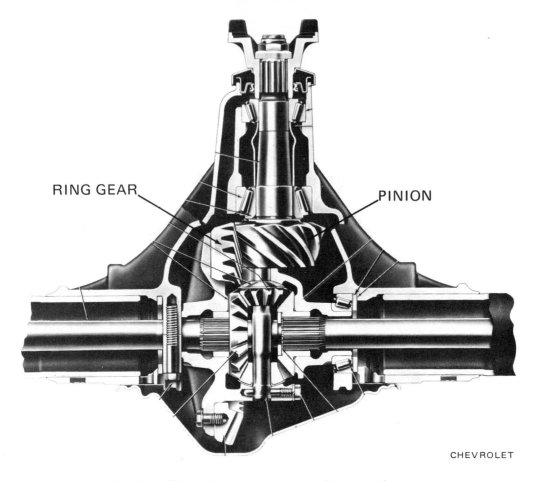

RING GEAR   PINION

CHEVROLET

Fig. 7-8 A differential gear arrangement as used in automotive
rear-ends, ring gear, pinion

body and frame through the rear springs. As the car moves over
bumps, the differential will move up and down with the action of
the springs and independently of the up-and-down motion of the
transmission. The *universal joint* (Fig. 7-9) accommodates this
motion. This unique coupling, an invention of Leonardo de Vinci,
operates somewhat like a chain link as it is twisted. A certain
amount of misalignment may be tolerated, and rotary motion may
still be transmitted along the shaft. The relationships among these
various elements of the power train are shown in Fig. 7-10. A drive
shaft with universal joints at each end is shown installed on a car
in Fig. 7-11.

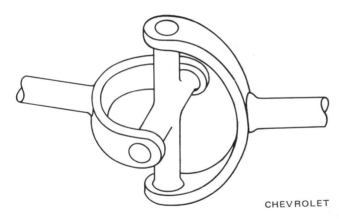

CHEVROLET

Fig. 7-9 Typical universal joint as used in drive shafts

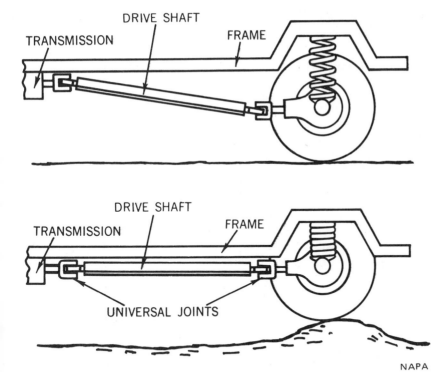

DRIVE SHAFT

TRANSMISSION

FRAME

DRIVE SHAFT

TRANSMISSION

FRAME

UNIVERSAL JOINTS

NAPA

Fig. 7-10 An illustration of the manner in which the universal
joint allows the drive shaft to move up and down with the action
of the springs

131

Fig. 7-11 Driveshaft with universal joints as they appear
on the car

PART 2—MAINTENANCE

Home *repair* of the automotive power train can be very difficult,
often requiring a hoist, special tools, or other generally inaccessible
equipment. There are a number of *maintenance* tasks, however,
that can be handled at home.

Each year the percentage of cars manufactured with automatic
transmissions increases. Some cars, however, especially sports cars,
are still manufactured with standard transmissions and clutches.

The Clutch

A "rough clutch" does not allow the car to move forward without some degree of jerking and bucking. This problem is usually
caused by a worn clutch plate, or faulty pressure plate and its solution falls into the category of repair, not maintenance. A rough
clutch, as well as an automatic transmission that does not seem to

be shifting properly, frequently can be traced to an engine that is not running well. An engine that needs a tune-up will not deliver a steady flow of power, and the result is a roughness similar to that caused by worn clutch components. To avoid unnecessary expenses, be certain the engine is properly tuned before taking the car to a garage for clutch repairs.

Adjusting the clutch pedal for the proper amount of "play" is usually a simple task, but the correct technique varies widely from car to car. Refer to the owner's manual or to the factory repair manual for detailed instructions. A squeaking or scraping sound may sometimes accompany the depressing of the clutch pedal, particularly on cars with high mileage. This sound usually indicates that a *clutch throwout bearing* must be replaced. This task is far beyond the scope of home maintenance. However, if clutch repairs are needed anyway, it will cost little more to have a new throwout bearing installed while the clutch is dismantled for the other work.

The Transmission

Both automatic and manual transmissions contain gears that are continually immersed in oil. The only required home maintenance on transmissions is a periodic check of the oil level. The oil level of most manual transmissions has to be checked from the underside of the car by unscrewing a plug and inserting one's finger in the hole from which the plug came to determine the oil level. Adding oil to a manual transmission is fairly difficult without special equipment, so if the oil level is found to be low, the car should be taken to a service station where it can be raised on a hoist and the necessary lubricant added. The fluid level in an automatic transmission is measured on a dip stick similar to the engine oil dip stick (Fig. 7-12). Follow the instructions in the owners manual.

The automatic transmission fluid is extremely important and must be checked occasionally, although it may need replenishing only rarely. (It is not necessary for the car owner to keep a supply at home.) If fluid is needed, however, it is very important that the proper type of hydraulic fluid be used. Different manufacturers use different types of hydraulic fluid, and different hydraulic fluids should not be mixed. The owner's manual specifies which type is to be used, and you should not permit a service station attendant

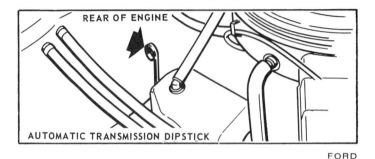

REAR OF ENGINE

AUTOMATIC TRANSMISSION DIPSTICK

FORD

Fig. 7-12 Dipstick is also used to measure automatic transmission fluid.

to add a different type. The same is true of power steering fluid (Chapter 10). Automatic transmission fluid, like engine oil, is available in quart cans. To add new fluid, it is frequently necessary to use a funnel with a long hose.

Tests have shown that if the automatic transmission fluid is drained and replaced yearly, the life of the automatic transmission can be prolonged far beyond that normally anticipated. This task is not significantly more difficult than changing the engine oil, but since it is done so infrequently it probably is best left to a service station. A competent service station mechanic can also adjust the transmission bands. While the latter is a relatively simple and inexpensive procedure for an experienced technician, only the more adventurous auto owner should attempt it.

universal joints

Greasing of the universal joints has long been considered part of the traditional "grease job" (Chapter 10). Many modern universal joints are packed and sealed for their life, however, and have no grease fitting or other means whereby grease can be added.

Servicing The Differential

The differential gears, like those in the transmission, operate in a heavy oil. About all the owner can do is check the oil level by removing the plug and inserting a finger in the hole. If the oil level is more than one-half inch or so below the level of the access hole, the car should be taken to a service station and the proper oil (typically 90 weight) added. As with all fluids used throughout the car, the reservoir should never be overfilled. If the differential is overfilled and the volume of the oil expands as its temperature rises, the excess fluid has no place to go except out through the seals, which normally prevent it from escaping from the ends of the rear axle where the wheels are attached. If the pressure becomes too great, these rear seals will be damaged, and oil will leak past them and drip onto the brake linings. Having to reinstall new rear-wheel bearing seals and clean the brake system can be very expensive. Most newer cars have "overflow vents" to avoid this problem. If your car's differential appears very greasy on the outside, check to see whether this condition is due to a leak or just to excess oil venting out the overflow.

The automotive electrical system

PART I—HOW IT WORKS

In very early automobiles, electricity was required only to provide the spark for ignition of the fuel-air mixture in the combustion chamber. This function was served by a simple device called a *magneto*. The increasing complexity and sophistication of the automobile, however, brought new requirements for electrical power, and to meet these needs, the automobile battery and its charging system were developed.

One of the most revolutionary applications of the new battery power thus made available was Charles F. Kettering's electrical starter system, introduced in 1911. In fact, Mr. Kettering is credited with putting women in the driver's seat, for his self-starter eliminated the difficult and often hazardous chore of hand cranking the engine to start it.

The automobile electrical power system, and the more important devices it serves, are discussed in this chapter; the ignition system itself is the subject of Chapter 9.

Basic Electrical Units

The *volt* is a unit of electrical pressure; *voltage* pushes electrical current through a wire and the device connected to it. Electrical *current* is the flow of electrons found in any material classified as a good electrical *conductor*. Nearly all metals are good conductors. Copper is one of the best choices for electrical wire; iron and steel are also suitable, as shown by the use of the automobile frame and body as the second "wire" for auto electrical circuits. (Electrical circuits require two wires to be complete.)

Voltage applied to an electrical circuit causes electrons in the conducting material to move. This movement of electrons is known as *current flow* and is measured in *amperes* (amps). All electrical conductors, even copper, resist the movement of the electrons to some degree. A poor conductor is one that strongly resists or opposes the movement of electrons in its structure. Such opposition, called *resistance*, is measured in *ohms*.

These three basic units of electricity—the volt, the amp, and the ohm—are related as follows. When one volt of pressure is applied to a circuit having a resistance of one ohm, one amp of electric current will flow in the circuit. Thus, the current flow (amps) in a circuit can be found by dividing the resistance (ohms) into the pressure applied (volts). This relationship is known as "OHM'S LAW."

The *power law*, another useful electrical relationship, states that the pressure (voltage) multiplied by the current flow (amps) in the circuit yields the electrical power, measured in *watts*, delivered to that circuit. Figure 8-1 shows the basic circuits of the typical passenger car.

Fig. 8-1 Schematic diagram of the basic elements of an automotive electrical system

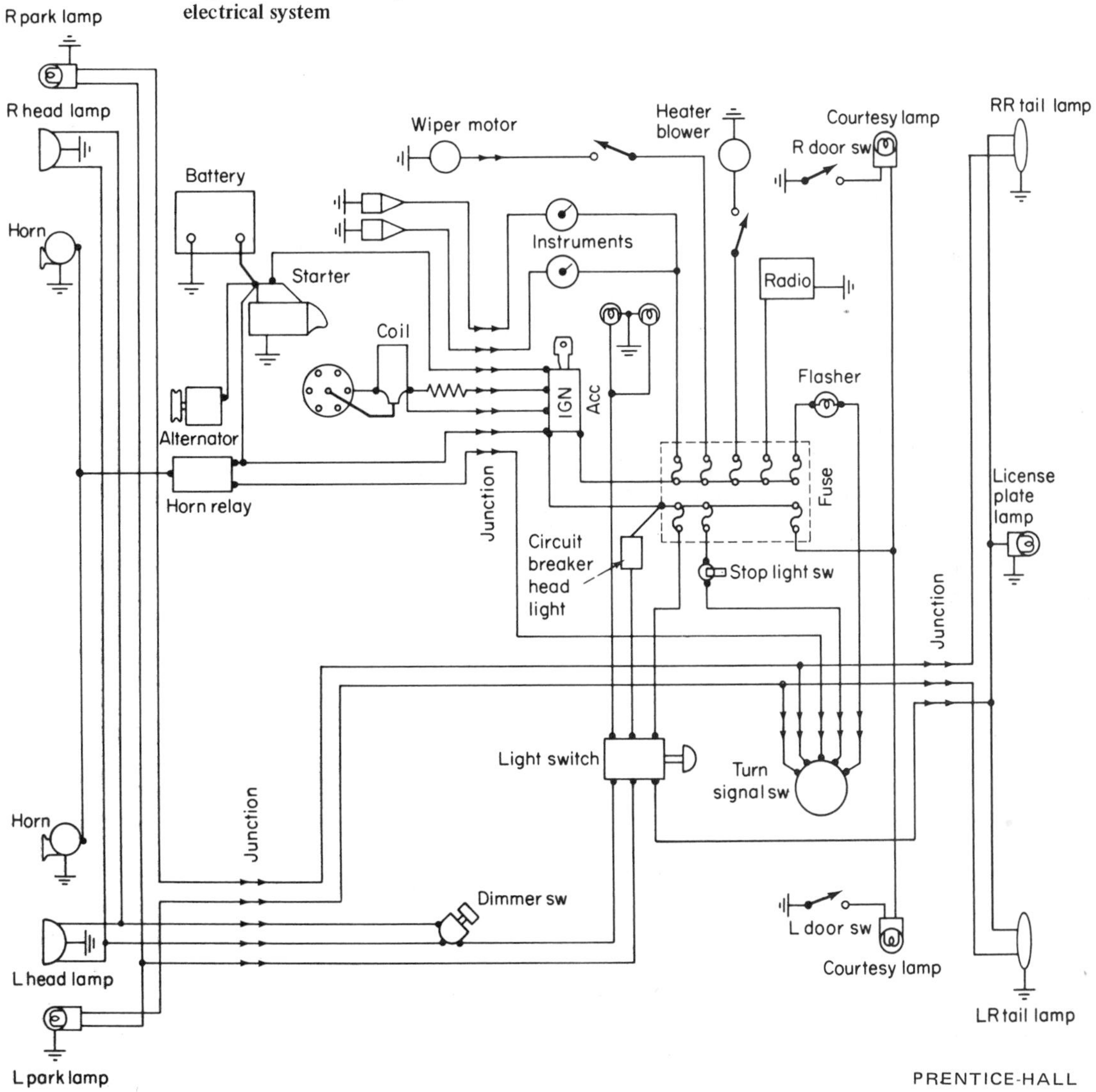

PRENTICE-HALL

PARTITION

PLATE
STRAP

ELEMENT

CONNECTOR

CHEVROLET

Fig. 8-2 Cutaway view of an automotive battery, showing its
construction

The Battery

The battery is the electrical power reservoir for the electrical
equipment in the car, just as the gas tank is the fuel reservoir for the
engine. An automobile battery consists of a number of 2-volt lead-
acid cells connected together to provide the required voltage. A
6-v battery has three cells, and a 12-v battery, the most common in
automobiles, has six cells. The connected cells are housed in a hard
rubber or plastic acid-resistant case which is filled with a dilute
solution of sulfuric acid, called the *electrolyte*. Figure 8-2 shows a
typical automobile battery.

When energy is applied to the battery, as when it is being *charged*, chemical changes occur which allow that energy to be stored. Then if the energy source is removed, the battery itself can serve as a source of energy, providing nearly the same amount as in the initial charge.

The capacity of a battery is expressed in *ampere hours* (AH). Battery manufacturers express this value as a 20-hour rate; thus, an 80-AH battery will supply 4 amps of current for 20 hours. Batteries are given a high ampere discharge rating also. For 12-v batteries, the high amp discharge rate is 150 amp. Batteries are expected to deliver this level of power for 5 to 15 seconds only, the maximum starting time for a properly tuned engine in good condition. To demonstrate starting capability under severe conditions, high amp discharge tests are made after battery temperature has been held at 0 degrees for 24 hours. Batteries usually are identified by number, as to case size and ampere hour and high ampere discharge rates, and months of warranty.

The Alternator

A battery cannot supply all of the electrical power required to operate the engine, the associated equipment, and the accessories in the car for very long. Even if the battery was used to power the ignition system alone, it would supply sufficient energy for a few hundred miles only. The *alternator* generates a steady supply of electrical power to charge the battery when the car is being driven (Fig. 8-3). Mechanical energy from the engine is transferred through a drive belt to the alternator where it is converted to electrical energy. The alternator is usually located at the front of the engine on one side or the other.

The Voltage Regulator

The amount of energy generated by the alternator depends, among other things, on the speed of the engine. Since engine speed does not remain constant, the voltage output from the alternator does not remain steady. To overcome this problem, a *voltage regulator* (Fig. 8-4) measures the voltage from the alternator and

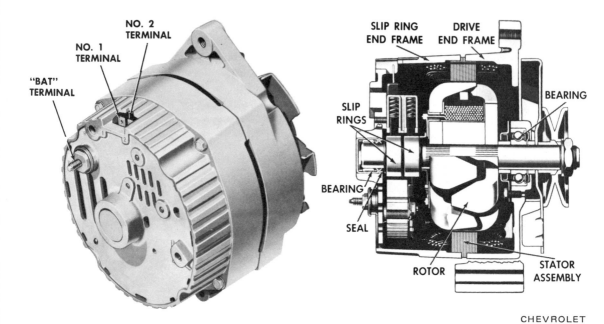

SLIP RING END FRAME   DRIVE END FRAME

NO. 2 TERMINAL

NO. 1 TERMINAL

"BAT" TERMINAL

BEARING

SLIP RINGS

BEARING

SEAL

ROTOR

STATOR ASSEMBLY

CHEVROLET

Fig. 8-3 General view of the alternator used in automotive service

PRENTICE-HALL

Fig. 8-4 Typical regulator units, usually located on the firewall above the level of the engine

compares it with the battery voltage. If these two voltages are nearly equal, indicating the battery is at full charge, the regulator stops the alternator from further charging the battery; if the voltage from the alternator is too low, the regulator automatically increases it. If the battery voltage exceeds the alternator voltage as when the engine is idling, the battery current tries to flow back through the alternator, in which case a "cut-out" or automatic switch disconnects the alternator.

The Starting or Cranking Motor

The motor that starts or "cranks" the engine is similar to the motor that powers a sewing machine, refrigerator, or fan. It must deliver a great deal more power, however, for it must rotate heavy automobile engine parts against the high compression of the cylinders (Chapter 2). To accomplish its task, the starter motor shaft is made to turn at a very high speed, many times that of the engine shaft. A speed reduction, which is achieved by a reduction gear between the starter motor and auto engine shafts, results in an increase of the power supplied by the starter motor.

The outside rim of the engine flywheel is completely ringed with a set of gear teeth, typically 180 to 200. A small gear on the starting motor shaft has 10 to 12 teeth that match those on the flywheel *ring gear*. Thus, the starter motor shaft can turn 15 to 20 revolutions for each rotation of the engine shaft and thereby deliver a great amount of power to turn over the large engine. As soon as the engine starts, an *overrunning clutch* disengages the starting motor gear from the driven flywheel ring gear. A typical starting motor is shown in Fig. 8-5.

Starting Motor Power

The starter motor must develop high power and therefore must draw high current. It would be awkward and ineffective to try to switch this high current *off* and *on* directly with the ignition key switch. A more practical method is through the use of a *relay*,

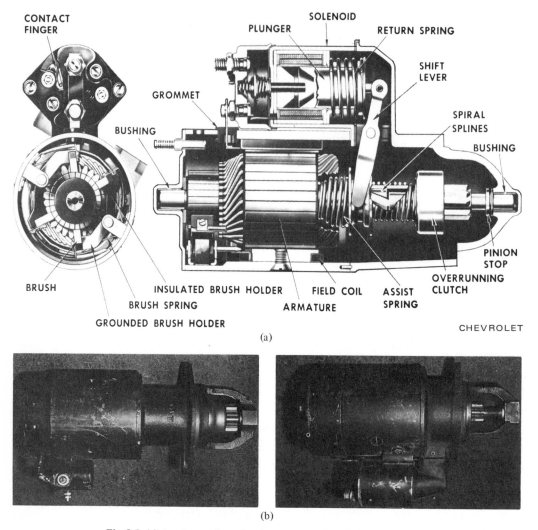

CONTACT FINGER

PLUNGER

SOLENOID

RETURN SPRING

SHIFT LEVER

GROMMET

SPIRAL SPLINES

BUSHING

BUSHING

PINION STOP

OVERRUNNING CLUTCH

BRUSH

INSULATED BRUSH HOLDER

BRUSH SPRING

GROUNDED BRUSH HOLDER

FIELD COIL

ARMATURE

ASSIST SPRING

CHEVROLET

(a)

(b)

Fig. 8-5 (a) A cutaway view of a starter motor, showing the solenoid engage system, usually located low on one side of the engine, at the back, and mounted on the flywheel housing. (b) typical starting motors

which is simply an electromagnet operating a big switch. The relay magnet circuit can be operated with very little current, and through its contacts can handle the very high starter motor current (Fig. 8-6). In almost all starter motor systems, the starter button or the starter contacts on the ignition switch operate a relay that turns the starter motor off or on.

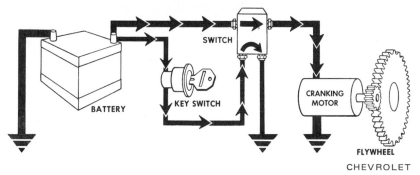

Fig. 8-6 Schematic diagram, showing how low-current relay
can be used to control the high current needed by the
started motor.

Severe damage would result if a starter motor gear engaged the
flywheel gear when the engine was already running. For this reason,
cars equipped with automatic transmissions must be in "neutral"

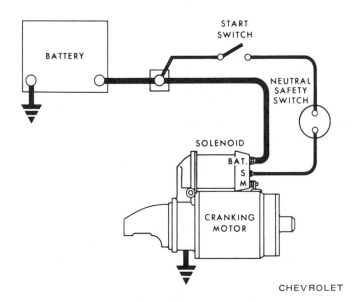

Fig. 8-7 Starter with neutral safety switch

or "park" before the starter can be activated. As an added precaution, many engines are provided with *vacuum switches*. When the engine is running, a vacuum exists at the carburetor intake; a vacuum-operated switch placed in the starter circuit makes it impossible to switch the starter motor on while this vacuum exists or while the motor is running. Some cars have "safety switches" that prevent the operator from moving the ignition key to *start* from *drive* without going to *off* first. Figure 8-7 shows the complete starter motor circuit, incorporating the neutral safety switch and vacuum safety switch.

Lights

headlights

Headlight circuits are simple and reliable. Power to operate the headlights comes from the battery/alternator system. Each sealed-beam lamp in a 12-v system is approximately equal to a 60-watt bulb used in the home. Thus, dual headlamp systems with four sealed-beam units require about 240-W of power from the car's electrical system.

The sealed-beam headlight is used in motor vehicles all over the world. Basically, a sealed-beam unit is a light bulb and a reflector assembled into one unit. Most units have two light sources, or filaments, working in the same reflector. The reflector directs all the light forward, which explains why the 60-W auto headlamp appears so much stronger than a 60-W household bulb.

The two filaments in the headlight are positioned in front of the reflector in such a way that when one filament is lighted, the beam is directed ahead of the car and far enough down the road for safe driving. When the other filament is lighted, the light is focused lower down on the road and closer in front of the car. These two arrangements constitute the high-and low-beam system. All these components are sealed inside an airtight glass bulb, which prevents the silver reflector from tarnishing and the filaments from quickly burning out. Figure 8-8 is a cutaway view of a typical sealed-beam headlight unit.

Fig. 8-8 Cutaway view of a typical sealed-beam headlight unit

headlight switching system

The headlight system requires considerable current and is therefore often relay-controlled. The circuit is arranged so that the switch on the dash panel need carry only a small current to operate a relay that is located close to the headlamps, under the hood of the car. When this relay is activated, it closes a second switch, which has contacts large enough to carry all of the current needed by the headlights.

A *dimmer switch* controls the high-beam and low-beam filaments. In most U.S. automobiles, it is a foot-operated, heavy-duty switch, usually located on the floorboard near the normal position of the driver's left foot. In many foreign cars, a hand switch mounted on the steering column is used to operate the headlight relay.

the light switch

In modern automobiles the light switch incorporates several sets of contacts which do various jobs. The typical lighting control is a pull-switch that has three different positions. In the first position, all the way in, all lights are off. The second position, halfway out, activates the instrument panel lights and all exterior lights except headlights. In third position, full out, the switch activates the instrument lights, the exterior lights, and the headlights.

Many light switches incorporate rheostats, which control the brightness of the instrument panel lights as the switch is rotated. A rheostat, or variable resistor, impedes the flow of current in a circuit by an amount that is proportional to its setting. A separate rheostat is often used to control the fan speed on the automobile heater or air-conditioner.

panel lamps

Myriad small lamps behind the instrument panel illuminate the speedometer, oil, temperature, alternator, fuel gauges, and other indicators. Accessories (radio, air conditioning controls, tape players, and the like) are also provided with small lights. On many cars, additional lights illuminate the ignition lock, cigarette lighter, and glove compartment.

tail lights and stop lights

The tail lights and stop lights, which are required by law, mark the rear of the vehicle and warn following traffic of the operator's intention to slow or stop. Normally, rear lights are not sealed-beam units. Most automobile manufacturers install fairly dull reflectors with a red lens on rear lights. Stop lights may be assembled into the same lens and reflector system as are the other rear-mounted lights, but stop lights are controlled by the brakes. A pressure-activated switch that turns on the stop lights when the brake pedal is pressed is commonly used. Most state laws require that lights at the rear of a moving vehicle be red except for those that illuminate the license plate.

turn indicator lamps

The turn signal is arranged so that a light flashes at the corner of the vehicle corresponding to the direction of turn. The bulbs for the turn signals resemble those for tail lights, but the bulb specified in the owner's manual *must* be installed or the system will not work properly.

IDEAL

Fig. 8-9 Flasher unit for turn signals and emergency lights

The *flasher* activates the turn signal circuit. This is a small device in a metal can that resembles a starter for fluorescent lights (Fig. 8-9). The flasher opens and closes a switch about once a second, causing the signal light to flash. The overall control for the turn light circuit is the turn signal switch, usually a small lever located on the steering column. When the lever is moved up (right) or down (left), it locks in position and closes a switch that directs power to the flashers for the appropriate amber light on the front of the car and for the red lamp on the rear of the car.

Turn signal operation is displayed to the driver by a flashing light on the instrument panel. In some cars, the dash light indicates the side on which the signals are flashing. When a turn is completed and the steering wheel is brought back to center position, a "trip" on the turn lever releases, returns the lever to *off* position, and the turn lights stop flashing.

license and back-up lights

Most automobiles come equipped with a small, low-intensity white light mounted near the license plate bracket. This light makes the license plate readable and is activated by the light switch in the dash. The *back-up lights* are two small white lights positioned on the rear of the car near the tail lights. Although these lights serve as a miniature headlamp system when the car is driven in reverse, they are not as bright as normal headlights and are not usually sealed beam units.

interior, trunk, and hood illumination

In most cars, interior lights, known as courtesy lights, come on when a panel switch is hand operated or automatically when a car door is opened. This last may be a great help when trouble is encountered on the road after dark.

Nearly all of the automatic light systems operate like the glove compartment light. A spring-type switch is held in *off* position while the door, trunk lid, or hood is closed; when the door, lid, or hood is opened, the spring pressure moves the switch to *on*, and the lights come on. This switch arrangement is similar to the light control in a refrigerator or oven.

Horn System

The horn is usually mounted inside the hood and in front of the radiator. The electric car horn is similar to a telephone buzzer. To make the horn loud enough, however, high current must be forced through it. For this reason, it is usually relay controlled. The horn relay, which is often mounted directly on the horn assembly, is activated by the center button or ring on the steering wheel. When the relay closes, it allows high current to flow directly from the battery to the horn. The relay resembles a headlight relay in appearance.

The Fuel Pump

The fuel pump, like other devices on a car, can be operated either by mechanical drive from the engine or by electrical power from the battery. On most domestic automobiles, the fuel pump is mechanically driven by the cam shaft. Electric fuel pumps are

AUTOPULSE

Fig. 8-10 Detailed view of an electric fuel pump

used on many European and Japanese cars. One type of electric fuel pump is shown in Fig. 8-10.

Electric fuel pumps offer two major advantages: (1) as soon as electrical power is applied, fuel is delivered immediately to the engine; thus, the heavy engine need not be cranked for several revolutions to pump fuel into the carburetor float chamber, (2) an electric fuel pump can be positioned at any point in the fuel line and can be used to combat vapor lock. It is virtually impossible for vapor lock to develop in cars with electric fuel pumps located inside the fuel tank.

Electric Clutches

A few European cars have electric clutches in the drive train. The most common electric clutch in U.S. made cars is the drive clutch. This activates the air-conditioning system, compressor and fan control clutch which, on some cars, connects the radiator cooling fan to the engine only when the engine starts to run hot.

All the electrical equipment in the automobile depends on the battery for power. Without some protective measure, if a failure occurs in a system so that the battery is shorted, all of the electrical power in the automobile is lost. Further, since wires that are short-circuited get hot, a fire hazard results.

A common device to protect against these possibilities is the *electrical fuse*. In essence, a fuse is a short length of fine wire that is used as a connection in an electrical circuit. Depending on its size, a fuse carries current up to some maximum level; if the current exceeds that level, however, the wire gets hot enough to melt. When the wire melts through, the circuit in which it is connected will be turned off, just as though a switch had been turned off. Electrical fuses can be made to deactivate a circuit (or "open" it) at almost any current level. They are rated by the amount of maximum current they will carry.

The typical automobile fuse is a short glass tube of 1/4-in. diameter with a metal cap at each end. The fusible wire runs through the center of the tube. The metal caps serve as connections. The fuses are grouped in a *fuse block*, which is usually located under the hood or behind the instrument panel. The owner's manual should indicate the location of the fuse block. A typical fuse block is shown in Figure 8-11.

When a fuse works as it is intended, it destroys itself; that is, it "blows." The only way that power can be restored is to replace the fuse with a new one of the same type. Although these small fuses are not expensive, it is sometimes difficult to find the right replacement just when you need it. In some cars, space for spare fuses is provided in the fuse block.

The *circuit breaker* is by far the best solution to this problem. A circuit breaker is a special type of heat-sensitive switch that will turn itself *off* if overloaded with current. After the overload condition has been corrected and the circuit breaker has cooled, the device can be turned back *on* and the circuit will work again. Circuit breakers protect against fires that might result from overload. They eliminate the need to carry spare fuses and replace a blown fuse after its failure. Figure 8-12 shows some fuses that are commonly used in automotive service.

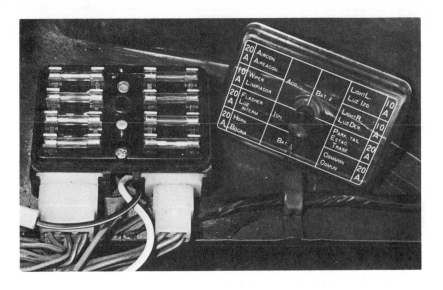

Fig. 8-11 A typical fuse block, showing the fuses and the circuits that they serve

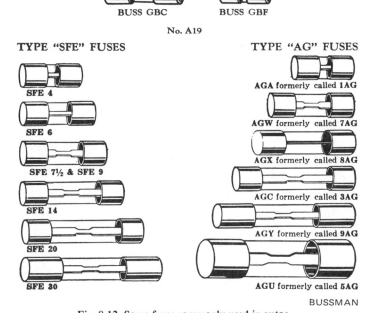

BUSS GBC   **BUSS GBF**

No. A19

TYPE "SFE" FUSES

SFE 4

SFE 6

SFE 7½ & SFE 9

SFE 14

SFE 20

SFE 30

TYPE "AG" FUSES

AGA formerly called **1AG**

AGW formerly called **7AG**

AGX formerly called **8AG**

AGC formerly called **3AG**

AGY formerly called **9AG**

AGU formerly called **5AG**

BUSSMAN

Fig. 8-12 Some fuses commonly used in autos

"He screamed, rolled on the floor, and threw a laughing fit . . . And that was only the estimate!"

PART 2—MAINTENANCE

According to the American Automobile Association (AAA), battery problems account for most road service calls. Battery failure is even more common than running out of gas. It is possible to extend battery life by frequent and correct maintenance. Other, less common, causes of electrical malfunctioning include burned out fuses and faulty wiring.

Battery Maintenance

Good maintenance consists of more than simply adding distilled water to each battery cell when the water level gets down to the level of the plates. While adequate water is important, particularly in warm weather or when the car is started frequently, the main cause of battery failure is corrosion at the terminals. Corrosion insultates the contacts and prohibits the battery from delivering enough power to the starter. Corrosion at the terminals is caused by acid and fumes from the battery cells reacting with the metal posts and the cables. It is not always obvious to the eye. Corrosion occurs in the area between the battery posts and the cable clamps where it is difficult to detect until it builds up and forms a greenish crust. Some of the new batteries have terminals on the side of the case so they avoid the fumes emitted from the battery cells.

For most batteries the auto owner should perform routine maintenance, as follows, several times each year.

For your own safety, *remove all rings, bracelets, or wrist watches* before beginning work on the battery or electrical system. There is no danger of an electric shock, because the battery voltage is low, but the battery is so powerful that it can turn a watch or a ring *red hot* instantly, causing a serious burn. *Do not neglect this personal safety rule.*

Using open-end wrenches, remove the cable clamp attached to the *negative* battery post. In most cars, this cable is the one that goes directly to the frame or engine block. (Some batteries show the negative post by a minus sign, and the positive post by a plus sign). It is important that the negative cable be removed first, because it is grounded. (Exceptions to this standard "negative ground" hook-up include some tractors, industrial and specialty vehicles.)

If the nut and bolt on the cable clamps do not loosen readily, it may be necessary to use a vise grip wrench or, preferably, a battery terminal nut wrench. The nut wrench provides effective squeezing action so even those nuts that are badly "chewed up" can be removed. If the cable itself does not come off easily, do not hammer it or pry it with a screwdriver. This could break the posts that extend down inside the battery. The proper tool to use is the battery clamp remover, shown in Figure 8-13.

After the negative cable clamp has been removed from the battery, remove the positive cable clamp. Then clean both battery posts carefully, using steel wool or a metallic household scouring pad until each terminal shines. Clean the cable clamps in the same manner. A convenient cleaning device that performs these tasks quickly is shown in Figure 8-14.

After the clamps are cleaned, examine them carefully. If any of the wires leading to the clamps is broken, or if the clamps themselves are cracked, it will be necessary to install a new cable or a new clamp. Replacement clamps and cables are available at an auto parts store (Fig. 8-15).

Fig. 8-13 Battery clamp remover

Fig. 8-14 Battery post and clamp cleaning tool

It is not necessary to remove the battery from the car for cleaning unless it is very dirty or it is mounted under the rear seat or in the trunk. If the battery is greasy or covered with corrosion, loosen the hold-down clamp and remove the entire battery from the vehicle. Wash off the battery as best you can, using a garden hose. Sprinkle the washed battery with baking soda (bicarbonate of soda) and let this bubble for a few minutes. Repeat the washing and bubbling soda process several times until the battery is clean again. Clean the battery brackets in the same fashion.

Install the clamps back on the battery posts, *positive* terminal first, pushing them all the way down, and tightening the nuts

Fig. 8-15 Battery cable with terminal

securely. Coat the terminals and clamps generously with clear petroleum jelly. This keeps air away from the connections and reduces
the corrosion rate. These simple battery maintenance steps can
extend the working life and vigor of your car's battery. The importance of this half-hour routine is seldom realized until that cold
morning when you are running late and the car won't start.

Checking for a Weak Battery

If nothing happens when the ignition key is turned to start, try
the horn to see if it honks loudly. If it does, then the battery is
probably all right. If it doesn't honk loudly, try the headlights. If
they don't light brightly, the difficulty is probably with the battery, and it will be necessary to push-start the car (if possible) or
start it with jumper cables if the transmission is automatic.

If the horn, headlights, and other electrical circuits work, but
the starter does not turn over the engine, then the difficulty is
probably in the starter circuit.

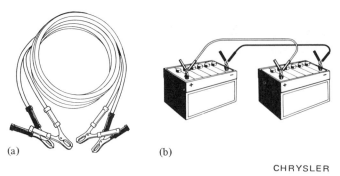

(a)   (b)

CHRYSLER

Fig. 8-16 (a) Jumper cables (b) jumper cables connected
to batteries

Jumper Cables

If the ignition starter does not turn the engine over rapidly or does not turn it over at all, the difficulty may be a weak battery, corroded terminals, or both. Whichever, the car must be started, but one with an automatic transmission often cannot be started by pushing, so it is necessary to "borrow" electric power from another car battery by means of jumper cables. Jumper cables, or "jumpers" are inexpensive and easy to use. They come in several lengths and it is wise to buy the longer ones (Fig. 8-16a).

To start a car with jumper cables, drive the operating vehicle up close to (but not touching) the disabled one, run one jumper cable between the negative (−) terminals, then run the second jumper cable between the positive (+) posts. The operating vehicle can be left running, but racing its engine above a fast idle does no good. Switch on the ignition key and start the disabled vehicle (Fig. 8-16b). Don't run the starter for more than 30 seconds without allowing it several minutes to cool off or you may burn it out. As soon as the disabled vehicle starts, disconnect the jumpers.

Two precautions are in order when starting a car in this manner. First, be sure that both cars have the same voltage systems. Some older cars still have 6-volt systems; the application of 12 volts could cause severe damage. Second, some cars have the positive battery terminal grounded rather than the negative terminal. As mentioned before, this is common in tractors, industrial, and some speciality vehicles. Be sure the jumper cables connect negative to negative and positive to positive.

A common maintenance item easily handled by the car owner is replacement of burned-out headlights, parking lights, tail lights, brake lights, running lights, and interior map and dome lights. Fig. 8-17 shows a typical tail light assembly. If your weekly vehicle inspection discloses a burned-out bulb, simply remove the red or yellow lens (typically held in place by two or three screws) and remove the burned-out bulb. In some cars these bulbs are removed by opening the hood and pulling out the bulb and socket assembly from the inside of the engine compartment instead.

Fig. 8-17 Tail light assembly

Fig. 8-18 Tail light bulbs have special retaining pins to assure proper positioning

Most auto bulbs do not screw out like ordinary house light bulbs. Instead, the entire bulb must be pushed in and rotated counter-clockwise at the same time. Take the burned-out bulb with you to the auto supply store and buy a new one that has the same number on it as the old one. Install the new bulb by inserting it in the socket, pushing it forward, and turning it clockwise.

Fig. 8-18 shows that the retaining pins on the bulb may be positioned so that the bulb can only be put in the socket one way. By looking closely at both the bulb and the socket before installation, it is easy to determine which is the correct way to install it. Many bulbs have both a stop light and tail light inside the glass envelope, and since the stop light is much brighter than the tail light, the base of the bulb is purposely made this way so it must be properly installed. The same is true of combination parking and turn signal bulbs. Bulbs inside the car are generally handled the same way, except that to get at the dome light bulb it is frequently necessary to pull the chrome rim which holds the lens off of the light fixture, since internal bulb fixtures often are not held in place by screws.

A burned-out headlight can usually be changed at home. First remove the chrome trim ring which surrounds the burned-out head lamp. It is held in place with one or two screws. After removing this ring you will see two more screws, typically above and to the side of the bulb. The screw on top of the bulb is for the purpose of aiming the bulb higher or lower, and the one to the side for adjusting the aim of the bulb to the left and to the right. *Do not touch these screws.*

By close inspection you should find the screws which fasten a clamp that holds the bulb in place. Remove these screws, and the bulb will come forward. Unplug the socket from the back of the bulb and remove it. The bulb will have a number molded into the glass. Buy a new one identical to it from a parts house and install the new headlight by doing just the opposite of what you did when you took the old bulb out. If you have not touched the two aiming screws, the bulb replacement will probably be complete. If, however you note that the new bulb is not aiming light at the same place on the road that the old lamp did, you may have to take the car to a service station and have the headlight adjusted, or do it yourself. Some states have official headlamp inspection stations, where a certificate or sticker must be obtained from time to time certifying that the headlights are properly aimed.

Other Units

The advent of electric turn signals was considered a remarkable innovation, but like all innovations, created some necessary maintenance. If a turn signal does not work, the problem is usually caused by a burned-out bulb or faulty flasher unit.

Flasher units are simply and inexpensively replaced at home, as in most cars they simply plug in. The flasher unit is found near the fuse cluster or speedometer usually, underneath the dash. In some cars, one flasher may be used both for the turn signals and the emergency flasher system. In other cars, two separate flasher units are used.

Electric defrosters are built into the rear window of a few cars. If the rear defroster does not work, check first for a blown fuse, and second for a loose or broken wire. If neither of these is the problem, then it is best to take the car to a garage for professional attention. The same is true of the horn.

Windshield wipers are driven by an electric motor in many U.S. model vehicles. The motor itself rarely needs attention, but the blades need frequent replacement, (See Chapter 13) particularly in a hot, dry climate or smog area where there is rapid cracking of the rubber. An automobile owner can usually save at least half the cost by purchasing and replacing the wiper blades himself. These are available from auto supply stores.

Fig. 8-19 The fusible link, in the smaller wire, part of the starter circuit wiring between the battery and starter

Fuses

Nearly every car has a fuse block, as described earlier, and almost all electricity that flows to the various parts of the car must flow through a fuse in the block. If something electrical is not working, then first check its fuse. A fuse is burned out if the metal inside has been burned up. This can be seen through the glass of the fuse container. Be sure to replace a bad fuse with one having the same amperage value. Using a fuse of a higher value can lead to an automobile fire.

One fuse that is not usually located in the fuse block is the *fusible link*, which is part of the starter circuit wiring. This device carries a strong current to the starter solenoid and is placed directly in line between the battery and starter (See Fig. 8-19).

If honking the horn and trying the headlights indicate that the battery is delivering electricity properly, yet the car cannot be cranked, the problem could be due to failure of this fusible link. The solution is to replace the link. However, when this link fails, the cause is usually a more serious problem somewhere in the starter system.

Loose Wires

Frequently a car can be seen parked alongside the road, hood open, with the driver looking—usually unsuccessfully—for a "loose wire." Loose or broken wires do occur, but if an automobile is given proper weekly inspection, these will be found and corrected more conveniently at that time.

The automobile ignition system

The ignition system generates the sparks that ignite the air-fuel mixture in the engine. The generation of a spark requires a very high voltage, typically 20,000 volts, far beyond the capability of the 12-volt car battery alone. Thus, the ignition system must increase the low battery voltage sufficiently to cause the sparks. In addition, the system must provide the sparks at exactly the right time. This timing factor is a critical consideration in ignition system design and adjustment.

The Spark Plug

The spark plug is the element that delivers the high voltage to the combustion chamber and creates the spark. The spark plug screws into a hole near the top of the cylinder. A hook fastened to the bottom end of the spark plug extends horizontally toward a wire through the center of the plug, ending near but not in contact with it, as shown in Fig. 9-1. The small space between these two electrical conductors forms a gap across which the spark jumps when the high voltage is applied through the spark plug wire at-

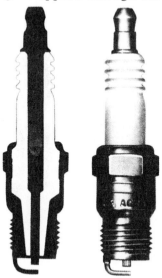

CHEVROLET

Fig. 9-1 Sectioned view of a regular spark plug

tached to the threaded terminal at the top of the plug. In the spark plug circuit, the wire down the center serves as one connection, while the engine (into which it screws) serves as the other, completing the circuit.

Spark plug operation varies with combustion chamber temperature, which in turn depends on the type of engine and the driving conditions. The normal temperature range for proper ignition is between 650°F and 1500°F. Below 650°F, the plugs will tend to foul; that is, deposits of carbon will collect inside the plug around the gap and the insulator, and weaken the voltage by allowing current flow through the fouled region rather than through the spark at the gap. This condition usually develops in cars driven infrequently or at low speeds in normal traffic, resulting in operating temperatures that are lower than average. If plug fouling occurs, the use of "hot" plugs is indicated—that is, plugs that transfer heat relatively slowly from the combustion area into the engine cooling system.

At operating temperatures above 1500°F, "pre-ignition" will occur, with its telltale engine rattle, and can cause engine damage. In cars operated at high speeds, over hills, or heavily loaded, high combustion chamber temperatures necessitate the use of "cold" plugs, which transfer combustion heat into the cooling system more rapidly than "hot" plugs.

Medium temperature plugs are used for the vast majority of cars operated between these extremes. Manufacturers specify the appropriate spark plug heat range for their engines, and it is best to follow their recommendations when making replacements. Examples of hot, medium, and cold spark plugs are shown in Fig. 9-2.

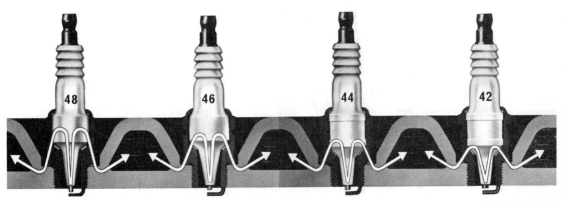

AC SPARK PLUG

Fig. 9-2 Examples of hot, medium, and cold spark plugs

The *ignition coil* is a special kind of *transformer*. It is used to transform the low battery voltage into the high voltage needed to cause the spark at the spark plug gap. As shown in Fig. 9-3, the coil consists of a *primary winding* of a few turns of wire on an iron bobbin or core, and a *secondary winding* of thousands of turns of fine wire. The two windings are separated by insulation to prevent their "shorting" together. The high-voltage terminal of the ignition coil is connected by the ignition wires to the spark plugs. When the flow of current in the low-voltage winding (of few turns) is interrupted, a high voltage flashes out of the second winding (of many turns) for an instant. This instant is long enough for the spark to jump across the gap at the plug and ignite the fuel-air mixture.

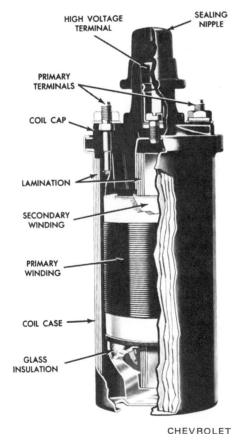

CHEVROLET

Fig. 9-3 The ignition coil

The low voltage to the primary part of the coil is interrupted, or turned off, by means of a spring-loaded switch, something like a doorbell button, called the *points* (Fig. 9-4). The two electrical contact points are made of tungsten or a hard alloy that will withstand heat and will not bend out of shape or break as they operate. Each time they open, they interrupt the flow of current to the primary winding of the coil, thus causing the spark required for ignition. At the same time, however, a small spark is caused at the points themselves; as a result, a bit of the metal comes off one contact and is deposited on the other contact.

If sparking at the points is not minimized, "pitting" and "build-up" can render the points inoperable in a short time. The device used for this purpose is the *condenser*, a sandwich-like arrangement of paper or plastic insulation laid between two slices of aluminum foil and rolled up in a small metal cylinder (Fig. 9-5).

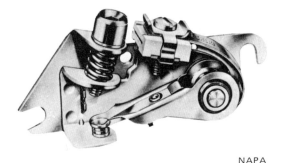

NAPA

Fig. 9-4 A set of contact points

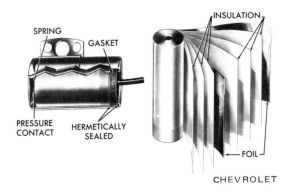

CHEVROLET

Fig. 9-5 Ignition condenser with mounting bracket

The condenser behaves like a small battery. As the points open and the small spark starts to form, the energy that would sustain the spark is diverted to "charge" the condenser. As the points close again to ready the coil for the next ignition cycle, the diminished charge on the condenser is let out through the closed points. As a result, sparking at the points is nearly eliminated, substantially extending their life.

The Ballast Resistor

The battery provides 12 volts in most cars. The coil is designed to operate on an average of 7 to 8 volts. It is necessary, therefore, to limit the voltage delivered to the coil to the lower value. To do this a resistor is connected in series with the coil. A resistor is a device that uses up electrical energy by converting it to heat. The resistor that does the job in the ignition system is called the "Ignition Resistor", or the "Ballast Resistor".

During start-up, the heavy load of the starting motor reduces battery voltage to about 10 volts. When the starter is operated, a system of contacts allows this current to flow to the coil without passing through the resistor. This insures a very "hot" spark at starting time when it is needed. The slight excess voltage for the short time needed to start the car does not damage the coil. If the resistor is by-passed while the engine is running, however, full output from the alternator—14 volts—will be applied to the coil; it will quickly overheat and in a short time will burn out completely.

The Distributor Assembly

As its name implies, the distributor directs, or *distributes*, the high voltage from the ignition coil to the spark plugs at the engine cylinders. The parts of a distributor are shown in Fig. 9-6. The moving parts of the distributor are powered by a rotating shaft that extends down inside the engine and couples to the engine camshaft by means of a gear.

operation of the points

Inside the distributor, one contact point is fastened firmly in place while the other is allowed to move. The movable contact has a plastic or fiber member that acts like the push rod in the valve

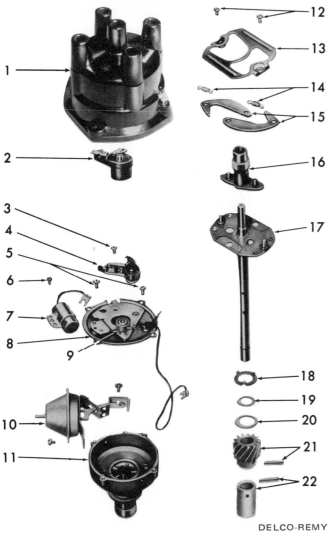

DELCO-REMY

1. Distributor Cap
2. Rotor
3. Contact Point Attaching Screw
4. Contact Point Assembly
5. Breaker Plate Attaching Screws
6. Condenser Attaching Screws
7. Condenser
8. Breaker Plate Assembly
9. Cam Lubricator
10. Vacuum Advance Control Assembly
11. Distributor Housing
12. Weight Cover Attaching Screws
13. Weight Cover
14. Weight Springs
15. Advance Weights
16. Cam Assembly
17. Distributor Main Shaft
18. Tanged Washer
19. Flat Washer
20. Shim (as required)
21. Drive Gear and Roll Pin
22. Damper and Roll Pin

Fig. 9-6 The parts of a distributor

system. The points are operated by a *breaker cam*, which has a number of lobes corresponding to the number of cylinders in the engine. The breaker cam is part of the distributor shaft and rotates with it. As each lobe of the breaker cam comes around, the points are pushed open; they then are allowed to close until the next lobe comes around. The points create a spark at the high-voltage terminal of the ignition coil, as described earlier, each time they are pushed open. The distributor shaft rotates one time for each two engine revolutions, thus, there is a high-voltage spark generated for each cylinder when the engine crankshaft rotates twice, allowing one spark for every other piston *stroke*.

The low areas on the breaker cam are comparatively long and flat, while the lobes have relatively sharp corners, so the points remain closed for a longer time than they are held open. The *dwell angle* refers to the number of degrees of (circular) rotation of the cam during which the points remain closed—that is, in contact. Dwell angle affects the *point gap*, that is the space between the points when they are open. If the dwell angle is too small, the points will be open too long, resulting in a weak spark and poor combustion; if the dwell angle is too large, the points will not be separated long enough, sparking will occur at the points, and the engine may misfire or "backfire." Dwell angle may be set with a *thickness gauge* or a *dwell meter,* both of which are described later in this chapter. Figure 9-7 illustrates the dwell angle concept.

the distributor cap and rotor

Sparks generated by the points and transformer must be directed to the proper spark plug at the proper time. This task is accomplished by the *distributor cap* and *rotor.* The distributor cap is made of plastic or some other good electrical insulating material. There are pieces of metal, called *conductors* spaced evenly, one per cylinder, circling around the outside top of the cap. These carry the high voltage from inside the distributor cap to the outside. Each of the outside conductors protrudes a short distance down inside the cap and may have a flat surface facing toward the center. An additional conductor with a spring-loaded contact is located in the center of the distributor cap. The contact may be made of carbon and resembles the retracting button on the top of a ball-point pen.

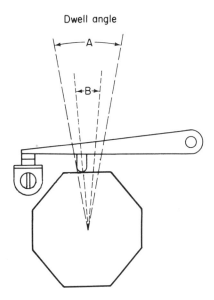

Dwell angle

Fig. 9-7 The dwell angle concept

All the electrical connections on top of the distributor cap terminate inside short tubular extensions, giving the cap the appearance of a castle turret. Each extension provides a connection into which the high-voltage cables can be plugged. The high-voltage cable from the ignition coil plugs into the center connection. The coil itself has a plug connection similar to those on the distributor cap. Each connection around the edge of the distributor cap accepts the cable to a spark plug.

When the distributor is assembled, the *rotor* is fitted above the point assembly on top of the distributor shaft so it will rotate with the shaft. High voltage from the ignition coil travels through the spring-loaded contact of the center conductor to the rotor conductor and out to the rotor edge where this voltage is able to travel to the spark plug leads. When a piston is in position to fire a particular cylinder, the high voltage is directed to the spark plug serving that cylinder.

Ignition Cables

Most of the wire used in the automobile electrical system is similar to electrical wiring used for lamps, radios, and high-fidelity systems. There are two major exceptions, however. One is the heavy-duty wiring that connects to the battery and some of the high-current systems such as the starter motor. These cables are easily distinguishable by their size. They are about a half-inch in diameter and have very heavy terminals for connection.

The other exception is the ignition wire, which is about 3/8 inch in diameter; the wire itself is very fine but is encased in extremely thick insulation (Fig. 9-8). Ignition wire is used to connect the high-voltage terminal of the ignition coil to its counterpart on the distributor cap, and each of the output terminals of the distributor cap to the spark plugs. The thick insulation keeps the electrical sparks from jumping off to places on the engine that the wire may touch en route to the spark plugs (Fig. 9-9).

GLASS YARN = Processing Strength-Above 100 Pounds

CONDUCTIVE DUOPRENE G = Rubber-Like, Resilient, and Continuous

GLASS BRAID

INSULATING RUBBER = High Dielectric Strength

HYPALON JACKET = Heat, and Oil Resistant

CONDR. = (7) Strands Copper Covered Steel

INSULATION = Synthetic Rubber = High Dielectric Strength

JACKET = Hypalon-High Quality Ignition Cable For General Use

NAPA

Fig. 9-8 Cutaway showing construction of standard ignition cables

PRESTOLITE

Fig. 9-9 Spark plug wiring (middle area) with terminals at the end. Protective nipple is shown at right

Most ignition wires have a carbon-impregnated thread instead of a metallic wire conductor. This arrangement permits delivery of the voltage to the spark plugs while reducing the radio interference noise that ignition circuits sometimes cause.

**Electronic Ignition
Systems**

Transistors are finding increasing application in the automotive field. Because of their high reliability and accurate timing capabilities, they have become very popular in ignition systems. There are a large number of different electronic ignition systems, all of which have advantages over the more conventional system described here.

The Chrysler Corporation's electronic ignition system warrents particular attention. Many so-called "electronic systems" make use of the points to turn a transistor circuit on and off. Pure electronic ignition, on the other hand, involves a special arrangement that eliminates the points altogether. The ballast resistor and the coil are the only items of the conventional ignition system that have been retained. In the distributor, the points have been replaced by a fixed coil-and-magnet assembly and a rotor called a *reluctor*, which resembles a gear. The rotor has one wide tooth-like protrusion for each spark plug; these teeth, evenly spaced around the rotor, correspond to the cam-lobes on the old distributor. As each tooth passes the fixed magnet-and-coil, it disturbs the magnetic field and causes a small voltage to develop. This voltage switches on a transistor in the electronic ignition system, causing a high voltage to develop and be directed to the proper spark plug. Figure 9-10 compares the electronic and conventional ignition systems.

The advantages claimed for electronic ignition systems are more accurate timing, improved gasoline mileage, and greatly increased mileage between tune-ups. Some cars with electronic ignition systems have operated for over 50,000 miles without need for a tune-up, a job that conventional ignition systems require about every 5,000 to 10,000 miles. Some cars have factory-installed transistorized ignition; others have this feature added after manufacture. In most cases, there is little a driver need know about the internal operation of the transistor ignition system except that the car is equipped with transistorized ignition and what the specific type is.

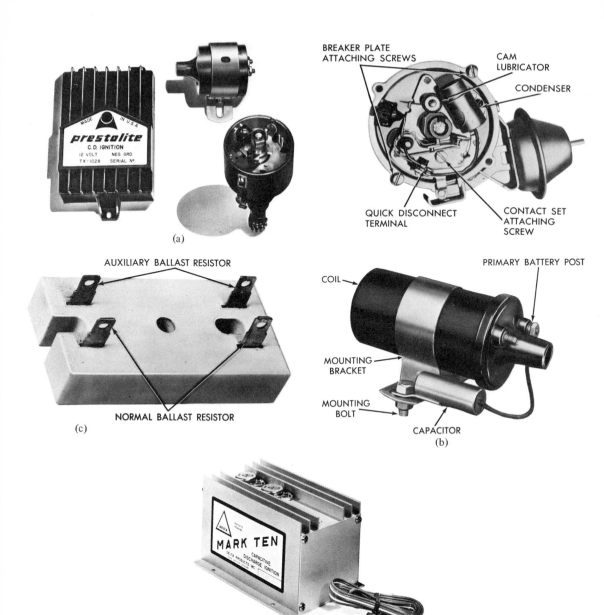

BREAKER PLATE ATTACHING SCREWS

CAM LUBRICATOR

CONDENSER

QUICK DISCONNECT TERMINAL

CONTACT SET ATTACHING SCREW

(a)

AUXILIARY BALLAST RESISTOR

NORMAL BALLAST RESISTOR

(c)

COIL

PRIMARY BATTERY POST

MOUNTING BRACKET

MOUNTING BOLT

CAPACITOR

(b)

MARK TEN
CAPACITIVE DISCHARGE IGNITION
DELTA PRODUCTS INC.

(d)

PRESTOLITE/CHEVROLET/CHRYSLER/DELTA PRODUCTS INC.

Fig. 9-10 Electronic and conventional ignition systems.
(a) typical all-electronic ignition components (b) typical
conventional ignition components (c) ballast resistor
common to both systems (d) typical add-on capacitive
discharge ignition unit

174

"I hate to see his bill for this job."

PART 2—MAINTENANCE

With smog controls becoming more stringent and fuel prices steadily rising, it becomes increasingly important to keep the car's engine in good "tune." As a result of wear or deterioration, certain engine components, nearly all of them part of the ignition system, need replacement or adjustment about once a year on full-sized cars and about every six months on smaller cars. With a modest one-time investment in the extra tools and test equipment needed, the complete tune-up can easily be performed as routine maintenance at home by the car owner. Without the proper tools and test equipment, however, it is a frustrating and fruitless exercise, usually ending up with the car in a local garage for professional attention, and no savings of either time or money.

Tune-up Tools and Test Equipment

In addition to the standard tool kit outlined in Chap. 1, the following special tools and test equipment are needed for tuning the engine.

Fig. 9-11 Ignition wrenches

ignition wrenches

A small inexpensive set of ignition wrenches is needed to change the breaker points and condenser (Fig. 9-11).

spark plug socket

This extra deep socket should be purchased with the same drive size (3/8 in. or 1/2 in.) as your regular socket set. The socket should have a rubber insert built in it so it will grip the spark plug and keep it from falling (Fig. 9-12).

sparkplug gap gauge

This gauge is needed to measure the gap between sparkplug electrodes so they can be adjusted accurately (Fig. 9-13).

Fig. 9-12 Spark plug socket

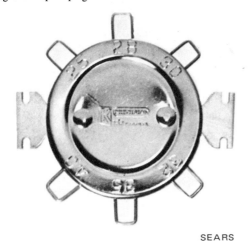

Fig. 9-13 Spark plug gap gauge

dwell tachometer and point gap gauge

The dwell meter is an essential piece of electrical testing equipment usually combined with a tachometer (Fig. 9-14). It is used for measuring the number of degrees the points dwell closed (discussed earlier in this chapter); the tachometer indicates how fast the engine is running. The point gap gauge (Fig. 9-15) is used to "rough" set the point gap prior to inspection with the dwell meter.

timing light

The timing light is an essential tester for setting the spark timing to ensure that the electric spark ignites the fuel at the proper time (Fig. 9-16).

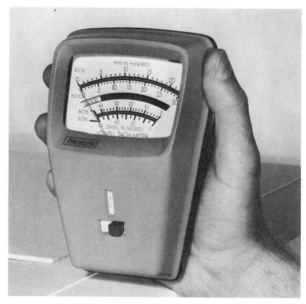

Fig. 9-14 Dwell meter and tachometer

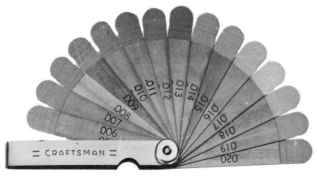

Fig. 9-15 Point gap gauge

distributor locking bolt offset wrench

On a few cars, it is almost impossible to reach the distributor locking bolt. In such cases, the offset wrench is used in conjunction with the rachet wrench, and therefore must have the same size drive hole (3/8 in. or 1/2 in.) as your regular socket set (Fig. 9-17).

Fig. 9-16 Timing light

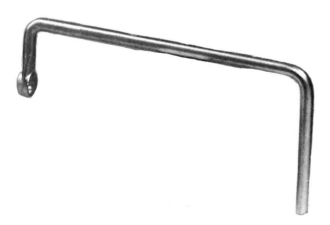

Fig. 9-17 Offset wrench used with ratchet wrench
to unlock the distributor

The routine engine tune-up involves replacement of parts if wear or deterioration cause degraded engine performance.

spark plugs

The proper number of the spark plug used is listed in the owner's manual, or it can be determined by the supplier from the type, year, and size of engine involved. For normal driving, a "medium" spark plug should be used, but a "hot" or "cold" plug may be desirable, depending on the conditions discussed earlier. Always buy *new*, top grade spark plugs. About half the retail price of the plugs can be saved at discount houses and department stores.

breaker point set

To buy the proper set of "points," it is necessary to specify *exactly* which engine your car has (Fig. 9-18).

condenser

Modern condensers rarely fail, but since they are inexpensive and easily installed, they are usually replaced at the same time as the points (Fig. 9-19).

rotor and distributor cap

The inexpensive electrical *rotor* and the *distributor cap* should be replaced as part of every second tune-up (Fig. 9-20).

high-voltage wiring

High voltage wiring is subject to the deterioration caused by high engine temperatures, oil, and the constant bombardment of pulses of high voltage. In some cars, the original wiring may last the life of the car; in others, particularly those with modern high-temperature engines, the high voltage wiring may have to be replaced as often as the rotor and distributor cap.

Fig. 9-18 Breaker or contact "points"

Fig. 9-19 Condenser used in ignition system

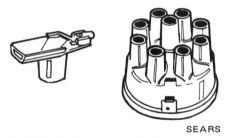

Fig. 9-20 Distributor cap and rotor

Tune-up Procedure

Work on the engine when it is cool so that you will not get burned on the exhaust manifolds. An inexpensive pair of cloth gardening gloves will help prevent skinned knuckles, as well as keep your hands clean for working with the electrical parts.

replacement of spark plugs

Adjust the new spark plugs to the gap specified in the owner's manual. The type of gap gauge shown in Fig. 9-13 is preferred for this purpose. It has a bending tool to make the process simpler.

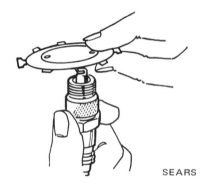

Fig. 9-21 Checking the plug gap with gauge

Never attempt to bend the center electrode of the plug, only the curved one, as shown in Fig. 9-21.

Unless you are very familiar with the car's engine, it is preferable to remove and replace spark plugs one at a time, so their wires won't get mixed up. Grasp the wire (or its connector) firmly close to the spark plug and pull it off. Using the spark plug socket, the ratchet handle, combinations of socket extensions as necessary, and perhaps a universal joint, remove the spark plug by unscrewing it counterclockwise. In those few cases where the spark plug is simply too tight to loosen with the ordinary 3/8 in. drive ratchet, it may be necessary to replace the ratchet handle with a large breaker bar (Chap. 1). If the old spark plugs have copper gaskets on them, be sure to replace them with new plugs having similar gaskets. Some cars (such as some Fords) use plugs that do not require a gasket.

Replace the old spark plug with a new one, being careful not to bump the end of the new spark plug when locating the spark plug hole, or the gap might be changed. Always start the new plug into the hole by hand. Be sure the new plug screws in easily for several turns before applying the wrench. Since it usually is not possible to see both the spark plug and the hole at the same time, the plug can be threaded in crooked, resulting in severe thread damage to the engine and potentially expensive repairs.

When the plug is properly threaded, tighten it very firmly in place with the ratchet handle and accessories. While many manufacturers specify use of a torque wrench when installing spark plugs, experience has shown that a person of average strength cannot overtighten a spark plug using a standard 3/8 in. ratchet handle.

The plug must be screwed in place tightly to withstand the very high cylinder pressures. Push the spark plug wire connector back over the metal tip of the spark plug, being sure that it is firmly attached. If it does not fit snugly, it may be necessary to bend the connector slightly with a pair of pliers.

Follow the same procedure for each of the four, six, eight, or twelve spark plugs in your particular car. This completes the spark plug replacement.

distributor cap

It sometimes is necessary to pull several wires out of the distributor cap to gain easy access to the parts beneath it. For this reason, it is wise to make a sketch noting which wires plug into which holes in the cap, unless this is covered by a photograph or diagram in the owner's manual.

Most distributor caps can be removed by inserting a screwdriver between the clips on either side and twisting. Other types (General Motors V-8) are removed by pressing down and turning each of the two screws found on either side of the distributor cap. Carefully lift the cap off of the distributor. After drawing a sketch unplug the wires from the cap as needed by pulling on them firmly.

the breaker points

Removing the Rotor. Usually the rotor must be removed to gain access to the breaker points. On many cars, the rotor is removed simply by pulling on it firmly. In some cases, it is stuck so tightly that it breaks in the process. Don't be alarmed if this happens, however; rotors are very inexpensive, and it obviously is advisable to have a spare rotor on hand, or better yet, another car available for going after parts. On some cars (General Motors) two screws must be removed to allow the rotor to be lifted off. Note the underside of this rotor as it is removed; it can be replaced in only one position. Don't force the square peg into the round hole when reinstalling.

Replacing the Points. Unhook the electric wire(s) going to the points, using the ignition wrenches as necessary. Loosen the screws that hold the points in place. Some cars require complete removal of all screws to remove the points, while others only require the removal of one and the loosening of the other(s). Do not remove more than is necessary, and be *extremely careful* that no screws are dropped or fall into the distributor. If they do, professional help may be necessary to retrieve them. This part of the procedure has proven to be a particular hazard for novice mechanics working on the "slant-six" engine used in many Chrysler products.

Remove the old points and set them aside. Remove the condenser and replace it. In some engines (like some Volkswagens) the condenser is mounted outside the distributor, so it is necessary to push out the dust-plug before removing the old condenser and its wire.

Install the new points by reversing the procedure used to remove the old ones.

the points dwell angle

There are numerous methods of setting the points dwell angle, but many of them require the facilities of a well-equipped garage. This is clearly the most difficult adjustment for the home driveway maintenance technician until it has been performed several times. That should not deter you, however. Two methods suitable for the auto owner working at home are outlined here.

The Gap Gauge. This method requires that the rubbing block on the breaker points be positioned on the tip of one of the distributor cam lobes. See Fig. 9-22. There are two ways of achieving this: (1) Loosen the distributor clamp and, after scratching a reference mark so it can be returned to its original position, rotate the entire distributor assembly until the rubbing block and a cam lobe are properly oriented; or (2) with the distributor assembly in its original position, rotate the *engine* and stop it at such a point that

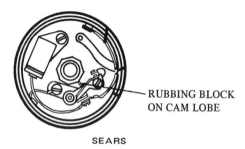

RUBBING BLOCK
ON CAM LOBE

SEARS

Fig. 9-22 Breaker points on lobe of distributor cam

the distributor (which is geared to the engine) stops with the rubbing block sitting atop one of the cam lobes. This is easy on small engines which can be turned over by hand (such as Volkswagen). Cars with manual transmissions can be put in "high" gear and the entire car pushed back and forth a bit until the rubbing block and a cam lobe are properly positioned. On cars having large engines and automatic transmissions, it is necessary to turn the engine over by engaging the starter by turning the key and hoping the engine stops at the proper point. The obvious disadvantage is that you may have to engage the starter many times before the engine stops at just the right point.

A third alternative is to mark the distributor's position as in (1), then loosen the clamp and remove the entire distributor from the car, where it can be worked on. This alternative is NOT for the beginner, unless he knows how to reinstall this particular distributor and will not have to resort to professional help to complete the tune-up.

With the cam lobe and rubbing block properly positioned, use a feeler gauge of the proper thickness, and adjust the point gap using the gauge and screwdrivers. When the points are properly adjusted, the feeler gauge should fit snugly between the two open points. The proper point gap and dwell angle will be given in the owner's manual or listed at a parts store.

The Dwell Meter. The dwell meter is connected as shown in Fig. 9-23. The "ground" lead can be hooked to any solid clean metal part of the car, and the "hot" lead clipped onto the small wire from the coil that is connected to the distributor.

Use two screwdrivers, one to adjust the point gap and the other to lock the set screw when the proper point gap setting is reached. Observe the dwell meter while someone else cranks over

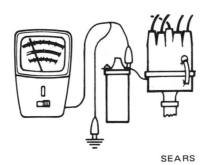

SEARS

Fig. 9-23 Showing the connection of the dwell meter

the engine with the ignition key. The engine cannot start, of course, since the distributor cap is removed, and high voltage cannot reach the spark plugs. After the dwell has been set, tighten all breaker-point holddown screws, replace the rotor, the distributor cap and any wires which were removed from it, and start the engine.

With the engine running, note the dwell angle on the dwell meter. If it is not within the tolerance prescribed, shut off the engine, remove the distributor cap, remove the rotor, and readjust the points as follows: (1) If the dwell meter indicated that the points were closed too long (dwell reading too high), using two screwdrivers, loosen the set screw very carefully, *slightly* open the points, and tighten down the set screw. (2) If the dwell meter indicated that the points were not closed long enough (meter reading too low), using the two screwdrivers loosen the set screw, move the points *slightly* closer together, and tighten the set screw.

When the procedure is completed, install the rotor, distributor cap, and loose wires, start the engine, and read the dwell angle again on the meter. If you adjusted the points carefully the dwell angle should have moved closer to the required setting. Repeat the procedure until the dwell angle is correct.

General Motors cars have a unique feature that *greatly* simplifies dwell angle adjustments. Follow the directions that come with the new points. Typically they instruct as follows:

> After installing the points, use the enclosed hex wrench and turn the dwell adjustment fully clockwise until snug. From this position, turn the dwell adjustment counterclockwise one-half turn. Install the rotor and the distributor cap and attach the dwell meter. Open the "window" in the side of the distributor cap, insert the hex wrench, start the engine, and adjust the dwell as measured on a dwell meter to the angle indicated. This completes the dwell setting.

It's really easy!

spark timing

The final step in the tune-up is checking the spark timing. Connect the timing light as shown in Fig. 9-24. If the owner's manual does not indicate which is the number 1 cylinder, this information can be obtained through charts at any service station, dealership, or parts house. Mark note of such information for future tune-ups.

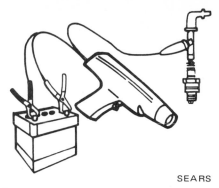

Fig. 9-24 Connecting the timing light to check
correct spark timing

From the same source, find out the proper timing setting for
your engine. Most pre-1970 engines were set so each spark plug
fired a few degrees before the piston rose all the way to the top of
its stroke, thereby igniting the fuel a little early and giving it a head
start toward delivery of energy during the power stroke. Setting
the engine to fire BTDC (before top dead center) causes it to run
better, deliver more power, and use less gas. Such an engine setting also produces more smog, so most engines manufactured
after 1970 require the spark to be delivered either when each piston is at TDC (top dead center) or even a few degrees after TDC.
This lessens smog but greatly reduces engine performance. Cars
built in 1975 and later with the catalytic converter can be timed
BTDC.

With the timing light attached, start the engine and—*being very
careful to avoid the moving belts and cooling fan*—shine the flashing
timing light so that the marks on the flywheel and engine block
can be observed (Fig. 9-25). If these two lines appear to be lined
up, the engine timing is correct.

If the two lines do not align, turn off the engine and loosen the
distributor clamp (Fig. 9-26). Restart the engine and, observing
the two lines with the timing light, rotate the entire distributor
assembly slightly in one direction or the other until the two lines
are opposite one another. Tighten the distributor clamp and recheck both the dwell meter reading and timing setting. If it was
necessary to rotate the distributor some distance it may be necessary to readjust the point dwell slightly. On many engines, it is
difficult to see the timing marks on the flywheel and the block.

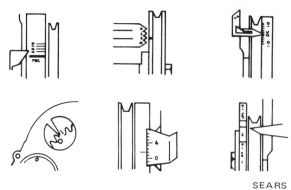

Fig. 9-25 Aligning the timing mark on the fan belt

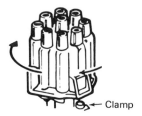

←— Clamp

Fig. 9-26 Locating the distributor clamp

Applying a line of fluorescent paint on the flywheel pulley and another line at the proper spot on the engine block helps. Ordinary blackboard chalk can be used in a pinch.

idle speed setting

When the engine has warmed up, set the dwell/tachometer to "tach" position and read the engine speed in revolutions per minute (rpm). On many pre-1970 cars, it is possible to adjust the carburetor air/fuel mixture with the engine idling.

Watching the tachometer, adjust the idle mixture screw first in one direction, then in the other, leaving it set where the idle speed is highest. Finally, observing the provisions specified in the owner's manual (e.g., air conditioner on or off, transmission in neutral or drive) adjust the idling speed to the rpm's specified. See the owner's manual for location of the idle air/fuel mixture and idle speed adjustment screws. These adjustments complete the engine tune-up.

Engine tuning has such an effect on pollutants emitted from the tail pipe that significant changes are being made in the ignition system. Many post-1970 cars have "breakerless" ignition systems—that is, they have no ignition points. Nor do they have a condenser. In these cars, the dwell never has to be set, so timing adjustments are not necessary.

Spark plug manufacturers are developing spark plugs with unusually long life. In the future perhaps only one or two plug changes may be required during the life of the car.

As such improvements are built in more cars, the need for the tune-up described here will decrease and, in time, may be eliminated altogether. "Tune-ups" of the future will probably have less to do with electrical system deterioration, and be increasingly directed toward the maintenance of pollution control systems. Of course, the tune-up is only one of many maintenance procedures required for optimum auto life and performance, so even with simplification or elimination of the conventional tune-up, the routine care and maintenance described in earlier chapters must still be performed.

Chassis, suspension, and running gear

Like a house, an automobile must have some kind of foundation. A house foundation is fixed, and there is no requirement for it to be moved. The automobile foundation, or *chassis*, on the other hand, must be completely mobile and still serve as a firm base that will support the rest of the car.

In early cars, the chassis was simply a framework to which the rest of the car was attached. The entire upper body could be removed and the car still operated because the power train and running gear, still attached to the chassis, were complete and operational. In recent years, this type of construction has given way to the *unitized body* in which the body itself becomes the chassis. The body, stamped out of steel, has certain stiffening members welded, bolted, or riveted in place to provide the required strength and rigidity. Most of the strengthening attachments are under the car or in the engine compartment. In some cases, a partial frame is provided at the front to support the engine and to strengthen the front end. Figure 10-1 shows some typical body and frame arrangements.

Suspension Systems

The chassis, which supports the rest of the car, is supported in turn by the suspension system. In general, suspension refers to the chassis, body, engine, and power train being suspended above the wheels. The suspending members are the front and rear springs, assisted by the shock absorbers.

spring suspension

Suspension systems vary widely, but those most commonly used for passenger cars are the independent coil spring and the leaf spring systems. Some cars have *independent coil spring suspension*—that is, coil spring suspension on all four wheels. A more

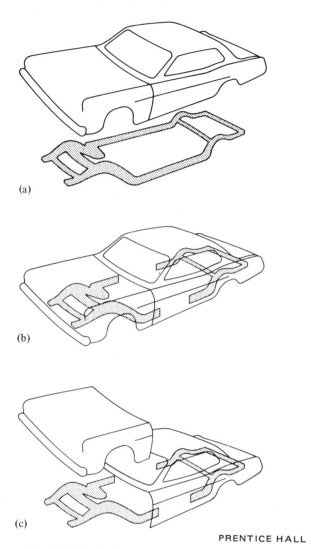

(a)

(b)

(c)

Fig. 10-1 Typical body and frame arrangements (a) separate body and frame, (b) unitized construction, (c) unitized body with steel front frame

common arrangement on domestic cars is the use of independent coil springs on the front and leaf spring suspension on the rear.

The objective in mounting the car on springs is to make the ride smoother and to cushion the passengers from bumps in the road. Spring suspension prevents severe jarring, which would damage the car. Figure 10-2 shows a typical, independent front suspension

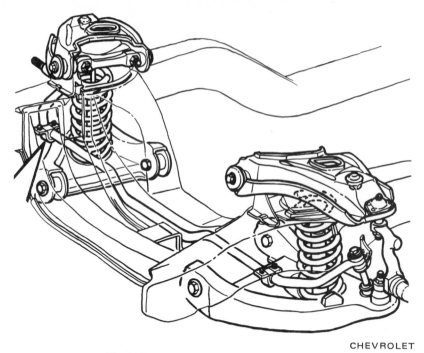

CHEVROLET

Fig. 10-2 Typical independent front suspension

arrangement; Fig. 10-3 illustrates solid-axle leaf-spring rear suspension. A typical coil spring suspension is shown in Fig. 10-4. The wheel is mounted to the small axle protruding at the right. As it moves up and down over uneven places in the road, the spring compresses and expands to accommodate those variations. In this manner, the action of the spring absorbs the jolts and jars that would otherwise be transmitted through the frame to the car and its passengers.

torsion bars

In some cases, a different type of spring, called a *torsion bar,* is incorporated into the suspension system. In essence, this device is a spring that is not coiled. It is a long shaft attached at one end to the frame of the car and at the other end to the wheel mount in such a way that as the wheel moves up and down the bar twists. The bar is of hardened steel and resists the twisting action. When the force that causes the twist is removed, the bar untwists and

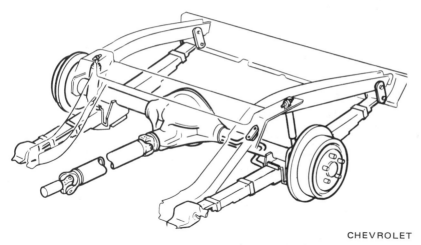

Fig. 10-3 Solid axle, leaf spring rear suspension

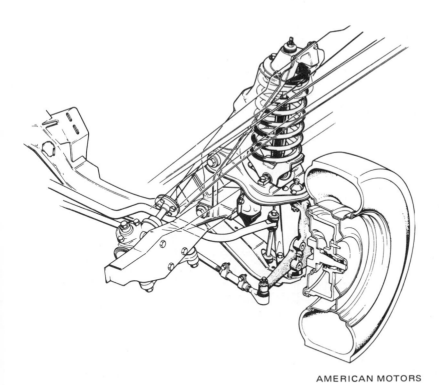

Fig. 10-4 Typical coil spring suspension, cutaway for clarity

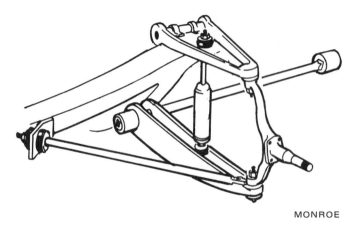

MONROE

Fig. 10-5 Torsion bar arrangement used on front suspension system

returns to its original position. Figure 10-5 shows a typical torsion bar suspension. In some cars, the torsion bar is used alone; in others, it is used in conjunction with a common spring.

suspension joints

Suspension systems must flex to do their jobs, therefore, a certain amount of movement is required at the joints. Two common types of flexible suspension joints are the *ball joint* (Fig. 10-6*a*) and the *rubber suspension bushing* (Fig. 10-6*b*). Bushings

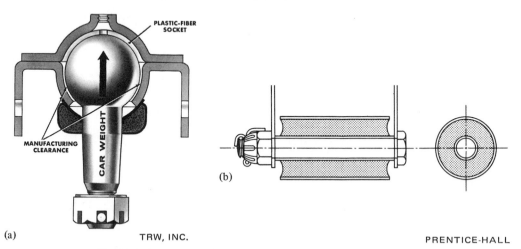

(a) TRW, INC.

PRENTICE-HALL

Fig. 10-6 Two common flexible suspension systems (a) a ball joint, (b) a rubber bushing

are used wherever a single hinge-type action is involved. Ball joints are used where multidirectional freedom is needed, as in front-end suspension, up and down, and in steering, right and left.

stabilizer bars

Cars that are softly sprung—that is, have very flexible springs—give a good ride but sometimes have a tendency to roll from side to side when traveling over uneven roads. A stabilizer bar is often used to minimize this effect. This bar is attached across the front of the car and connects the two front suspension systems. When both wheels move up or down at the same time, the stabilizer simply moves with them. When only one wheel is affected, the action is transmitted to the other wheel by the stabilizer bar so that even though only one wheel may strike a bump, such as a chuck-hole, the bump will be felt by both wheels, thus overcoming the forces which could cause a rolling action. Figure 10-7 shows a stabilizer bar installed in a car.

Fig. 10-7 A stabilizer bar installed on the front suspension, shown in white

If a car with good springs strikes a bump, the car will bounce up and down. Once past the bump, the car will continue to bounce, as a rubber ball, with each bounce a little less pronounced than the previous one until, eventually, a smooth ride is achieved once again. Unless this tendency is prevented, it is possible that with numerous irregularities in the road, the car would always be reacting to some sort of spring action and a smooth ride would never be achieved. Aside from the discomfort that this might cause, it is difficult to steer a car when the weight on the front wheels varies widely as it would under these conditions. *Shock absorbers* correct this situation. Shock absorbers may be installed either inside the springs (Fig. 10-4) or external to the springs. In either case, the shock absorbers are connected to the same mounting members as the springs.

A shock absorber may be compared to a bicycle pump or a garden sprayer of the hand-operated type. If either of these devices is operated too quickly the plunger will not respond until some air has escaped from the cylinder through the nozzle or hose. If these openings are partially blocked, movement of the plunger will be more difficult. The same type of action takes place in the shock absorber. In the bicycle pump, air absorbs the energy of the plunger. In the shock absorber, oil is the working medium, hence, the name *hydraulic shock absorber*. The oil does not escape to the atmosphere as does the air in the tire pump; rather, it is worked back and forth between two chambers inside the shock absorber housing. The size of the hole, or aperture, between these two chambers determines the response of the shock absorber. The physical size of the shock absorber determines the overall capacity because the energy absorbed is converted to heat, and a larger mass will absorb more heat and cool more readily than a small one. Figure 10-8 is a cutaway view of a shock absorber.

Steering Systems

The steering wheel inside the car is coupled through a small, specialized transmission to an arm, which connects to both front wheel mounts in such a way that movement of the arm causes equal movement of the front wheels. The wheels turn in the same

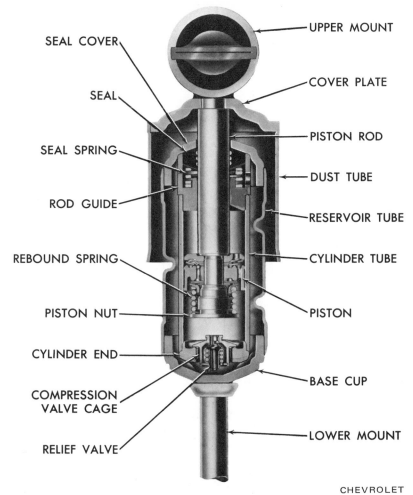

SEAL COVER

SEAL

SEAL SPRING

ROD GUIDE

REBOUND SPRING

PISTON NUT

CYLINDER END

COMPRESSION
VALVE CAGE

RELIEF VALVE

UPPER MOUNT

COVER PLATE

PISTON ROD

DUST TUBE

RESERVOIR TUBE

CYLINDER TUBE

PISTON

BASE CUP

LOWER MOUNT

CHEVROLET

Fig. 10-8 A cutaway view of a typical automotive shock absorber

direction and just the right amount to "track" around a curve. Compensation for left and right turns is automatic so that the inside wheel will properly follow a smaller circle than does the outer wheel.

steering ratio

If the steering wheel were connected directly to the front wheel steering mechanism, it would be almost impossible to steer the car. A child's pedal car is arranged this way, and steering in these light-

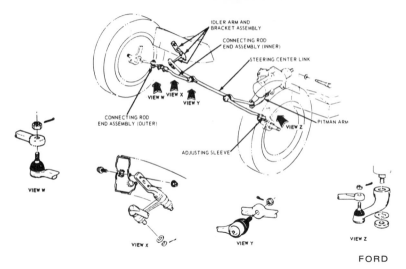

IDLER ARM AND
BRACKET ASSEMBLY

CONNECTING ROD
END ASSEMBLY (INNER)

STEERING CENTER LINK

VIEW W VIEW X
VIEW Y

CONNECTING ROD
END ASSEMBLY (OUTER)

PITMAN ARM

VIEW Z

ADJUSTING SLEEVE

VIEW W

VIEW X

VIEW Y

VIEW Z

FORD

Fig. 10-9 A manual steering system: shaft, gearbox, pitman, idler and intermediate arms, tie rods, and steering knuckle

weight and slow-moving vehicles is extremely erratic. Such problems with high-speed motor cars would be intolerable. The steering transmission provides a gear ratio that gives the driver a mechanical advantage and also slows the rate of turning so that directional control is achieved. Figure 10-9 shows a typical manual steering system. The gear ratio might provide for four turns of the steering wheel to turn the front wheels from full left to full right or from "lock to lock". Gear arrangements vary, but the one shown in Fig. 10-10 is typical.

power steering

Manual steering is satisfactory for light cars and cars with rear mounted engines. On heavier cars and in cars driven in tight traffic conditions, power steering is nearly indispensible. Actually, power steering is *power-assisted* steering: if the power system fails, the car can still be steered manually. Because of the very low gear ratio used in power steering systems, however, manual steering in the event of system failure requires a great deal more physical effort on the part of the driver. The steering system gets its power from the engine through a belt-driven pump; the effect of losing the power assist can be observed by steering a slowly moving automobile with the engine off.

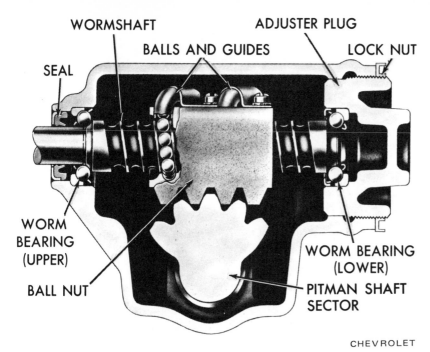

WORMSHAFT   ADJUSTER PLUG

BALLS AND GUIDES   LOCK NUT

SEAL

WORM BEARING (UPPER)

BALL NUT

WORM BEARING (LOWER)

PITMAN SHAFT SECTOR

CHEVROLET

Fig. 10-10 Typical gearing arrangements as used in the steering system (recirculating ball)

In most power steering systems, a hydraulically driven piston pushes the wheels to the left or right depending on the position of valves controlled by the steering wheel. Pressure to operate the piston is provided by the belt-driven pump, which usually is mounted on the engine. Often it is powered through the belt that drives the fan.

When the car is being driven straight ahead, pressure on both sides of the actuating piston is equal and the wheels do not turn left or right. If the steering wheel is turned to the left, the pressure is reduced from the left-hand side of the piston and applied to the right-hand side, and the piston is forced to the left. The range of travel or the distance that the steering mechanism moves is governed by the position of the mechanical gear system. The position of the gears is controlled by the driver through rotation of the steering wheel.

If the steering wheel is turned all the way to the left or right and held there, fluid pressure acting on the piston will drive the power system against the stops and an automatic bypass valve will release the excess pressure. Operation of the bypass valve usually

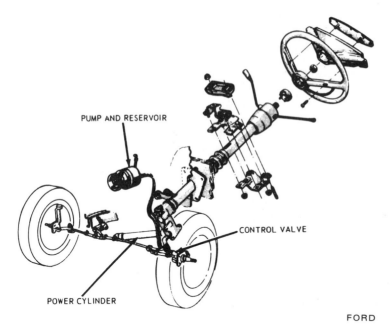

PUMP AND RESERVOIR

CONTROL VALVE

POWER CYLINDER

FORD

Fig. 10-11 A power steering system installed on a car:
component locations are typical

is accompanied by a high-pitched squeaking noise, which persists until the wheel is returned far enough so that the bypass valve can close. Figure 10-11 shows the complete power steering system installed in a car.

safety and comfort features

To prevent injuries from the steering column in the event of accidents, many cars are equipped with *collapsible steering columns*. These columns collapse or telescope if the driver is thrown forward violently, as in a forward collision. There are a number of systems for this purpose.

An optional feature is the tilting steering wheel, which allows the operator to position the steering wheel at the angle affording the greatest comfort in driving. This is shown in Fig. 10-12.

There is a wide variety of power steering, collapsible column, and tilting steering wheel systems. The owner's manual indicates which of these features is provided on a given car and usually includes a discussion of how they work and how to maintain them.

UNLOCKING
LEVER

CHEVROLET

Fig. 10-12   One example of a tilting steering wheel

Front End Alignment

The entire system that holds the front wheels to the car and connects the steering mechanism is called the *front end*. It is a relatively sensitive part of the car, and must afford considerable flexibility of movement and adjustments under widely varying driving conditions. The front wheels must be free to turn right or left so that the car can be steered. They must be able to roll so that the car can move, and they must allow for up and down motion. The front wheels must assume new positions to compensate or adjust for changes in the load carried by the vehicle. This adjustment is in the form of an inward or outward movement where the tires touch the ground. The front wheels also must be kept in the proper position with reference to the rest of the car to prevent abnormal tire wear, unsafe steering, or uncomfortable vibrations.

The process of adjusting the front wheel system is called *alignment*, or *front end alignment*, and it involves four main adjustments: *toe-in*, *toe-out*, *caster*, and *camber*.

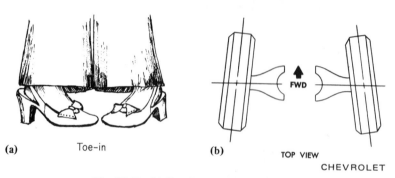

CHEVROLET

Fig. 10-13 (a) Sketch showing "toe-in" (feet) (b) sketch showing "toe in" of automobile front end

toe-in

Toe-in is a condition that also might be described as "pidgeon-toed." The front of the tires as viewed from above point slightly toward one another to allow easier steering. The angle is adjusted so that the car will remain stable and the tires will roll with minimum tread wear when the car is moving at highway speeds (Fig. 10-13).

toe-out

Toe-out, which is the reverse of toe-in, must be achieved as the car turns. The tire on the outside as the car turns must follow a larger circle than the tire on the inside; hence, the inside wheel must be turned a little bit more than the outside wheel. This condition as achieved by arranging the steering mechanism so that when the front wheels are turned either left or right, the inside wheel will turn about three degrees farther than the wheel on the outside of the turn (Fig. 10-14).

caster

Caster refers to the position of the *steering knuckle* relative to the front wheels. The steering knuckle is a hinge with one side fastened to the car and the wheel attached to the other. It permits the front wheels to turn right and left for steering. If the steering knuckle is attached straight up and down, the wheels have a tendency to "wiggle" as they roll. If it is adjusted so that there is

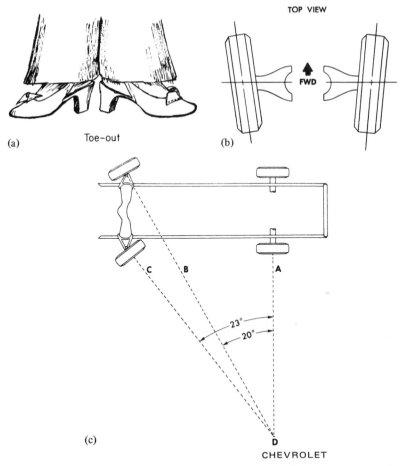

(a)   Toe-out   (b)

FWD

C   B   A

23°
20°

(c)   D

CHEVROLET

Fig. 10-14 (a) Sketch showing "toe-out" (feet) (b) sketch showing "toe-out" of automobile front end (c) sketch showing diagram of angles

a slight angle either to the front or to the rear, the weight of the car tends to keep the wheel stable. This effect is similar to the behavior of the wheels or casters on furniture or shopping carts. Furniture casters usually trail, or follow behind, the supporting leg. On automobiles, some front ends are aligned for *positive* caster, which sets the wheels into a slight trailing position; others are adjusted for *negative* caster, which sets the wheels into a position slightly ahead of a line drawn from the axle to the ground (Fig. 10-15). The owner's manual indicates the direction and degree to which caster needs to be adjusted on a given auto.

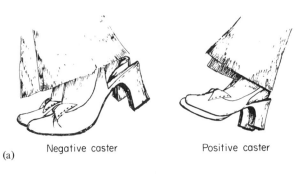

(a)

Negative caster   Positive caster

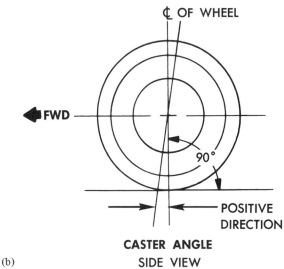

₵ OF WHEEL

◄FWD

90°

POSITIVE
DIRECTION

CASTER ANGLE

(b)   SIDE VIEW

Fig. 10-15 (a) Sketch showing caster attitude (feet) (b) sketch
showing caster of automobile front wheels

camber

Camber describes the angle that the front tire leans outward
at the top. This angle varies with the load being carried. As more
weight is added and the springs compress, the top of the wheel will
be pulled inward toward the frame of the car. If the wheels on an
unloaded car were vertical, as the load increased the front wheels
would angle in toward the car and the tires would roll more or less
on the inside edge. With positive camber, the tire leans outward at
the top when the car is unloaded. When weight is added, the top of

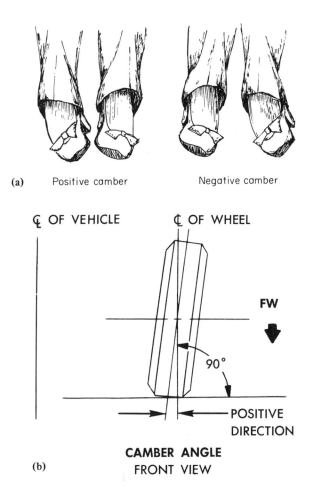

(a) Positive camber   Negative camber

Ȼ OF VEHICLE   Ȼ OF WHEEL

FW

90°

POSITIVE
DIRECTION

CAMBER ANGLE
FRONT VIEW

(b)

Fig. 10-16 (a) Sketch showing camber attitudes (feet) (b) sketch showing camber of automobile front wheels

the wheel is pulled inward so that when the car is rolling along the road, the wheels are very nearly straight up and down and the full tread of the tires touch the ground (Fig. 10-16).

Braking Systems

The braking system is an extremely important part of any motor vehicle. Usually an automobile has at least two independent braking systems, the *foot brake* and the *emergency*, or *parking brake*. In many cases, the front and rear brakes operate independently of each other although both are activated by the same foot pedal. Increasing numbers of cars have some form of power-assisted brake system. The two common brake systems on passenger cars are *drum* brakes and *disc* brakes.

drum brakes

The most common system on most U.S. cars is the drum system in which a drum is attached to the wheel and rotates along with it. The drum resembles a round cake pan, but it is of much heavier construction and has a 2- to 3-inch rim. Inside the drum, but not rotating, are two pie-shaped segments that can be pushed outward and jammed against the rim of the drum. When enough pressure is applied, these segments or *brake shoes*, can be held against the rim tightly enough that the wheel cannot turn. The contact surfaces of the segments are covered with an asbestos material, the *brake lining,* that enables them to build up friction without grabbing and thus stop or slow the car gently.

The force to push the brake shoes against the drums is provided by hydraulic pressure from a cylinder actuated by the foot pedal. Springs are provided to pull the brake shoes away from the drums when pressure on the foot pedal is released. Figure 10-17 illustrates a brake drum. The shoes and wheel cylinder which operate inside

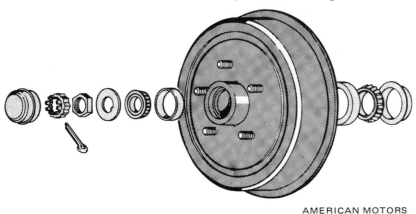

AMERICAN MOTORS

Fig. 10-17 Expanded view of a typical drum brake system

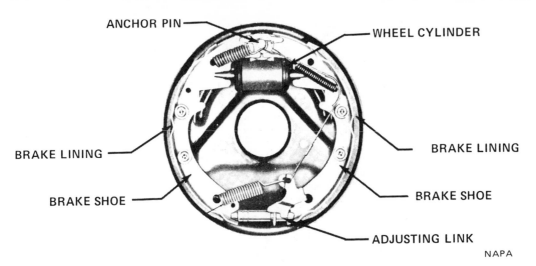

ANCHOR PIN

WHEEL CYLINDER

BRAKE LINING

BRAKE LINING

BRAKE SHOE

BRAKE SHOE

ADJUSTING LINK

NAPA

Fig. 10-18 Brake shoes and wheel cylinder as they appear from below

the drum are shown in Fig. 10-18. There is one brake assembly for each wheel of the car, although the front and rear assemblies are not necessarily the same size.

disc brakes

Drum brakes have a characteristic that can be considered a safety deficiency in some aspects. When the drums become heated, as they will after the brakes have been on for a long time as in descending a long hill, they tend to "fade." Brake fading is a tendency for the brakes to lose their hold. Because of this characteristic it takes longer to stop a car with drum brakes if prior use has generated heat in the drums. One means of overcoming this deficiency is the use of disc brakes (Fig. 10-19), in which a flat, round disc replaces the drum. Like the drum, the disc rotates with the wheel. An assembly called the *caliper* is positioned over the edge of the disc so that the pads, or linings, can grasp the disc on opposite sides and squeeze it between them. The action is as though the disc were clamped in a vise. Obviously, if it is clamped tightly enough the wheel cannot turn. Since the greater part of the surface of the disc is exposed to the air, it cools more effectively and fading does not occur. Brake fade is practically

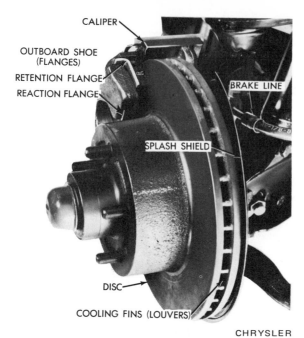

CALIPER

OUTBOARD SHOE
(FLANGES)

RETENTION FLANGE

REACTION FLANGE

BRAKE LINE

SPLASH SHIELD

DISC

COOLING FINS (LOUVERS)

CHRYSLER

Fig. 10-19   A typical disc brake assembly

nonexistent with disc brakes.   Like the shoes or a drum brake assembly, the calipers are hydraulically actuated.   Because the contact area of the calipers is small compared to the contact area of the shoe and drum system, it takes much more pedal pressure to obtain braking action with disc brakes than it does with drum brakes.   As a consequence, disc brakes are almost invariably operated with power brake systems.

hydraulic brakes

The *hydraulic* brake system has been in almost universal use on passenger cars since the thirties when the last of the mechanical brake systems was finally abandoned.   The typical hydraulic brake system consists of a *master cylinder* and *reservoir* for the hydraulic fluid and an actuating cylinder or *wheel cylinder* at each wheel. When the foot pedal is pressed down the piston of the master cylinder pushes hydraulic fluid out through the brake lines to each of the wheel cylinders.   The fluid enters the wheel cylinders at the

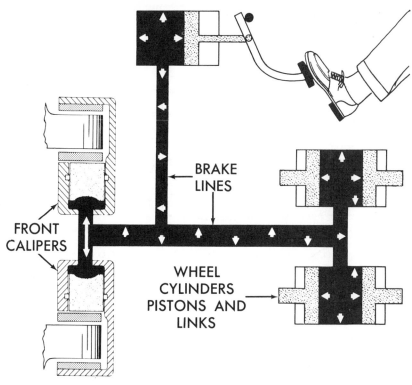

FRONT
CALIPERS

BRAKE
LINES

WHEEL
CYLINDERS
PISTONS AND
LINKS

CHEVROLET

Fig. 10-20 Schematic drawing of a typical hydraulic brake system

center between two pistons. These pistons are forced apart and since the outside end of each piston is in contact with a brake shoe, the brake shoes are forced outward until they come in contact with the brake drum.

Pressure for all four wheels comes from the master cylinder and is equalized throughout the whole system so that braking action will be similar at all four wheels. New cars must have two independent master cylinders, one for the front wheels and one for the rear, both actuated by the same foot pedal. In these cases, each system will equalize within itself and the two systems must be adjusted to operate effectively together. Figure 10-20 demonstrates how a common four wheel hydraulic brake system operates. Figure 10-21 shows a dual master cylinder with an integral reservoir of the type that is becoming increasingly popular due to its inherent safety features.

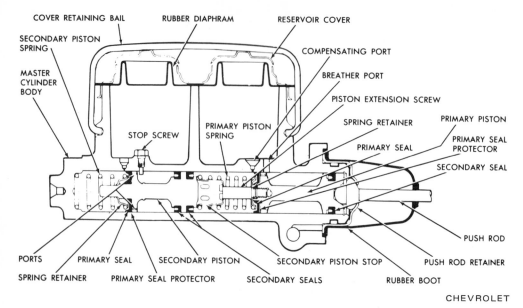

Fig. 10-21 A cross section of a typical brake system master cylinder. Dual master cylinder is used to increase safety; failure of one system does not result in total loss of brakes

emergency or parking brakes

Emergency or parking brake systems are not well suited to stopping the car in the normal driving situation. On some cars, a cable is brought into the brake shoe system so that tension on the cable will force the shoes into contact with the drum (Fig. 10-22). Other cars have a totally different brake system in which a friction brake siezes the drive shaft.

Power Brake Systems

Power brake systems are used with both disc and drum brakes. One popular arrangement is disc brakes on the front wheels and drum brakes on the rear. The term *power assist* used to describe power steering systems applies equally to power brakes. Should the power brake system fail, the driver still has normal hydraulic braking capability but more effort is required to achieve effective braking action.

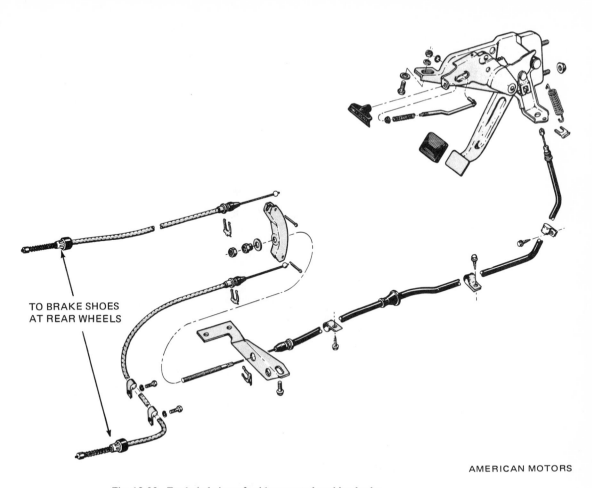

TO BRAKE SHOES
AT REAR WHEELS

Fig. 10-22   Exploded view of cable operated parking brake

The most common power assist units operate from the engine vacuum. A typical power assist unit, with the master cylinder attached, is shown in Fig. 10-23. Figure 10-24 is a cutaway view of the power assist unit. A large diaphragm is attached to the plunger on the master cylinder. When the brake pedal is pressed, a valve is actuated in the power assist unit which causes a vacuum on one side of the diaphragm and atmospheric pressure on the other. The diaphragm then moves in the direction of the vacuum pushing on the master cylinder plunger with considerable force. This force supplements the force being applied by the driver through foot pressure. When the master cylinder plunger is pushed in this manner, the hydraulic brakes will operate.

Power brakes provide a mechnical advantage in applying the necessary pressure to stop the car. The mechanical advantage is derived from the engine vacuum and little effort is required from the driver to maintain control of the car. If the power-assist system does not work, the brakes will work as normal, unassisted hydraulic brakes.

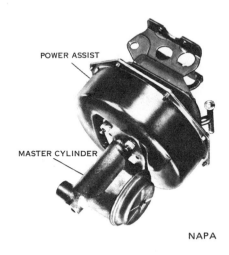

NAPA

Fig. 10-23 A typical power assist unit for automotive brakes with master cylinder

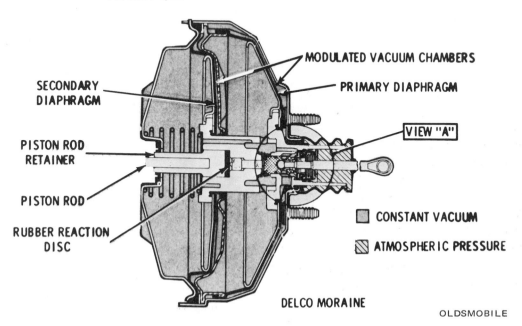

Fig. 10-24 Cutaway view of a power assist unit

Wheel Bearings

Low-friction, well-lubricated bearings are required to allow the wheels to roll as freely as possible; otherwise, friction would soon generate enough heat to damage the wheels or axles. Some form of roller or ball bearings are used on the wheels of all automobiles. A roller bearing is a series of small, round metal rollers arranged in a ring, called the *bearing race,* which usually is made to fit the machined surfaces around the hub and axle. As the wheel spins, the rollers roll freely, thus eliminating the friction between the two surfaces. Figure 10-17 is an exploded view of a complete front wheel assembly with the bearings shown in their relative positions; Fig. 10-25a shows the type of bearing used. Ball bearings some-

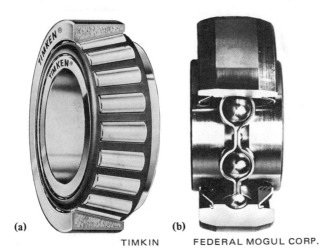

(a)   (b)

TIMKIN   FEDERAL MOGUL CORP.

Fig. 10-25 (a) An example of a roller bearing as used in automobile wheels (b) An example of a ball bearing, sometimes used in automobile wheels

times are used particularly in small, lightweight cars. They are arranged much like roller bearings except that the rollers are replaced by steel balls held in the race by specially formed retainers (Fig. 10-25b). Ball bearings have a smaller contact area and therefore usually allow less friction than roller bearings.

Wheel bearings need to be kept well lubricated, and grease is used for this purpose. Front wheel bearings usually are easily removed, along with the wheels, making lubrication a fairly easy task. Lubrication of rear wheel bearings, however, is more difficult, since removal of the rear wheels usually requires a special tool called a *wheel puller*.

Once the bearings are lubricated, tightly fitting synthetic rubber discs or washers pressed against them on either side serve as grease seals to contain the lubricant even when the heat of friction tends to make it more fluid.

Bumpers and Energy-Absorbing Systems

The front and rear bumpers are attached to cars to prevent damage should the car inadvertently bump against another car or some fixed object. In early cars, the bumpers protruded well in front and behind the vehicle and were made of tough steel to take the punishment that driving conditions of the times subjected them to. Gradually, as driving conditions improved, bumpers were considered less necessary and style took on greater importance than function, then bumpers of thin metal stampings, chrome-plated for appearance sake, became little more than stylish accessories.

It has been proven that properly designed bumpers can do a lot to minimize damage in accidents. The trend now is to more functional bumpers that afford a reasonable degree of protection. In many cases, both front and rear bumpers incorporate energy-absorbing systems that absorb some of the impact of collision. Figure 10-26a and b shows a typical energy absorber in the extended and collapsed positions. Note the resemblance to a standard shock absorber. Figure 10-27 is a view of the energy absorber installed on the frame member under the car with the front bumper attached. Installations on rear bumpers are much the same.

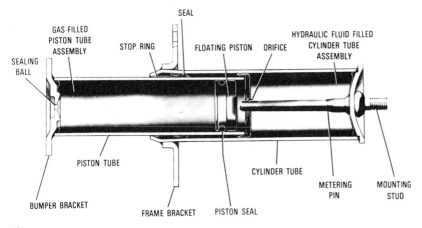

(a)

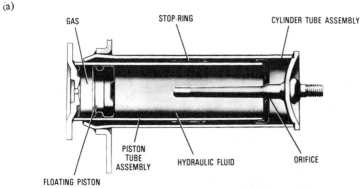

(b)

CHEVROLET

Fig. 10-26 Energy absorber as used on automobile bumpers—
a safety feature (a) energy absorber extended, (b) collapsed

AMERICAN MOTORS

Fig. 10-27 Energy absorber installed on an automobile

The Chassis

The chassis or frame of the vehicle requires virtually no maintenance. About the only useful thing that can be done is to examine the frame from time to time for cracks and to see if any of the items attached to it, like brake lines, electric wiring, hoses, or pipes, have come loose. Anything found rubbing on the frame should be corrected.

Suspension Systems

lubrication

The days of the old-fashioned "grease job" are pretty well gone. Older cars (and a few newer ones) had a great number of grease fittings, called *zircs,* to which a grease gun (Fig. 10-28*a*) could be attached. Prepackaged grease cartridges (Fig. 10-28*b*) make grease handling clean and convenient. Through these fittings,

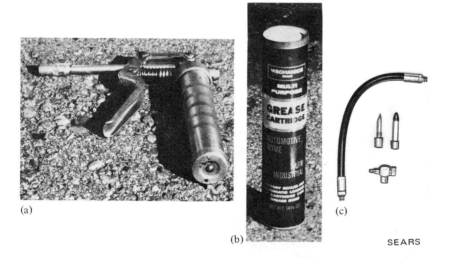

(a)

(b)

(c)

SEARS

Fig. 10-28 (a) Grease gun used to grease zirc fittings
(b) typical grease gun cartridge filler (c) plastic or metal
plugs can be removed, then a grease gun with a special
adaptor used to lube the suspension

grease could be added periodically to parts of the suspension system that rub against one another—for example, ball joints, king pins, universal joints, other moving parts, and sometimes leaf springs. In nearly all modern cars, these areas are enclosed in rubber boots or protected by other means to ensure that the grease does not escape and require replacement.

As a result of recent improvements, today's greases last much longer than older types. A modern car thus may require a complete "grease job" only two or three times in its lifetime, instead of every thousand miles, as before.

It is still possible to perform the "grease job" at home when necessary. Some new cars are equipped with zircs, and several "shots" of grease from the grease gun at the recommended intervals will do the job. Most other cars have plastic or metal plugs instead of zircs. These plugs can be removed, and grease can be forced into the appropriate areas by means of a grease gun with a special adaptor (Fig. 10-28c). The owner's manual or shop manual indicates the parts of the suspension system that should be lubricated, and at what intervals. Service stations also have lubrication charts showing points requiring lubrication and recommended intervals for most cars in common use.

Because of new grease technology, greases cannot be used interchangeably. There are two general categories of grease: (1) chassis grease and (2) bearing grease. Chassis grease has historically been of lower quality. Its main characteristic is slipperiness, and little attention has been given to its ability to withstand high temperature or high pressure. Bearing grease, on the other hand, must be capable of retaining its lubricating qualities at high temperature and high pressure for long periods of time. The standard bearing grease for many years has been *Lithium-based long-fiber grease*. Like most bearing greases, it also is suitable for use as chassis grease; on the other hand, chassis grease, is not of high enough quality normally to be used for bearings.

A high quality grease, *molybdenum disulfide*, is now being used as the standard grease for both bearings and chassis in many new cars. Although it is not much more expensive than the older lithium-based greases, it is of much higher quality, and its use significantly extends the time between greasing of both the bearings and the chassis. It does not mix well with lithium-based grease, however, and mixing with another type of grease can result in destructive chemical reactions. Molybdenum disulfide, called "moly" grease, may replace most other greases in use today.

A modern vehicle's suspension system contains many rubber bushings that absorb road shock and prevent parts from rubbing against each other. As these rubber bushings age, they dry out and become more brittle, so can be the cause of very annoying squeaks. Leaf springs, commonly found at the rear of the car, sometimes have rubber spacers built into them to minimize squeaky springs. Overload springs, which are wound around shock absorbers and are commonly found on station wagons and other vehicles that pull trailers, sometimes have rubber guides that can cause squeaks (Fig. 10-29). Another common source of squeaks is the rubber bushings found at the points where shock absorbers are attached. Rubber lubricant applied to these rubber surfaces will usually eliminate this annoying problem. If no rubber lube is on hand, brake fluid will do nearly as well.

shock absorbers

The condition of the shock absorbers, and on some cars the steering vibration damper (which is nothing more than a shock absorber mounted horizontally), significantly affects the way a car rides and steers, and its safety at highway speeds. The simplest test to determine the condition of shock absorbers is to bounce the front of the car (if the front shocks are being inspected) up and down violently. Good shock absorbers will bring the bouncing to a halt almost immediately. If the car continues to bounce, it may be assumed that the shock absorbers are bad and should be replaced, always in pairs. The same procedure may be followed with the rear of the car.

A second test of shock absorber condition is a visual one. Shock absorbers that show signs of leaking oil are probably bad and should be replaced. The third (and ultimate) test of the operation of a shock absorber is to remove one end of a shock (or both ends, if necessary) and pump it back and forth by hand to see if it strongly opposes such pumping action. If the plunger moves back and forth easily, or when changing from pulling to pushing it moves even part of the distance easily, the shock absorber should be replaced. Chapter 18 provides information on how to avoid being sold shock absorbers unnecessarily.

Unfortunately, the life of the original shock absorber on new cars often is not even as long as the automobile warranty period. Shock absorbers do need occasional replacement, a job that can be done at home. If the bolts and nuts that hold the shock absorbers in place are muddy and rusty, application of a "penetrating oil" for a few minutes before trying to loosen them should simplify the process. The purchase and home installation of "heavy-duty" shock absorbers can afford considerable dollar savings.

ball joints

A favorite (and expensive) sales gimmick of some shady operators is to try to sell major repairs of the front suspension and steering mechanism. "Evidence" of serious wear is shown the customer by raising the car up on a hoist and showing how loose the steering mechanism is, frequently by prying around with a rod or a pipe. The fact is that if a brand new car is raised off the ground, an apparently alarming amount of "play" can be found in the steering mechanism. This condition is quite normal and is eliminated when the weight of the car is let back down on its wheels.

Front-end wear does occur, particularly in the ball-joint and king-pin areas, as discussed earlier. It is not possible, however, to indicate here how much "play" is tolerable for each make of car. The use of modern high-quality greases, and adherence to the manufacturer's prescribed maintenance schedule, should prevent the need for major front-end repairs until near the end of the vehicle's useful life.

It is a good idea to have the front suspension and steering safety-checked every year or so by a competent mechanic whose judgment you trust. Caster, camber, and toe-ing cannot be adjusted at home without special equipment and skills. See Chapter 11 for visible signs of misadjustment in these areas.

trailer towing

When engineers design a car, they design a suspension system for that particular type of vehicle and distribution of weight. About the only simple thing a car owner can do to vary the handling characteristics is to change the tire pressure or buy a new type of tire design (Chapter 11). If the car is to be used for some purpose outside its design capability, such as pulling a heavy trailer, it may be necessary to modify the suspension system, either temporarily by means of a special load-leveling hitch when the trailer is attached, or by more permanent means such as the installation of overload springs.

Since the topic of trailer-towing could easily fill a book, all that can be said here is that if your car is going to be used to tow a heavy trailer, its suspension system should be modified to compensate for the difference in weight distribution. If not changed, the handling characteristics of the car could be dangerously affected. Owners of heavy station wagons, whether they pull trailers or not, frequently replace the rear shock absorbers with overload shocks (Fig. 10-29), which prevent the rear of a heavily loaded vehicle from "hitting bottom" when it goes over a bump. Overload shocks do result in a little firmer ride when the vehicle is carrying only one or two passengers.

Because of the strain on the suspension system of a vehicle used to pull a heavy trailer, it is advisable from time to time to check to see that the vehicle is still level with respect to the ground. This is most easily done by parking the car on a level stretch of street and measuring the height above ground of a certain spot on

SEARS

Fig. 10-29 Overload shock absorbers and springs with rubber fittings at ends.

each of four points on the car, for example the top of each fender opening, with a yardstick. If one side of the car is higher than the other, usually an indication of weak springs, a mechanic can correct the problem with relatively simple adjustments of the torsion bars or springs.

The condition of front wheel alignment and tire balance is indicated by the wear patterns of the front tires, as discussed in Chapter 11. Here we deal with routine maintenance and care of front wheel bearings and brakes.

front wheel bearings

The bearings on which the front wheels rotate are under a great deal of stress and may operate under very high temperatures. It is usually necessary to remove the front wheels and their bearings once a year, clean the entire assembly, and repack the bearings and races with high-quality bearing grease. Failure to do this can result in severe bearing and bearing assembly wear and, in the extreme case, loss of a front wheel while driving.

While the process of "repacking" the front wheel bearings is a fairly simple one, because of the safety implications the car owner should decide whether to do the job himself or have it done by an experienced mechanic. Virtually the entire cost of a front wheel bearing repack is labor, the cost of the grease being insignificant. On cars having disc brakes, it is necessary to partially disassemble the brake assembly; for this reason, it is recommended that the average car owner leave front wheel bearing maintenance to an experienced mechanic. The interested car owner should learn the steps involved in repacking wheel bearings by actual experience under the direct guidance of a competent instructor.

brakes

Numerous accidents are caused by improperly adjusted brakes, so an increasing number of states are requiring that brake work be performed only by persons licensed to do so. The average auto

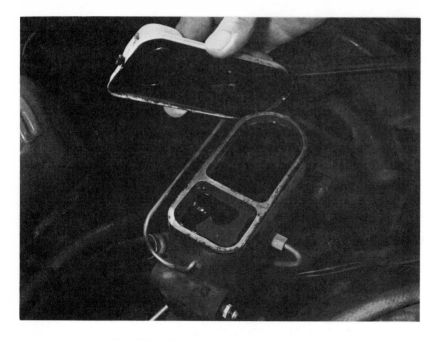

Fig. 10-30 Checking fluid in brake fluid reservoir

owner is therefore not encouraged to perform repairs or maintenance in this area. From the standpoint of safety and economy,
however, an understanding of how to assess the condition of the
vehicle's brakes is helpful.

Brake linings in a modern car should last at least half the life of
the vehicle unless the brakes are used excessively or abused. Because the linings are made of asbestos and they do wear, it is necessary to have the brakes "set up" from time to time. This is a fairly
simple and inexpensive process, but should be performed only by
those who are competent to do so.

The auto owner, as part of the weekly inspection, can check
the level of the fluid in the brake fluid reservoir (Fig. 10-30).
Although this fluid level should be checked regularly, it should
rarely be necessary to add fluid. If it becomes necessary to add
fluid frequently, there is a leak in the system, and the vehicle
should be taken to a garage for further inspection.

There are different levels of quality of brake fluids, and only
the top quality should be purchased. If the can specifically states:
"For use in cars with disc brakes," the fluid may be assumed to be
of a high enough quality for use in any car. Some brake fluids of

lower quality have been known to boil under the high pressures of emergency braking, lose their effectiveness, and the car loses its braking ability. When in doubt, check the owner's manual.

If the car does not have power steering, there is a gear box under the hood, not too far off the ground, at the opposite end of the steering column from the steering wheel. The grease level in this gear box must be checked from time to time, and grease added when necessary. This grease is actually a very heavy oil and should not be confused with chassis and bearing greases previously discussed. Check the owner's manual for the proper weight of steering gear box oil or grease. The steering grease level can usually be checked by removing a large plug, which resembles a bolt (Fig. 10-31).

On cars with power steering, it is necessary to check the power steering fluid level, usually by means of a dip stick (Fig. 10-32) or

Fig. 10-31 Checking the gear box grease in the steering system

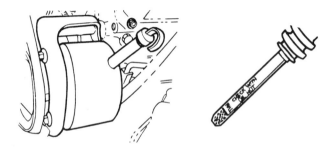

Fig. 10-32 Checking the power steering fluid with a dip stick

by removing a cap similar to the radiator cap. Since different manufacturers use different types of power steering fluid (hydraulic fluid), just as different manufacturers use different automatic transmission fluid (hydraulic fluid), the owner's manual should be consulted to determine the appropriate type of fluid for the power steering system. Hydraulic fluid is not expensive, but using the wrong fluid could result in improper operation of the system or greatly reduce the life of the pump or steering cylinder seals and gaskets.

Frequently, service stations do not have the special hydraulic fluid needed for a specific system of each specific car. It is wise therefore, to keep a can of each on hand as part of your home servicing car care kit. In the case of automatic transmissions and power steering systems, it is especially important that you resist the claims of some service station attendants that all hydraulic fluids are the same. They are not all the same. Failure to observe this simple precaution can be expensive. As in the case of engine oil, add only enough power steering fluid to achieve the level prescribed by the manufacturer.

Since some of the hydraulic fluids required are available only from automobile dealerships, and dealers are often closed on weekends, it is wise to carry small supplies of special hydraulic fluids when taking a trip.

Tires

tire construction

There are several different types of tire construction. An understanding of their differences will aid in the selection of the best tire for the particular vehicle and anticipated driving conditions.

bias ply tires

Bias ply tires have a traditional design that has been used for decades. The only major changes in their construction have been from cotton plies to rayon and then to nylon, which is the strongest. They are available in multiples of two plies (Fig. 11-1a). Two large plies (or layers of construction material) can have more strength than four small ones. Some tires with more plies may have higher load-carrying capacities, but they are more susceptible to overheating as the plies rub against each other during travel. Truck tires with many plies must be kept inflated to very high pressures to prevent excessive flexing and heating.

The standard 2- or 4-ply nylon bias ply tire is a good general duty tire and is the least expensive. It usually is wise to avoid tires having *only* rayon cord plies because of their reduced strength. Nylon ply tires may have an annoying "nylon thump" caused by flat spots that form on the tire bottoms while the vehicle is parked, but after a few blocks of driving the flat spots smooth out and the tire runs normally.

Belted bias tires are similar in construction to the regular bias tire but have greater strength and stability provided by additional

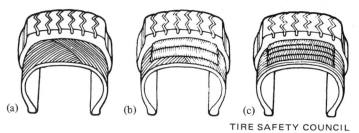

TIRE SAFETY COUNCIL

Fig. 11-1 Bias ply tires of various types (a) bias ply construction (b) belted bias (c) radial

belts of fiberglas or polyester around the circumference (Fig. 11-1*b*). While the belted bias tire offers significantly longer tread life, there have been serious manufacturing problems and numerous tire recalls. In some cases, it has been impossible to keep the tires balanced as the belts move around and change their weight distribution. These tires are more expensive than the regular nylon bias ply tires. They are furnished as original equipment on many new U.S. cars.

Radial ply tires have main plies that run radially around the tire (Fig. 11-1*c*) and additional circumferential belts to give sidewall flexibility and very great strength. This is the U.S. tire of the future, although it has long been in common use in Europe. Nearly all new French, Italian, and British cars, as well as an increasing number of U.S. cars have radial tires as standard equipment. They are exceptionally strong, suitable for continuous high speed driving, and give very long tread life. A car equipped with radials handles noticeably better at highway speeds than one with regular tires; however, radials do tend to be a bit noisy at low speeds. They are two to three times more expensive than regular bias tires, especially if the circumferential belts are of steel mesh, which makes them virtually puncture proof.

These general observations should be considered when selecting tires. Choose new tires according to your actual needs. Do not mix different types on one car, or its handling characteristics may become unsafe. If you are going to switch from one type of tire construction to another, install all four new tires at the same time.

The standard nylon bias ply tire can be purchased in "special" sales very reasonably and is suitable for older cars that are used primarily for short-distance commuting at moderate speeds. If you are willing to accept "blemished" tires, those having imperfect white sidewalls perhaps but no structural problems, additional savings can be made. For long-distance driving at expressway speeds, radials will be the better buy.

As you consider purchasing tires with long anticipated life, bear in mind that this long life can be realized only if the front end alignment and tire balance are regularly checked and the tires regularly rotated. Just a few days of steady high speed driving with faulty alignment, balance, or shock absorbers can seriously reduce the tread life of any tire.

Fig. 11-2 Sidewall of tire showing the tire load/pressure, ply, size, and construction information

Manufacturers' Specifications

All tires sold in the United States bear certain information required by the Department of Transportation (DOT). Figure 11-2 shows how the information discussed below is arranged on the tire sidewall.

manufacturer's name

The actual manufacturer is determined from the DOT number on the tire. A chart is needed to identify the manufacturer from this DOT number, which also includes the date of manufacture, and other information. Discount houses can buy tires with their own name on the sidewalls if they buy in large quantities.

This information really doesn't mean much as there is no industry-wide standard for the use of the work *premium* or any other term implying relative quality.

maximum load and pressure

These are important figures. Never buy a tire with a maximum load-carrying capacity lower than that of the original tires on the car. Slightly larger tires are alright, provided they do not rub against the fenders. A change to a larger tire size will cause the speedometer and odometer to read low. "Load range B" means the same as the old "4-ply rating" and is standard for autos. Load ranges C and D are for trucks or for severe off-highway use.

ply information

Rayon cord is sometimes used for the sidewalls in belted and radial tires, where there are additional belts of stronger materials below the tread.

tubeless

Virtually all auto tires are now tubeless. If the tire is of radial construction it must be so designated.

F78-14

This is the size identification sequence used on bias and belted bias tires. Radial tires have this sequence plus the letter R (for example, FR78-14). The letter F indicates the load-carrying ability. The higher the letter the larger the tire, with A being the smallest and L the largest in common auto use.

The number 78 means that the tire's height is 78 percent of its width (Fig. 11-3). The three common ratios are 78, 70, and 60 percent with 78 being "standard." The others are referred to as "low-profile" tires. Older tires might have the designation 7.75

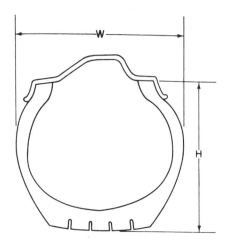

Fig. 11-3 Tire aspect ratio (see text)

instead of F78. The number 7.75 refers to the tire width—7.75 in.
—but tells nothing of the height-to-width ratio.

The —14 means the tire fits a rim (wheel) of 14 in. diameter.
Most radials made outside the United States have a semi-metric
designation such as 195-14, which is read as "195 millimeters
width, to fit a 14-in. diameter rim."

Recapped Tires

When truck and aircraft tires wear out their tread, it is common
practice to have them "recapped." Recapping consists of taking
the old tire and molding a new rubber tread cap on it. Tires made
for recapping have many plies and can be recapped a dozen times
or more. The regular auto tire, however, was not meant to be recapped. It was built to be sold as cheaply as possible and discarded
when worn out.

This does not mean that all recaps should be avoided. If most
of your driving is around town, at relatively slow speeds, recaps
may be adequate. By careful shopping, however, you can often
buy new bias ply tires for just a little more. Recaps with snow
treads make good snow tires where they are run at low speeds and
the snow keeps them cool.

Recapping companies must mold an identification number into recapped tires. This identification is found on the side of the tire in the edge of the new cap. Look carefully when buying tires to be sure you are not paying for a new tire and receiving a recap. The quality of recapped tires depends on many things, including the condition of the old tire casing and the integrity of the recapping company. It would be unfair to say that auto recaps are unsafe, but let the buyer beware.

Snow Tires and Chains

The chief difference between snow tires and regular tires is in the tread pattern. Snow tires grip packed snow for better traction, but tests have shown that they are not as effective on ice as regular tires. Snow tires can be purchased with steel studs imbedded in the rubber tread so they will grip better on icy roads. Many states are outlawing the use of studded tires, however, because they cause serious road damage. Check your state's laws regarding studded snow tires before you buy.

The tread on a snowtire does not lose heat as readily as a tread on a regular tire, therefore, snow tires operated at high speed on warm days wear out very rapidly. They also run more noisily due to the tread pattern.

Do not use snow tires on the front of a car unless absolutely necessary as they tend to make steering unstable. Even on the rear of the car, snow tires may cause handling to become mushy, making high speed operation dangerous.

For traveling on icy roads, tire chains should be used on the rear wheels. By all means, purchase them long before you reach areas where they are required. Prices have been known to go as high as 10 times the regular price in areas where supply is limited. The rental for a set of chains (a common practice when they are needed only to get over a mountain pass) may be as expensive as buying your own set. If desired, service stations will install and remove them for a reasonable price.

Do not drive fast with chains on. If a link breaks, it could go right through a fender or do other damage. Remove the chains as soon as it is safe to do so, for they wear out on bare pavement in a very few miles.

AMERICAN CHAIN

Fig. 11-4 Tire chains with "claws" for winter weather driving

When buying tire chains be sure they are the right size to fit your tires and look for those that have "claws" for better gripping on ice (see Fig. 11-4). Learn how to install them before they are needed and, after they are removed, wipe them with an oily rag to prevent rusting.

Tire Maintenance

Good tire maintenance is one of the easiest but most overlooked ways to save money on your car.

proper tire pressures

The major cause of premature tire wear and failure is improper inflation. Underinflated tires wear out along the edges, as shown in Fig. 11-5a; if the internal air pressure is too high, the tire will

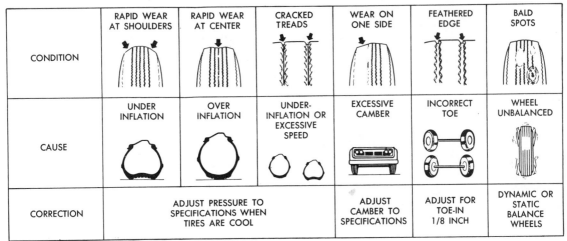

	RAPID WEAR AT SHOULDERS	RAPID WEAR AT CENTER	CRACKED TREADS	WEAR ON ONE SIDE	FEATHERED EDGE	BALD SPOTS
CONDITION						
CAUSE	UNDER INFLATION	OVER INFLATION	UNDER-INFLATION OR EXCESSIVE SPEED	EXCESSIVE CAMBER	INCORRECT TOE	WHEEL UNBALANCED
CORRECTION	ADJUST PRESSURE TO SPECIFICATIONS WHEN TIRES ARE COOL			ADJUST CAMBER TO SPECIFICATIONS	ADJUST FOR TOE-IN 1/8 INCH	DYNAMIC OR STATIC BALANCE WHEELS

CHRYSLER

Fig. 11-5 Six typical tire problems, cause and correction

bulge and wear in the center, as shown in Fig. 11-5b. The optimum tire pressure for a given car depends on such factors as the weight of the car and whether the tire is to be used on the front or the rear. A certain amount of experimenting is needed to determine just how much air pressure should be carried in each tire.

The owner's manual gives the manufacturer's recommended tire pressures for a particular car. These suggested pressures are good starting values. Remember, however, the manufacturer wants the car to ride soft so you will be pleased, therefore the recommended values are often on the low side, resulting in premature tire wear.

Tire gauges attached to air hoses at service stations are frequently very inaccurate. You should invest in *your own* gauge, carry it in the car at all times, and check the tire pressures yourself. Figure 11-6 shows a typical tire pressure gauge.

The correct time to check pressures is when the tires are cold. As tires roll along the road they flex, and the flexing causes them to heat. This tire heat causes the air inside to heat and expand, increasing the pressure. The pressure in a hot tire may be significantly higher than when it has cooled. Drivers sometimes fear that the high hot-tire pressure will cause a blowout, so they remove some air. This only makes the situation worse, however, for when the tire cools, its pressure will be too low, more flexing will occur, and

Fig. 11-6 Tire pressure gauge

the tire will heat up even more—and it is heat that weakens and destroys tires.

For trips when the car is fully loaded, pulling a heavy trailer, or traveling at expressway speeds, it is advisable to *add* 3 to 4 pounds of pressure to each tire before starting out. The added pressure will result in a bit rougher ride because the tires will not flex as much, however, they will not heat as much, so the rise in internal air pressure will not be as great. Obviously, tires under higher pressure will wear more in the center, but this is a penalty that has to be paid for heavy loading or prolonged high speed driving. Never put in more air than the maximum rated pressure printed on the sides of the tire (normally 32 pounds per square inch when measured cold), and be sure to reduce the tire pressures to normal after they have cooled down and the trip is over.

tread wear patterns

Tires should be inspected weekly. The tread wear patterns indicate whether the tires are being driven overinflated or underinflated. On some cars, such as heavy station wagons and those with engines mounted in the rear, it is necessary to have the rear tire pressures very high and the front pressures rather low in order to maintain good road handling characteristics. Improved handling,

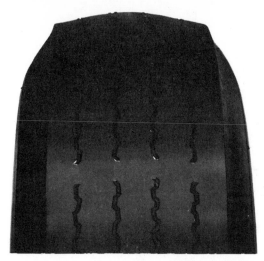

Fig. 11-7 Tire tread wear indicator

in this case, is achieved at the expense of poor wear patterns. To extend their life, the tires should be rotated back and forth from front to rear, adjusting the pressures accordingly, equalizing the wear. On large cars, tires should be rotated every 5,000 miles or so; on smaller, lightweight cars, every 10,000 miles is often enough.

To enable drivers to readily determine the tread condition of each tire, manufacturers must include *wear indicator bars* in the tread pattern of each new tire. These bars are sometimes referred to as "Nader bars" after the consumer advocate of that name. When the tread wears down to the indicator bar at any point, that tire is considered worn out. In some states, the highway patrol will issue a citation to the driver whose car has a tire with a wear bar showing, on the basis that he is driving an unsafe vehicle. Figure 11-7 shows a tire worn down to the indicator bars.

The Flat Tire

A flat tire is a readily identified problem with an obvious solution. However, if a tire loses air as the car is traveling, the problem might not be as obvious but is much more dangerous. Modern tires tend to lose air more slowly and not blow out as frequently

"I don't think we'd prove anything by changing his tires for him."

as earlier ones did. Leaking tires sneak up on the driver in a treacherous way. It is possible to spot a low tire when driving if you know the normal handling characteristics of your car. To get the "feel" of your car, drive on a straight length of highway and gently "whip" the steering wheel from side to side and note how long it takes the car to respond. A small sports car will respond very quickly; a large heavy car will respond relatively slowly.

When a tire has been punctured or otherwise caused to leak air, the handling of the car becomes "mushy"—that is, it does not respond as quickly as you have previously noted. It may take a period of minutes, perhaps longer, to become apparent, depending on how rapidly the tire is losing air. If you suspect a low tire, again gently "whip" the steering wheel back and forth. If the car "turns like a battleship," stop and inspect the tires. If one of them is low, you then have the choice of driving on it or changing it. Normally, the defective tire should be replaced with the spare, but other factors sometimes come into play. If a tire goes flat on a long narrow bridge, on a busy freeway, or within sight of a service station, you may decide to drive on it, knowing that by so doing it will be ruined. If it is driven over a mile or so, the steel rim on which it is mounted may also be ruined.

Sometimes the cause of an apparent "leaking tire" is just a leaking valve inside the valve stem. Tire valves (Fig. 11-8) allow air to be added to the tire but keep the air from coming back out; screw-on valve caps keep dirt out. It is common practice when in-

Fig. 11-8 Tire valve in tubeless tire rim

stalling new tubeless tires to also install new valve stems as they become weather rotted after a few years. If you suspect a leaking valve, remove the valve cap and cover the air hole with water or saliva. If air bubbles appear, have the inexpensive valve core replaced at a service station.

Studies have shown that tires that are nearly worn out account for the overwhelming majority of flats and blowouts. Tires that still have some tread on them suffer less damage than bald ones when driven over nails and glass; they also run much cooler, lessening the chance of a blowout. An old tire, or one that is more than half worn, may not be worth the cost of patching and rebalancing. Once it has been repaired it is still the same worn tire, and the money spent on the repair might well have been better spent toward a new one.

types of jacks

Changing a tire can be dangerous, because it is necessary first to lift a great deal of weight, often with a very cheaply designed jack. Recently, over 50,000 cars were recalled by a major manufacturer because of failures in the jacking system. Automobile owners have long been plagued by problems resulting from the use of jacks

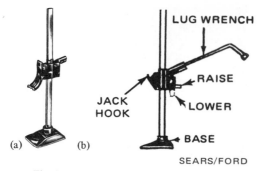

SEARS/FORD

Fig. 11-9 (a) bumper jack (b) parts of bumper jack

furnished with their cars; these have ranged from cracking of the windshield to bending of the main frame. Jacks can slip, causing the car to fall, and if you are underneath, the results can be serious. Also, when a jack slips, it can be sent flying with deadly force. So, learn how to operate your specific type of jack, but don't trust it very much.

The common *bumper jack* (Fig. 11-9a) consists of several pieces and has a mechanical lever for setting the jack to raise or lower the car as shown in Fig. 11-9b. This type of jack has a special bracket designed to fit into the car's bumper. If properly used, it should not damage the car. Be very careful not to install the bracket upside down or the car will almost certainly slip off and fall.

If the owner's manual or other instructions do not indicate where to attach the bumper jack, run your fingers under the bumper to see if there is a notched area (Fig. 11-10). If none is provided, locate the vicinity of several chrome bolt heads that hold the bumper to the car and position the jack there. Check to be sure the ground below the jack is firm enough to support the weight of the car. The jack should be positioned straight up and down so it won't tip.

FORD

Fig. 11-10 Placement of bumper jack

Fig. 11-11 A plug-in jack shown in position

The jack shown in Fig. 11-11 is often used on foreign cars. It plugs into a hole in the side of the car and lifts that entire side off the ground. It is generally much safer than the bumper jack, provided the jack is firmly pushed into the socket hole provided. Some of these jacks have two holes for the handle, one to raise and the other to lower. Other types have only one hole and a selector switch for "raise" or "lower."

The *scissors jack* shown in Fig. 11-12 is used on both domestic and foreign cars of light to medium weight. In most cases, a specific notch or pad is provided under the side of the car where the jack presses, raising both wheels on one side off the ground. Some of these jacks are very convenient to use; others required the operator to lie down on the ground.

The *hydraulic jack* (Fig. 11-13) is more expensive than the others and rarely is supplied with the car. Properly used, it is far superior to the others. This jack is positioned directly under the frame or axle of the car. Usually, it is fitted into place with small blocks of wood because it does not move up or down very far. It

Fig. 11-12 A scissors jack

Fig. 11-13 A hydraulic jack

is most commonly used with trucks, camping trailers, boat trailers, etc. Service stations and garages use hydraulic jacks of varying design because of their great strength and ease of operation.

Replacing the flat tire with the spare tire is not difficult. It is best to have at least one practice session, however, to learn how to use the jack before the need arises out on the road, under possibly adverse conditions. The directions for changing a tire in your particular car, and with the jack furnished, will be either in the compartment with the spare tire or in the owner's manual. Some additional precautions are outlined here.

procedure for tire changes

Put the car in PARK position if it has an automatic transmission, or in FIRST or REVERSE if it has a stick shift. Lock the parking brake as tightly as you can. To prevent the car from rolling, place a wooden block or large rock at the tire diagonal to the one to be changed, as in Fig. 11-14. Remove the spare tire and anything else you might need from the trunk before lifting the car. Even a small movement could cause the car to fall. Do not allow passengers to remain in the car.

Remove the chrome wheel cover with either a screwdriver or the pointed tip of the jack handle. Lay the cover upside down on

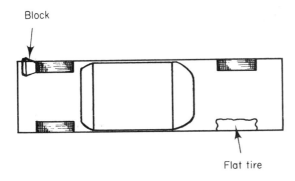

Block

Flat tire

Fig. 11-14 Correct way to block a car to keep it from rolling when a flat tire is changed

the ground to hold the wheel nuts or bolts as they are removed. Jack up the car so as to take most of the weight off the flat tire, but not enough so the wheel can rotate. It is easier to loosen and remove the nuts when the wheel is immobile.

Using the wrench provided, loosen each nut about half a turn. This sounds easy, but it is the point at which many tire changing attempts come to an end. Often the wrench provided with the car is too small or fits too poorly to permit loosening of the nuts, which may be rusted in place or tightened too vigorously by a service station attendant using a powerful air driven or electric "impact wrench." Overzealous use of these impact wrenches sometimes ruins the wheel nuts and there may be no way of removing them with the tools on hand. If this is the case, refer to Chapter 18, and call for help.

If the lug wrench does fit well, but it is impossible to loosen the nuts with normal pressure, position the wrench as shown in Fig. 11-15; stand *carefully* on the end of the wrench, and bounce up and down. This method will usually break the nuts loose.

On some cars (including most earlier Chrysler vehicles), the wheel nuts on the left side of the car have what are called *left-hand threads;* that is, they must be turned clockwise to remove and counterclockwise to tighten, just the opposite of regular threads. It is a fine safety feature. Usually an "L" or other mark is stamped on these nuts or the stud onto which they screw.

When all the nuts are loosened, jack the car up far enough that the tire clears the ground and remove the nuts, placing them in the wheel cover so they don't get dirty or lost. Remove the wheel from the car, bottom end first. Be *very careful* not to rock the car or it could fall. Always work in such a position that you cannot be

Fig. 11-15 One method of breaking loose stubborn wheel lugs

caught under the car if the jack should slip. Never put a hand or foot directly under or over the tire.

Lift the spare tire into place top end first (to get it under the fender). Since the spare tire is inflated, it will be a little larger than the flat one, so you might have to jack the car up a little higher in order to get it in place. BE careful not to rock the car as you lift the tire to fit over the threaded studs (or into position so you can put the bolts in place). A heavy tire can be raised by placing the jack handle under it and using the handle as a lever.

Install all the nuts and lightly tighten them with the wrench. Lower the car to put some weight on the wheel, and then tighten the nuts *very tightly*. Step on the wrench if necessary to get the nuts tight. Unless you are very strong, there is little danger of over-tightening the wheel nuts or bolts by hand. The more likely peril, of course, is that if they are not tight enough, the wheel could come off while you are driving.

If you are not sure the wheel nuts are tight enough, it's best to have them checked at a service station. The "star" wrench (Fig. 11-16) used at gas stations is a good investment if the car's original equipment proves unsatisfactory. These wrenches cost only a few dollars, and can make the difference between getting a flat

Fig. 11-16 A star or cross-rim wrench

tire changed on the road and having to call for road service.

Don't bother to put the chrome wheel cover back on. Just put everything back in the trunk and have the repaired tire reinstalled by the shop or service station personnel who fix it. They also will put the spare and jack back into place, and pound the wheel cover back on using a rubber mallet. This service usually is considered part of the tire repair.

Tire Balancing

Although tires are manufactured on a volume basis, they are essentially hand crafted. There are no two tires exactly alike. This being the case, tires are sometimes out of round, or do not have their weight distributed equally throughout. Almost every new tire must have small lead compensating weights added to the rim of its wheel so the wheel-tire combination will be balanced and not cause the car to vibrate as the wheel spins. There are two types of balancing techniques: *static* (or stationary) balance, and the *dynamic* (or spin) balance.

Static balancing relies on simply suspending the wheel at its middle point and moving weights around on the rim until a balancing bubble indicates that the weight is distributed equally. The static balancer shown in Fig. 11-17a is typical. The equipment is relatively simple to operate, and results are usually satisfactory for smaller, narrower tires.

Dynamic balancing is a much better technique because the wheel is balanced while it is spinning at highway speeds, either in

Fig. 11-17 (a) the Static tire balancer (b) dynamic tire balancer

place on the car or on a special machine. Any dynamic system provides wheel balancing under conditions that more nearly resemble operating conditions. In addition, a tire that is out of round will show up quickly while being spun.

Dynamic balancing involves equipment that is more expensive and requires greater operator skill. Wheels can be balanced by this method that cannot be balanced under static conditions and it costs little more. Some tire stores now have expensive new electromically controlled dynamic balancers that are very fast and accurate, even with the large, wide "low-profile" tires. It may take some hunting to find a service station or garage that has the right type of equipment. Figure 11-17*b* shows one type of dynamic balancer. For best results, new tires should be broken in at reduced speeds for about 50 miles and then balanced.

Tire trimming is needed when a tire is badly out of round. An out-of-round condition is similar in effect to a wheel out of balance in that the car shakes as the speed increases. By jacking up the car and spinning each wheel, you can quickly spot such a tire. The only way to salvage it is to have rubber cut away on a special tire trimmer to make it round. This rubber is removed right from the tread and reduces its life accordingly, but the tire can be salvaged. If a new tire is out of round, it should be replaced free by the manufacturer. If the faulty tire is an older one and no adjustment from the dealer is possible, weigh the cost of trimming and rebalancing against its remaining useful life.

Paint, trim, and upholstery

When the average buyer chooses a car, the exterior finish is largely a matter of aesthetics. Similarly, the interior appointments are chosen with an eye toward comfort and style.

There can be no doubt that exterior and interior furnishings are important to the beauty of the car, and give it a certain amount of "eye appeal" to attract the prospective buyer, however, their primary purposes are to protect the exterior metal from rust or corrosion, and to provide an interior compartment conducive to safe and comfortable driving.

The Exterior Finish

Exterior finish consists of two general categories: paint and trim, and undercoating. *Paint* and *trim* applies to all of the exterior coverings that fall into the general classification of "the paint job." *Undercoating* refers to a tar or asphalt like substance applied to the underside of the car to afford added protection from stones, moisture, and other harmful effects of driving.

paint and trim

When an automobile body is manufactured it is given a complete coating, often by submersing the entire body into a tank filled with the coating liquid, called the *prime coat, primer,* or *base coat.* Sometimes the coating is a regular metal primer such as red lead or a similar substance. An anodized finish or some other process for corrosion control may be applied to render the car body resistant to further rusting. These coatings are usually quite drab in appearance, do not accept pigments readily, and are often soft and subject to scratching or marring. Therefore, a second coat is applied, which gives the car its color and provides a protective hard surface over the prime coat. The final paint coat on an automobile might be enamel, lacquer, epoxy, acrylic, or any of the new finishes available.

Care of Exterior Finishes. Whatever the finish, proper care and protection will go a long way toward extending the life of the car. There is such a wide variety of automotive finishes that it would be impossible to give detailed information on the care of each one. The owner's manual for the individual car should be consulted for guidance. The manufacturer usually describes the type of finish used and recommends appropriate cleaning, waxing, and polishing methods. These usually consist of application of some type of cleaning agent followed by a wax treatment. Cleaning removes oil, dust, dirt, and road tar, as well as oxydized, or "dead," paint, which explains why your cleaning cloth may take on the same color as the finish of the car. It is essential that the old paint be removed because it prevents the adherence of wax to the surface, thus reducing the effectiveness of the protective coating. Moreover, oxidized paint usually is water absorbent, and the moisture it holds on the surface can penetrate the coat of paint and cause rust.

Once the body has been thoroughly washed and cleaned with a good car cleaner, a new coat of wax should be applied. The owner's manual is the best guide on the type of wax to use. A thorough cleaning and waxing at frequent intervals will help to stave off rust and will enhance the appearance of the paint.

Vinyl and Simulated-Wood Finishes. Many cars incorporate vinyl or other plastic materials into the exterior finish. These finishing techniques provide protection against rust and road damage and can contribute substantially to appearance. If the vinyl covering comes loose, however, it can provide a place for water to collect, and unless corrective measures are taken, rust will quickly follow. Vinyl is applied to the surface with a cement similar to the contact cement used to secure veneers and formica-type materials to kitchen counters and tables.

If an area of vinyl does not adhere tightly to the surface, the necessary adhesive must be injected through the covering. A hypodermic needle can be used for this purpose, or the adhesive can be forced in through an incision made with a razor blade or exacto® knive. Once the glue is injected, the loose area can be pressed down, working from the edge inward toward the opening through which the adhesive was introduced. Trapped air will be expelled through the opening as the covering is pressed down into the adhesive. Should moisture be trapped under the vinyl, the area must be thoroughly dried before the application of the adhesive. Drying can sometimes be accomplished by holding a lamp close to the area or pressing down on it with a hot iron; caution should be taken to avoid softening, burning, or stretching the material. In obstinate cases, it may be necessary to remove a patch of vinyl surrounding the damaged area so that the car body underneath can be prepared to accept the adhesive. With a little care, a patch job can be virtually undetectable. Major repairs are best left to a qualified body and fender shop.

Simulated wood trim is often applied on the sides of the car where it is subjected to the hazards of rocks thrown up from the roadway by passing vehicles and minor impacts from doors of other vehicles in the parking lot. The treatment and repair of plastic simulated wood paneling is the same as for vinyl except that the plastic material is much thinner and more delicate. Care must be exercised to avoid tearing the plastic during repairs. Because of the difficulty of matching grain in simulated wood, the repair of large areas usually entails replacing the entire panel.

Resilient plastic finishes may prove more durable than ordinary paint. Whether the finish is wood grain, vinyl, simulated leather, or regular paint, a good coat of wax is the best protection that can be provided. The techniques of applying wax to vinyl surfaces are similar to those used with regular paint finishes.

The thick vinyl roofing used on many cars may require a special treatment occasionally to prevent drying, which leads to cracking and rusting. There are many commercial products available designed to prolong the life of vinyl finishes. The types best suited to a particular car will be recommended in the owner's manual. Treatment should be given more frequently in dry, hot climates than in more temperate regions. If there are doubts about the best method of care for a particular plastic finish consult with a local auto body shop or upholsterer.

Chrome Trim. Many exterior body parts are plated with chrome, or other bright metals such as stainless steel, aluminum and nickel, all of which care characterized by durability and resistance to corrosion. The chrome is found on bumpers, grilles, light fixture trim, window frames, door handles, and other areas subject to hard wear. General road dirt can accumulate and mar the beauty of the plated finish. The dirt can hold moisture, which does permanent damage, particularly if chemicals are involved. Many commercial chrome cleaners are available which will remove this dirt. Once clean, the bright metal surface should be given a coat of wax along with the rest of the car to protect the surface and to seal out moisture. Both chrome and nickel are plated over another less expensive metal. The plated metal coating is quite thin—less than the thickness of a sheet of paper. The slightest trace of moisture, if allowed to get between the base metal and the plated metal, will cause peeling. Once this happens there is no alternative except to replace the part or to send it to an electroplating shop to be replaced. Either is an expensive solution.

The problem is even more severe in the case of cast parts such as door handles, hood ornaments, some headlight rims, and most tail-light housings. These castings are often made from a special alloy called *pot metal.* It is easy to cast, inexpensive, and light weight, which recommends it for use in automotive applications. Unfortunately, the finish of pot metal is unattractive, so nearly all pot metal parts are either nickel- or chrome-plated. The pot metal is quite porous and even a small chip or hole in the chrome will admit enough water to destroy the chrome finish from behind. It is evidenced by the appearance of many small bubbles under the chrome, which eventually chip away and expose more area, allowing still more moisture in. Once this sort of damage is noted it is too late to take corrective measures, and replacement of the part is the only satisfactory solution. In the case of the chrome-plated parts (particularly pot metal castings) an ounce of prevention is truly worth a pound of cure. Keep a good wax seal on these parts and their life will be extended greatly. Good chrome will help to keep up the re-sale value of the car.

The strips along the sides of many car bodies not only contribute to the style or the lines of the car, but also protect the "paint job" from scratches and abrasions imparted by the doors of other cars in tight parking spaces or minor bumps against other objects. They are a mixed blessing, however. While they do provide protection against bumping, they also provide a place for water to collect and cause rust. Areas under the chrome are particularly vulnerable in coastal regions and in the cold climates where salt is used on the highways to control ice. Salt water often collects between the chrome and the body, and even after the water has dried, the salt remains to continue its attack on the body until it eventually rusts completely through. The best protection against this is frequent washing. The "Jiffy" car wash is not the answer; instead of removing the salt, it often merely coats the surfaces with wax, increasing the difficulty of removal later. There is no substitute for thorough hand washing. Hidden crevasses where salt is likely to collect should be subjected to a steady flow of water for thorough cleaning.

It is a good idea to remove chrome stripping, headlight rims, and, in some cases, door handles occasionally, and thoroughly wash and wax the areas underneath them. This treatment ensures the removal of accumulated dirt that may hold salt. In industrial regions, chemicals more harmful than salt can accumulate as a result of the discharge from factory chimneys. These are effectively removed in the same manner as salt.

A particular hazard stems from add-on accessories such as fender-mounted mirrors, radio antennas, and top carriers. The holes drilled for these devices are not protected by paint or primer, as are holes made by the manufacturer prior to applying the finish. These areas require special attention to prevent rust. When such accessories are installed it is best to give all exposed metal a coat of primer such as Rustoleum® or a similar product. In any case, such accessories should be removed along with the trim mentioned above so a good coat of wax can be applied to protect the areas beneath them.

Repainting. In spite of all efforts to prevent it, rust will eventually begin to show up. At the earliest sign, the area must be treated to remove rust already formed and to reapply a protective coating. This can extend from small touch-up painting to a complete new paint job. If a new paint job is called for, have the car repainted by a competent, reliable paint shop. Beware of the cut-rate paint shop. Although such shops usually charge much less than a regular paint shop, as little as 25 percent to 30 percent of the going rate, the work is usually inferior. Sometimes paint is applied over accumulations of road dirt and grease, which prevent the new paint from adhering. Bear in mind that while a good paint job will increase the value of a car, a poor paint job may reduce it.

With the wide variety of materials available today, the car owner can take care of most routine touch-up painting. Some manufacturers provide a small container of matching touch-up paint when the car is new. Matching colors can be obtained also from the dealer or most auto supply houses.

The paint on any car is identified by a number assigned at the time of manufacture. The number enables the painter to find the color that will exactly match that on the car when it was new. (A good way to check to see if a car has been repainted is to compare the actual color of the car against that identified by the paint number.) Allowances must be made for fading, and a perfect match cannot always be achieved. Even a poor match of paint is to be preferred over unsightly rust spots.

Touch-up paint is sold in small bottles, cans and spray containers. Instructions for the use of a particular finish are provided with container. Small spots such as rock chips may require nothing more than a dab of paint applied directly to the spot without previous preparation. When properly applied, such small touch-up jobs will be nearly invisible. Larger areas usually require that the surface be cleaned of old paint and rust and a prime coat applied under the new finish.

Other Areas Susceptible to Damage. There are certain areas of the exterior car body that are more susceptible to damage than others. Door edges, for example, are apt to strike against other objects when the door is opened. In some cases, particularly in two-door cars (which have wider doors than do four-door models), the lower corner of the door will often rake on the sidewalk or strike the curb. This area requires almost constant paint touch-ups to keep it in shape. An alternative and highly recommended approach is to apply a chrome strip to the edge of doors showing this type of damage. Chrome strips are manufactured specifically for this purpose and can be obtained from most auto supply houses at reasonable cost. They can be installed in minutes with few tools.

Another area needing special attention is around the fuel filler cap. It is often struck by the fuel nozzle and flooded with fuel by inattentive station attendants. Here again, a chrome-plated apron that covers the areas adjacent to the fuel filler opening may be purchased to fit nearly all cars. To minimize the effects of spilled fuel, this area should be cleaned and waxed at more frequent intervals than the rest of the car.

The area around door handles accumulates many small scratches resulting from fingernails raking across the paint. The best approach is frequent "touch-up" waxing to keep ahead of the damage. Chrome or plastic shields are available for some cars.

The front area of the car, grille, headlights, front bumper, hood, and fender leading surfaces are subjected to many impacts by small objects. For routine service, a little additional cleaning and waxing will be all that is required. For long trips a worthwhile preventive measure is the installation of a "bug screen" across the front of the car. Not only do these devices protect against insects, but they also ward off flying particles that can wreak havoc with the paint and chrome. These screens can be installed and removed in minutes.

The exterior surface of the car is usually made smooth and attractive and given frequent wax treatments, and is protected against the hazards of its environment. This is not true of the underside. The undersides of the fenders are bombarded with rocks and soaked with water thrown up by the wheels, but they do not receive the protection afforded by frequent washing and waxing. There are many creases, ridges, and channels underneath the car that can accumulate water and provide a spawning ground for rust. The most common, but unfortunately short-lived, protection for this area is the prime coat applied at the factory. Large chips soon appear in the prime surface, and water and salt begin to dissolve the car body from underneath.

The best way to combat this problem is to have the car *undercoated* with a tar- or asphalt-like substance, which is sprayed on the underside of the car. Undercoating protects the underside of the car from flying objects and moisture, and serves as a sound absorber, which makes a quieter ride. It should be applied with care to avoid blocking vents and drain holes, or from covering heat-radiating surfaces, which will interfere with normal operation. For maximum effectiveness, undercoating should be applied when the car is brand new, because after a very few miles oil and grease from the road will collect and will prevent the under coating material from adhering. Once rust is established, it will continue to attack the metal even though a coat of paint or undercoat is applied over it. The advantages of undercoating far outweigh the cost, and it is highly recommended.

Upholstery and Interior Trim

The inside of a car requires as much attention as the outside. Whereas the exterior is subjected to road hazards and is exposed to the weather, the inside must withstand extremely high temperatures and the constant wear and tear of passengers and driver getting in and out. As with the exterior finish, the life of the upholstery and interior trim can be prolonged through proper care and cleaning.

upholstery

Most upholstery for car seats and backs is similar to the materials used to upholster household furniture. Household cleaning materials can be used in the car as well. Most manufacturers identify the particular material used in a car and recommend the best cleaning agent and method of application. Of equal importance are warnings against using some cleaning products which could damage the material. This information is found in the owner's manual.

The most commonly used upholstery material is vinyl, which is relatively easy to keep clean. Most vinyl seat coverings can be washed with a mild household cleaner. Most common soil and mild stains can be removed from vinyl seat covers with the spray cleaners used to clean kitchen chairs or other furniture with vinyl upholstery.

Sunlight will often bleach the colors, and spills can bleach and stain the original upholstery. There are a number of commercial products available from upholstery suppliers or from automotive

"I'm afraid we got quite a bit of grease on your seats, so we installed a set of seat covers at 10% off the regular price." © DAVID BROWN FEATURES

supply firms that will restore the color to even severely bleached vinyl upholstery. All that is required with some products is to wipe them on and let them dry. Most contain a coating or penetrating material that inhibits cracking. If vinyl upholstery is punctured or torn the vinyl can be repaired with the same material that is used to repair vinyl tops.

Cloth upholstery presents another problem. It should be dry cleaned. Water should never be used because it will ruin the hard surface of the material and hasten wear. A good solvent-type cleaning agent should be used to remove soil. A word of caution here: many of the volatile solvents can create fire or health hazards, so follow the manufacturer's instructions when using these hazardous chemicals. When applying the cleaning agent, use a dampened surface to wipe away the soil. Do not soak the surface or the padding, as this will ruin the upholstery. Make sure that the solvent is completely dry before using the car.

Leathers or imitation leathers need only be washed with a neutral soap to keep them clean. Solvents, bleaches, detergents, or normal soaps should not be used on these materials. If door panels are upholstered with the same materials used for the seats, the cleaning process is the same. Extra precaution needs to be taken here because the padding is usually thin and the cleaning agent can pick up worked-in dirt from the backside and draw it up into the upholstery, making the situation worse than before. This type of damage is virtually impossible to correct, so use only a cloth dampened with the solvent to wipe away stains.

There are two areas of the car's interior that receive unusually harsh treatment. These are the top of the dash just below the windshield, and the rear deck just inside the rear window. Extremely high heat and strong ultraviolet rays from the direct sunlight coming in through the windows can cause the upholstery material covering the areas to dry, crack, and fade. There is little that can be done about the bleaching except to occasionally restore the color with one of the coloring products used on seat upholstery. Some of these products incorporate a softening chemical that will reduce cracking due to heat. If dual-purpose chemicals cannot be found, it will be necessary to treat the material twice, once for each problem. As a general rule the coloring agent should be applied first, as the softening material usually contains oil or grease, which will prevent the dye from penetrating or adhering to the upholstery.

Automobile floors are covered with carpeting or mats. Rubber or plastic mats may be cleaned with soap and water, but care must be taken to avoid soaking the padding underneath. This padding is quite thick and absorbent; it takes a long time to dry out and can promote rust and mildew. The best way to dry out a water-soaked mat is to remove it from the car and spread it out in the air.

Carpets used on automobile floors should be treated in the same manner as carpets in the house. They may be brushed, swept, vacuumed, shampooed, and colored by nearly all the same means as household carpeting. Once again, avoid soaking the carpet, for it takes a long time to dry.

The trunk has a tendency to become soiled more rapidly than the rest of the car. A frequent culprit is dirt brought in with a tire change or with equipment used in recreational activity. The trunk floor often is lined with the same material as the rest of the car interior and it needs the same care. If mud gets on a carpet it is best to avoid trying to wipe it away; this only forces it down into the fibers of the carpet and makes it more difficult to remove. Let the mud dry (avoid smearing it or stepping on it until it is completely dry), then pick up the large pieces by hand and vacuum up the rest.

windows and window trim

Windows need to be kept clean as a matter of general safety. The ammonia cleaners used on house windows are satisfactory for automobile glass. (Don't overlook the headlight lenses and mirrors when cleaning the windows.) Care should be used to avoid getting window cleaners on the metal parts of the car or on the finish, as they can cause corrosion or damage the paint. The rubber trim around the windows, particularly those that open and close need to be treated with a restorative agent and cleaned to remove dust and grit and road dirt which hardens the surface and destroys the sealing qualities. These areas need only be washed with mild soap and water to keep them clean. Sometimes a thin coating of petroleum jelly or silicone grease will help to keep the rubber soft and seal out water and annoying wind noises.

Car cleaning is not unlike house cleaning. The outside needs to be cared for in one way and the inside in another. The outside of the car needs to be treated with water and wax to keep it clean and free from corrosive chemicals, such as salt and the residue from manufacturing processes. The interior calls for the same attention as upholstered furniture in the home. A periodic cleaning of the interior of the car will prolong its life, maintain its appearance, and help to keep the resale or trade-in value high. With the cost of automobiles as high as it is, this constitutes a fairly high return for the little time spent.

Frequent inspection and care

THE WEEKLY WALKAROUND

Through routine inspection and maintenance proceedures, the observant automobile owner can greatly prolong the life of the car and obtain maximum satisfaction from it in day-to-day driving. Preceding chapters have covered the operation and periodic maintenance requirements of the various working elements of the automobile. Here we summarize indicators available to the driver for monitoring the condition of the engine and the performance of the car as a whole. Some of these indicators are apparent when the car is not in operation; others are provided by dashboard instruments and the handling characteristics of the car as it is being driven.

Preventive inspection and maintenance are meant to locate small problems before they become large ones. The little problems may remain hidden, but they do not go away; they eventually appear as major repair items, attacking the pocketbook with a vengeance. The careful car owner can reduce the chances of vehicle breakdown on the road, or the sudden emergence of a major problem, by devoting only five minutes a week (or a few minutes each morning when on a long trip. Chap. 18) to a preventive walkaround inspection and by taking whatever corrective action is dictated by the findings of this inspection.

In aviation, a preflight inspection is considered routine, regardless of how short the planned flight may be or how recently the aircraft was flown. Usually, such an inspection follows a checklist, sometimes many pages in length. Aviation procedures, of course, reflect the important fact that an aircraft in trouble can hardly pull off to the side of the road for repairs. However, truck and bus drivers also perform frequent inspections,—one impressive result being that engines in those vehicles routinely give good performance for up to a half million miles, five times the expected life of an automobile engine. This fact underscores the important benefits that can be realized through preventive maintenance.

external inspection

The weekly walkaround begins with inspection of the items set out in Checklist 1. Tire pressure should be checked with a gauge,

1. Headlights and taillights clean
2. Front tire wear pattern
3.   a. Worn on one edge: needs camber alignment
     b. Worn on both edges: underinflated
     c. Worn in center: overinflated
     d. Feather edges on tread: toe-in or toe-out needs adjustment
     e. Spot wearing: needs wheel balance, or brake drum or shock absorber care
4. Rear tire wear pattern (inflation)
5. Tail pipe deposits
     a. Black soot: needs carburetor adjustment
     b. Gray deposits, light: that's normal
     c. Rust: have the entire exhaust system checked
6. Windshield wipers: replace when hard or cracked
7. Paint chips: note for touch-up paint after next wash and wax
8. Axle grease leaks
9. Brake cylinder leaks
10. Flexible brake lines

wear patterns should be analyzed (Chap. 11), any cuts or embedded nails noted, and the sidewalls inspected for bulges or wetness.

If the inner sidewall of the tire is wet, take a sample with your finger. If the fluid is very thin and has a pungent odor, it is brake fluid; if it is thick and greasy, it is wheel bearing lubricant. In either case, the vehicle should have the prompt attention of a mechanic, as both conditions are potentially dangerous. As you move around the car, perform the same examination on each tire.

See that headlights, taillights, and parking lights are clean. Check each window for cracked glass, and the body for paint chips. The next time the car is washed and waxed, these minor paint chips should be repaired. Check the inside of the exhaust pipe for deposits; this will give some indication of the operation of the engine. Inspect the windshield wiper blades to see that they are still pliable, and the outside mirrors, radio antenna, gas cap, and license plates to see that they are securely in place and clean. A lusty push or two on each wheel with a foot may detect loosening wheel nuts. If everything has been found to be in order, this walkaround will have taken less than one minute. On the other hand, the discovery of a faulty tire, loose wheel or leaking brake cylinder may have prevented a serious accident.

CHECKLIST 13-2
Under-the-Hood Inspection

1. Radiator coolant: check when *engine* cold
2. Radiator pressure cap: if evidence of a leak, have cap checked
3. Radiator hoses: should be firm but not hard
4. Heater hoses: look for cracks
5. Battery cables: wash off corrosion with soda and water
6. Battery acid level: add distilled water if needed, up to indicator
7. Oil level: check dipstick before starting the engine
8. Fan belts: should have one-half inch play, not cracked or slick
9. Water pump: look for signs of water leaks
10. Drive belts for alternator, power steering, air conditioner: check for cracks and tension
11. Power steering oil level: remove cap or dipstick and add fluid if low
12. Power steering hoses: check for fluid leaks
13. Spark plug wires: keep clear of other wires and parts
14. Oil leaks: check the
    a. valve cover: a small leak is normal here
    b. Fuel pump mounting area: check for loose bolts and tighten if needed
    c. filler cap: if leak shows here, crankcase ventilator may be clogged
15. Fuel leaks: check the
    a. fuel filter
    b. fuel pump
    c. carburetor
16. Brake cylinder leak: check the
    a. master cylinder
    b. brake lines
17. Power brake hose: look for cracks, loose clamp
18. Core plug leaks: look for rusty water on side of engine
19. Auto transmission fluid level: color and smell okay?
20. Windshield washer fluid level

under-the-hood inspection

Lift the hood of the car and check the items in Checklist 2. After performing this inspection several times, you will establish a routine for checking the items in your particular car and will be able to spot quickly anything that does not look normal.

If everything looks all right from the top of the engine, get a flashlight, and check the underside of the engine compartment for possible damage to radiator hoses, power steering hoses, and flexible brake fluid lines. These could have been cut by a flying rock

BERRY'S WORLD

© 1973 by NEA, Inc. Jim Berry

"It's part of the new inspection procedures!"

or other object since the previous inspection. An easy way to check for a leak without crawling under the car is to reach down from the top side and run your fingers around to the bottom side of a hose. If the bottom of a hose or brake line is wet, something is leaking. Then check further for leaks from the engine, transmission, and differential.

CHECKLIST 13-3 Driveway Inspection for Fluid Leaks

Material	Area to Observe	Probable Fault	Probable Cause	Correction	Facility*
WATER	Small spots on radiator	Small leaks, soldered joints	Excess pressure	Commercial stop-leak fluid	S
Usually leaves red or brown stain	Large spots on sides	Split seam		Resolder	R
	Large spots on radiator	Rotted core	Corrosion	Replace radiator	G
	Radiator hoses	Worn, split or burst hose	Age, vibration, rust, or excess pressure	Replace hoses	S
				Check pressure cap	S
				Flush radiator	S
No smell, unless containing anti-freeze	Radiator hose ends	Hose clamps loose	Age, vibration	Tighten or replace clamps	S
	Engine block	Rusted "freeze plug"	Age, rust in engine	Replace "freeze plugs"	G
Forms globules on	Engine block	Blown head gasket	Loose head bolts, warped head	Replace gasket, repair head	G
oily surface		Cracked block	Freezing, overheating	New or rebuilt engine	D
	Engine head	Cracked head	Freezing, overheating	New head	D
	Overflow tube	Coolant overflow	Overfilled	Fill cold, leave 1 ½" below top	S
ENGINE OIL	Front or rear of engine	Front or rear main oil seal	Clogged vent, dirty oil	Replace seals, clean vent	G
	Fuel pump, distributor, rocker arm cover	Leaking gasket, loose bolts	Vibration, clogged vent	Replace gasket, clean vent	S
Brown or black	Oil filter	Leaking gasket, loose bolts	Faulty installation, vibration	Replace gasket, tighten bolts	S
non-evaporating	Filler cap	Clogged vent, crankcase pressure	Dirty oil	Clean vent, change oil often	S
			Worn piston rings	New piston rings	G
TRANSMISSION OIL	Front, rear transmission	Worn shaft seals	Vibration, age, dirt, heat	Replace seals	R/D
Lightweight, slow evaporating	Bottom edges	Loose bolts, worn gaskets	Vibration, age	Replace gasket, tighten bolts	G
Usually colored red	Dip stick spout	Excess pressure	Overfilled	Fill to "FULL" mark only	S
DIFFERENTIAL GREASE	Differential	Loose filler plug	Faulty inspection	Tighten	S
		Cracked case	Impact object	Replace	G
GASOLINE	Carburetor	Float bowl flooded	Wrong float level	Bend float support arm	G
Red or brown deposits	Connecting lines	Loose fittings	Vibration	Tighten connections	S
Evapoates quickly	Filter	Leaking gasket	Faulty installation	Replace gasket	S
Dissolves grease, oil	Fuel pump	Ruptured diaphragm	Age	Replace fuel pump	G
	Gas tank	Puncture, split seam	Impact object	Weld or replace tank	R
BATTERY ACID sharp, acid odor, corrodes metal, spots paint, burns flesh and cloth	Filler caps	Heat expansion	Overfilled	Wash off with soda water	S
				Fill to top of cell only	S
	Side of case	Cracked case	Battery loose in carrier	Replace battery, tighten hold-down	S
BRAKE FLUID	Master cylinder (Brake pedal)	Leaks past pressure cap and seals, or connections	Dirt, age	Rebuild cylinder	G
Lightweight, slow evaporating colorless (or black with dirt)	Wheel cylinders	Same as above	Dirt, age	Rebuild cylinders	G
	Flexible line	Cut or abrasion	Impact object	Replace line	G
	Solid line or fittings	Hole, or loose fitting nuts	Vibration, abrasion	Tighten fittings replace line	G
POWER STEERING OIL	Pump	Leaking seals	Age, dirt	Replace seals	G
	Steering post	Leaking gasket	Age, dirt, vibration	Replace gaskets, tighten bolts	G
	Fittings, hoses	Loose or worn	Vibration, age	Tighten fittings, replace hoses	S

*S = Service Station   G = General Garage   D = Dealer for your make of car   R = Repair Specialist

Many different fluids are used in the modern automobile, and driveways are typically spotted with drippings of one kind or another. The dark stripe in every lane of an older highway bears testimony to the many vehicles that have passed, leaking something, mostly engine oil, as they went. If your driveway or parking space is regularly cleaned with a commercial driveway cleaner, it will be easy to spot a fluid leak when it begins.

Checklist 13-3 details the most common vehicle leaks, their probable cause, and corrective action to be taken for each. When you back out of the driveway next time, observe the area where your car was parked. If a spot has formed on the driveway, it is usually a simple matter to locate the source of the leak. If the fluid source is not readily apparent, however, the car should be moved to a service station onto a lift so the leak can be investigated further.

An Ounce of Prevention is Worth a Pound of Cure

Once a week, perform the inspections outlined. If you are on a long driving trip and traveling many miles each day, perform these simple inspections daily. The cost in time is quite small, and expensive surprises on the open road will be largely eliminated. In the chapter, "Taking a Trip," additional hints on car care are discussed. Meanwhile, make an appointment with your car and set aside the same five minutes each week for your "weekly walk-around."

FROM THE DRIVER'S SEAT

Dashboard Indicators of Engine Condition

Drivers are constantly advised of approaching road conditions or possible hazards through signs posted along the roadway. Inside the car, dashboard instruments monitor the vital signs of the operating engine and signal trouble that may lie ahead. The speedometer

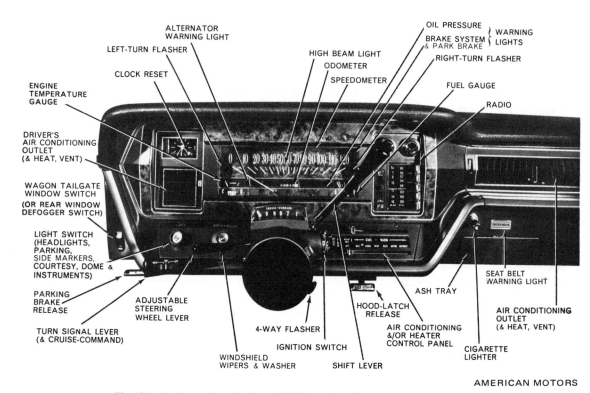

Fig. 13-1 Instrument panel of typical U.S. car, showing gauges and indicators

indicates how fast the car is going; the odometer tells how far it has gone. Meters or lights indicate whether the engine is running hot or cold, whether the battery is charging or discharging and whether or not the engine oil pressure is within tolerance. A gauge indicates the amount of fuel in the tank.

A fully instrumented dash in a modern automobile can be confusing. As the necessary measurements increase in number and importance, manufacturers began to substitute lights for meters as a means of reducing both the cost and the complexity of dashboard instrumentation. A typical instrument panel is shown in Fig. 13-1.

lights versus meters (or gauges)

Among those who profess expertise in the field of the internal combustion engine, there is continuing debate as to the relative merits of meters, or gauges, versus lights as indicators of engine operating condition. The basic difference between the two systems is quite simple. The gauge gives a constant indication of the condition being measured, including any changes, however small. The lamp is activated only when a predefined condition is reached, such as temperature too high, oil pressure too low, and so on, relative to the operating range specified by the manufacturer. Both systems are discussed briefly here, using the oil pressure indicator as an example.

A meter used to read oil pressure shows zero pressure when the engine is stopped. As soon as the engine is started, the pointer rises up the scale until it has reached the full pressure being developed by the oil pump at that engine speed and existing conditions. If a condition should develop that causes the oil pressure to lessen, the change will be reflected in the meter. For example, such conditions might occur if the reserve of oil in the pan was allowed to go below the recommended level or if the engine bearings were badly worn. Engine bearings that are gradually failing might show up on a dashboard gauge as a day-by-day lowering of oil pressure. The oil pump is designed to be able to develop pressure well above that required to deliver lubrication to the engine, and the regulator "bleeds off" any pressure above that point. Thus, the oil pressure shown on the meter is likely to remain relatively constant until the capability of the oil pump to continue to provide pressure is beginning to be exceeded. At that point, the engine would be in such poor condition that there would be many other symptoms that would warn the driver of imminent failure. Such indications would be rod knocks, bad oil leaks at the main bearing seals, and noisy rocker arms and tappets.

The oil warning light is connected to a pressure-sensitive switch, which "reads" the oil pressure at all times. Whenever pressure drops below the pre-set level, the switch operates and turns the light on. The light, when lighted, means that oil pressure has dropped below the minimum safe level and that continued operation will result in an inadequately lubricated engine. Continued operation under these conditions may result in the engine being ruined.

The indication from either the light or the meter is essentially the same. The meter will indicate the actual condition at any time. The light will only give a "go" or "no go" type of indication based on a preset level. The continuous reading provided by a gauge has the advantage of indicating a deteriorating condition in time for corrective action.

Features of any instrument cluster are pretty well standardized for each make and model of car at the time of manufacture. A wide variety of instruments are available that can be added to existing systems, ranging from individual gauges to complete instrument clusters. Once a driver is accustomed to the instrumentation on his car, he can interpret it easily. Whether the indicators are predominantly lights or gauges, they can tell you a great deal.

oil pressure

The oil pressure indication is one of the "vital signs" of the internal combustion engine. If the oil pressure light should come on or the gauge should fall below the safe minimum level recommended by the manufacturer, immediately turn the engine off. Any attempt to operate the engine under these conditions can ruin it, even in just a few blocks of driving. Many good engines that could have been repaired easily have been totally ruined by drivers who thought it would be all right to drive just over to the garage or to "get it off the freeway at least." If there is an indication that the oil pressure is below that specified by the manufacturer, turn the engine off immediately and seek competent mechanical help.

engine temperature

Engine temperature is another of the vital signs of engine operating conditions. Prolonged operation of an internal combustion engine at temperatures substantially above normal can result in serious damage and costly repairs. Engine temperature indicators are more varied than oil pressure instruments. The condition of concern in engine lubrication systems is low pressure, while engine performance is affected by both high and low temperatures, and both must be indicated in some manner. Many manufacturers provide a meter with a scale showing a "normal" range; temperatures below that range are too cold for proper engine operation and those above are too high. While excessively high temperatures are more likely to cause engine damage, low engine temperatures have the serious effects of poor combustion, loss of power, and an increase in smog-producing pollutants.

Some automobiles are equipped with a light system to monitor engine temperature. In some cases this is limited to a single light which warns of temperature above normal. In other cases two lamps are provided, one to indicate cold and the other hot engine conditions. Operating a car with a hot engine for an excessive time can result in serious damage, as can operation at high speed with a cold engine.

unsteady temperature indications

The amount of heat generated by the engine will vary with the load—that is, the work demanded of the engine. Thus, when a car is driven up a steep hill at a fairly low speed, the engine is laboring and a great deal of heat is generated. Under these conditions, some increase in engine temperature is to be expected and will be reflected in a higher reading on the temperature gauge. As long as the temperature remains within the normal range as prescribed by the manufacturer, there is no cause for alarm.

If the temperature indication goes above the normal range, some action is in order to reduce engine temperature. One approach is to shift to a lower gear so that the engine will turn faster. The water pump will then circulate the cooling fluid faster and the fan will turn faster, drawing more air through the radiator. Both of these measures will tend to reduce engine temperature. In addition, when the transmission is shifted to a lower gear and the engine turns at a higher speed, engine loading is reduced, which tends to reduce engine temperature.

On the downside of a hill, the opposite behavior is normal. As the car travels downhill, the load on the engine is reduced, resulting in lower engine temperature. It is normal for the engine temperature gauge to move to the low side of "normal" on long downgrades. If engine temperature drops significantly below normal under this condition, it might be an indication of a faulty thermostat.

When the engine is stopped after it has operated for some time it is normal for the temperature gauge to indicate on the hot side. This is because the water has stopped circulating, and the engine block takes time to cool. If the engine is started again, the temperature gauge should quickly return to normal. This condition is particularly prevalent during hot weather.

On a car equipped with gauges, these conditions can be observed as they develop and corrective measures may be taken ahead of time so that the engine will never reach an overheated condition. In cars with indicator lights, the signal is given only after the temperature has gone above or below the desirable range. After the cooling fluid has started to boil and the temperature has reached a level high enough to activate the light, corrective action may be too late, and the only cure for the problem may be to pull over and stop so that the engine can cool.

charging system

As a rule, the condition of the alternator or generator is indicated in a manner similar to engine temperature. A light may go on when the charging system is not charging enough, or the reading may be provided by a gauge or "ammeter," which shows the number of amps going into or being drawn from the battery. If the car is being driven at normal speeds and the charging monitor system shows a discharge, some part of the charging system has failed. The failure might be in the alternator or in the regulator system. It could be a poor connection. In any case, for some reason the charging system is not supplying sufficient energy to keep the bettery charged.

There is a possibility that the failure is not in the charging system itself but rather in the drive mechanism. In most cars, the fan belt drives the cooling fan, the water pump, and the alternator. *A broken fan belt might show up on the instrument panel as an indication of battery discharge followed by an indication of rising engine temperature.*

The possible consequences of a discharge condition are not as severe as those resulting from an oil system failure or overheated engine. As a rule, it can be assumed that the battery is not at fault because the discharge indication means that the battery is being used to provide all of the electrical power for the operation of the car. The fact that the battery is discharging into the system shows that it is, at least, operational.

If it is daytime and you are not far from home or help, there should be no problem in driving for a few miles to get aid. If a considerable distance must be traveled, it is advisable to turn off all electrical equipment not essential to operation of the vehicle to increase the distance that the car can be driven. Remember, under these conditions, the battery is providing all of the electrical power for the car and will in time become discharged to the extent that it can no longer even provide ignition energy for the engine. If possible, avoid turning the engine off, for the strain of turning over the starting motor can drain the battery to such a low level that the car can only be driven a few miles.

At night, power must be provided for the lights in addition to the ignition system and the battery can be expected to deliver power for only a few minutes under these conditions. Failure of the charging system at night requires that the car be stopped soon so repairs can be made. Once again, a gauge that indicates the constant condition of the charging system might predict failure by slowly dropping, whereas lamp monitors can only reflect that the system has gone below normal.

mileage and engine speed

Speedometer. All automobiles are provided with speedometers, which show how fast the car is going. The speedometer is always some type of gauge, because the driver must know the actual speed the car is traveling, within reasonable tolerances, at all times. The speedometer is located on the instrument panel directly in front of the driver. The reason for this is that the speedometer must be read from directly in front to get an accurate reading. If it is viewed from the right it will read low and in the unlikely circumstance that it is read from the left, it would read high. The speedometer reading is affected by tire size, and a reduction or increase in tire diameter will result in a corresponding error in speedometer reading.

Odometer. Most cars are equipped with odometers, which indictate the cumulative mileage driven. In some cars, a separate odometer is provided that can be reset to zero when the driver wishes to register trip mileage. In the absence of a separate instrument, trip mileage is obtained by simply recording the total mileage on the odometer at the beginning of the trip and subtracting that reading from the one after the trip.

Tachometer. Tachometers used to be limited to high performance engines and engines on trucks that require shifting of gears at precise engine speeds. They are found on increasing numbers of passenger cars, however, and can be quite useful for judging when to shift and for evaluating engine performance. It is customary for manufacturers to specify the maximum safe engine speed in rpm. This is referred to as "red line" and may be indicated by a red line on the dial face. While the speedometer is calibrated in miles per hour, the tachometer is calibrated in engine crankshaft revolutions per minute.

the ignition switch

Many drivers make a habit of getting into the car, turning the ignition switch full over to the start position and starting the engine. It is best to turn the key to the one position and inspect the instrument panel to be sure all indicators are functioning before starting the engine. In this way, the driver can be assured that those lamp indications which reflect a faulty condition by lighting a lamp are functioning properly. In some cars, certain lamps light in the "start" position of the key to provide a test of the system. Check the owner's manual for information pertaining to your particular car. A burned out indicating lamp will not show a low oil pressure condition, and such a failure can be quite expensive if not detected. If all the engine monitoring lights are functioning properly when the engine is not running, the fact that those same lights are extinguished after the engine is started, can be accepted as a safe condition.

The ignition switch should never be left on for a continuous period over a few minutes when the engine is not running. The least that can happen under these conditions is that the battery can be discharged so that it will not start the engine. Other consequences include a burned out ignition coil or coil ballast resistor, or both. The car will not start until the damaged parts are replaced. Most ignition switches are provided with an accessory position, which applies power to radio and other accessories but not to the ignition circuitry. The driver then can listen to the radio, when the engine is not running, without overheating the coil or resistor.

A final precaution in connection with the ignition switch involves its function as a starter switch. If the ignition key is held in the start position for a prolonged time after the engine has started, severe damage can result to the starter and the ring gear in a car not equipped with protective cutouts. Many cars have systems that turn off the power to the starter motor when the engine has started. Not all cars have this feature, however, and it is wise to check the owner's manual to be sure in each individual case. Furthermore, even though a car may have protective devices that prevent damage to the mechanical starting equipment, prolonged application of power through the ignition switch may cause sufficient heat to damage the switch itself. In any car it is advisable to avoid keeping the key in the "start" position longer than is necessary to start the engine.

On the Road: Handling Characteristics

Although the instruments provide the driver most information as to the condition of the car in operation, there are other sources of information that are quite helpful. The owner's manual usually spells out the conditions that are monitored on the instrument panel. An inspection of the engine will reveal which belts drive what systems and will enable the driver to evaluate dashboard indications of multiple failures.

A more subtle, but nonetheless important, indicator of automobile performance is how the car handles on the road. Each car takes a little bit of getting used to before a driver can evaluate normal versus abnormal performance. Once he is accustomed to the normal behavior of the car, however, it is not too difficult to determine when some abnormal condition exists. For example, a car with properly inflated tires, properly adjusted brakes, and well-lubricated and adjusted bearings, steering and suspension, should travel in a straight line on a smooth and level road. If the car pulls to one side or the other an abnormal condition in one of those features is likely.

A soft tire, that is a tire that does not have enough air pressure in it, will cause the car to pull to the side on which the soft tire is located. A front tire will cause a more pronounced pulling effect than will a rear tire. The same condition can result from a dragging brakeshoe. The latter can be differentiated from the former by touching the wheel in the area of the brake drum. Usually, a dragging brake is accompanied by a hot brake drum caused by the friction of constant rubbing. If the tire appears to be well inflated and there is no evidence of excessive heat at the brake drum, then it is reasonable to suspect a faulty wheel bearing. A bad wheel bearing may be indicated by heat at the end of the axle. A word of caution, however! These parts can be very hot and painful burns can result. If tires, brakes, and bearings are in proper condition and adjustment, and the car still tends to pull to one side or the other, suspension and alignment might be at fault.

One of the behavior patterns of the car that one gains a "feel" for is the proper braking reaction. If the car takes too long to come to a stop or requires excessive foot pressure on the pedal, the brakes need maintenance. As a rule, failure of the power system for power brakes is quite evident; the pedal pressure required to bring the car to a stop increases considerably and, usually, suddenly. In other cases, such as wear of the brake linings, the changes occur over a long period of time and the driver becomes gradually accustomed to the "feel" of the degrading system. The best way to overcome this is to periodically check the brakes as described in Chapter 10.

Grabbing brakes, or brakes that lock up under even the slightest pressure on the foot pedal, usually can be traced to a leaking oil seal. (Chap. 10). It is advisable to check the pressure relief valve on the differential housing whenever this type of failure is encountered with a rear brake.

Many diagnostic processes can be carried out by the driver who takes the time to really understand the car. The driver who spends a considerable time behind the wheel soon becomes an expert on its particular behavior in any circumstance. The driver becomes familiar with the sound and feel of the car as it is operating normally, and often can tell more accurately than even the most skilled mechanic when things are not quite right. Much time and perhaps a considerable expense can be saved if you can relay the symptoms accurately to the mechanic who works on your car.

Buying a new car

The cost of owning and maintaining an automobile is the largest single expense the average person assumes, except for a home. It is not unusual for a new nonluxury car to cost $5,000.00 or more, thus the buyer must shop carefully to find a vehicle that will provide maximum service and satisfaction per dollar. This chapter covers the purchase of a new car as a straight cash transaction and through a trade-in deal. New car warranties are discussed also. The purchase of a used car is covered in Chapter 15, and the long-term economic considerations of both alternatives are discussed in Chapter 16.

Buying a New Car for Cash

Most new cars are sold through franchised dealerships, which can actually be considered extensions of the factory. The manufacturer provides the dealer with considerable support such as advertising, training for his mechanics and sales personnel, warranty and guarantee support, and, in some cases, financing services. However, there is one major consideration that puts the local dealer in business for himself—that is, he must buy his vehicles from the parent company. The car in the showroom has been bought by the dealer and he has money tied up in it. When he sells the car, he must get cash with which to buy more cars and continue in business.

The expression "cash deal" refers to a sale where only money is involved, and the customer does not expect an allowance for his old car as part of the purchase price of the new car. It is a "cash deal" whether the full amount is paid in cash at the time of delivery or whether the purchaser makes a down payment and finances the balance through a lender. The important thing is that as a result of this type of sale, the dealer will receive the full amount in cash and need not wait for payments.

The dealer's profit in a *basic* new car is quite low and he must sell many of them to prosper. He can increase his profit margin by selling additional accessories, which yield a profit more nearly in line with other retail marketing ventures. Thus, the car dealer is highly motivated to sell as much optional equipment as the customer will buy. The wise buyer who is shopping for a new car should make a list of only those options really needed and that can be afforded.

Since the dealer's profit is on a percentage basis, he will make more money if he sells you a bigger car with a bigger engine than will if he sells you a smaller unit. He has additional incentive to sell you a "prestige" model because these cars usually come from the factory with all of the accessories (the trade term is "loaded"). The basic price for such a car is high, and the dealer enjoys the higher profit margin in the accessories.

Before you set foot in a dealer's showroom, think out exactly what you want in the way of an automobile. Then you will be able to tell the salesman exactly what you are looking for, and he will be less likely to show you something that you do not want or need.

negotiating a price

"Price shopping" is of little benefit in a new car cash transaction. Federal fair trade rules require that price data be displayed on all new cars sold. A basic car in one dealer's showroom will display exactly the same price as a similar basic car at another agency in the same area. But don't pay the sticker price! The dealer has considerable latitude to reduce the price without conflicting with either the federal rules or the trade agreements imposed under the terms of his franchise with the manufacturer. On standard size U.S. cars, there is usually a "pad" of many hundreds of dollars that enables the dealer to persuade a buyer that he is offering a high price for a trade-in. In a cash deal, however, no trade-in is involved, and the customer should be able to get the dealer to shave the price by that amount, usually 10 to 20 percent.

The sticker price of a new car includes a sufficient mark-up for the dealer to pay a commission to the salesman. When dealing through a salesman, the customer can expect to pay that amount unless the salesman can be persuaded to reduce his commission. One way to save on a salesman's commission is to buy the car through a small agency where the owner serves as his own salesman.

financing and insurance

Once a car has been selected and a price agreed on, financing arrangements are made. Down payments vary, but a common formula is one-third of the full price paid to the dealer, with the remaining two-thirds financed over a period of time. The dealer may make out the finance papers as part of his services, but the

"So that's your 'manufacturer's suggested retail price'? . . . Now would you like to hear my 'buyer's suggested retail price'?"

money nearly always comes from a savings and loan company, a credit union, a finance corporation, or a bank. When the customer has signed the papers, the dealer turns them over to the lending agency, which pays him the full amount in cash. Payments on the car are then made directly to the lending agency. The lending agency's profit in the transaction is the interest paid on the loan. The car becomes the collateral for the loan, thus the "loan value" of the car is an important factor in the financing arrangements. "Loan value" is discussed in some detail in Chapter 15.

In many cases, the financing transaction becomes a source of additional income to the dealer. In addition to the commission for selling the car, he may also collect a commission from the lending agency for bringing your business to them. The lending agency will demand insurance to protect their investment, and the dealer may collect a third commission as an insurance agent, provided he is a licensed agent, as a number of dealers are.

If the car agency is arranging for financing, be sure to check the interest rate, and do not pay more than is necessary. If it is difficult to establish a buyer's credit, the dealer may finance the sale through a "high risk" money lender whose interest rates may be exorbitant. The best way to circumvent this problem is to arrange financing through your own bank or credit union. Making these arrangements is not difficult. Many organizations are eager to lend money to the customer with a regular income and good credit. They are in the business of "renting money," and are always looking for new renters. Do not be fooled into thinking the lender is doing a favor in approving a loan. It takes two parties to make a deal, and the borrower may be doing the favor by renting money from one place instead of another. Shop for financing as carefully as you shop for the car.

The insurance coverage required by the lending agency, although providing adequate protection for agency interests in the deal, may not cover your risks adequately. A reputable insurance agent will arrange insurance coverage for both your interests and those of the lending agency. Many dealers will aid their customers in making arrangements with lending and insurance agencies of their own choice. It is not uncommon for dealers to provide financing at low rates and adequate insurance coverage for all parties involved. Since a commission is paid in any case, it makes little difference whether it goes to an insurance agent in an insurance office or to a car salesman doubling as an insurance salesman in an automobile dealer's office. The important thing is that the required coverage be obtained at the best possible price. Automobile insurance is discussed in greater detail in Chapter 17.

The Trade-In Deal

The purchase of a new car with an old car traded in as part of the deal is quite different from the cash transaction. As noted earlier, the sticker price on a new car includes considerable padding to enable the dealer to exaggerate the value that he places on your trade-in. The trade-in absorbs a portion of the "pad," thus limiting any potential reduction in the price of the new car. Some dealers occasionally have sales or other types of promotion that involve a reduction in the sticker price. It may be possible to persuade a dealer to lower the price a little, but the reduction will not be nearly as great as if there were no trade-in.

when to trade

Many different factors have a bearing on the decision to trade in an old car. For example: How many miles has the old car been driven? Has it been involved in an accident that might limit its usefulness? Do you still owe money on it? What is its current condition in terms of repair costs? On the average, a car that has been given reasonable servicing and has not been subjected to hard usage (such as taxi, rental, or racing activities) can be expected to give useful service for a hundred thousand miles.

the value of the trade-in

The dealer will allow a much lower value for a trade-in than the average owner will place on it. In fact, the difference is often a real shock to the owner, who might value the old car at a thousand dollars, for example, whereas a dealer might allow well under five hundred. The dealer has no emotional attachment to the car, as the owner perhaps does. To the dealer, it is simply a matter of dollars and cents, and the trade-in must bring a profit when it is resold.

Some owners try to sell the old car themselves. After paying for classified ads and giving up evenings and weekends to deal with prospective buyers, however, many end up trying to sell the car to a dealer outright (not as part of the purchase of a new car). In such cases, the seller certainly will not receive more than the average wholesale value of the car and possibly less than it would have brought as a trade-in on a new one. In view of the many problems that sometimes go with trying to sell a second-hand automobile through classified advertisements in the local newspaper, the best approach for most people is to dispose of the old car through a trade-in, and dicker for the best trade-in allowance the dealer will make.

The car dealer, in common with every other businessman, attempts to keep a good selection of merchandise that will meet the needs of a variety of customers. A dealer's best used cars, of course, are recent models with low mileage that have been traded in for reasons other than poor condition, damage, or obsolescence. He will be particularly anxious to get your recent low mileage car on his lot if he does not already have a similar car in his used-car inventory. If your old car fits the bill, you are in a position to hold out for the top dollar on it.

Warranties

The new car warranty is a sales device used by a manufacturer to attract buyers. It does not reflect any deep moral commitment or responsibility to the new car owner. A warranty is only as good as the manufacturer who offers it and the dealers who honor it.

basic warranty terms and omissions

A warranty is a guarantee of a car's performance covering a fixed period of time, or mileage, or both. Specific warranty provisions change significantly with changes in the automobile market, so, they are considered here in general terms.

As an example, consider a vehicle that is advertised as having a warranty for 12 months or 12,000 miles. Here's what that means: The manufacturer will reimburse authorized dealerships for repair of certain items that fail within 12 months or 12,000 miles following the purchase of the vehicle. When either one of these two conditions has expired, the warranty ceases to be in effect.

That warranty sounds simple enough to the prospective car buyer, but many important unanswered questions remain. For example:

1. Does the warranty cover both the parts and the labor required to make the repairs?
2. Where does the owner have to take the car to have it repaired? Does it have to go back to the dealer who sold it, or can it be repaired at any dealership connected with the manufacturer?
3. Does the warranty cover *everything* that goes wrong with the car, or are the tires specifically excluded? How about the

paint and the interior trim? Does it include such service items as spark plugs and ignition points, air filters, and oil filters?

4. Will the car be repaired promptly or will it be given a very low priority while cars which are not under warranty (and therefore bringing money into the shop faster) given priority?

5. If the dealer says nothing is wrong with the car, who determines whether repairs are to be made?

6. If the car breaks down on the road, who is responsible for the expenses of towing it to a garage for repairs?

7. When the repairs are needed, must they be made with new parts, or may the dealer use rebuilt or used parts?

8. Are the new repair parts warranted for an additional 12 months or 12,000 miles; That is, are the repairs themselves warranted?

9. Who is the judge of a job properly done, the garage or the owner?

10. Are certain items (like the upholstery) specifically warranted for a shorter or longer time than the rest of the car?

Clearly, the simple statement that a car is "warranted for 12,000 miles or 12 months" (or any other terms) leaves many issues unresolved.

new car problems

Buyers of new cars are often surprised to learn that their new purchase may not relieve them of the problems they thought they had left behind with the old trade-in. One study showed that, on the average, over two dozen items required correction under the warranty on a new car. It is unwise to take a new car on a long trip without first allowing a "shakedown" period of several weeks. The dealer who sold the car usually gives better and faster warranty service than a dealer in a strange town who knows he will not see the car again.

The new car owner should carry a pad and pencil and make notes of all problems that occur. Thoroughly inspect the car for faulty paint, missing or loose screws and bolts, poorly fitting doors and hoods, and similar defects. Also make note of all noises, however slight, and performance conditions that you suspect are not normal. After about a week, return the car with your list of accumulated defects, and expect it to be in the dealers's hands for several days while the necessary corrections are made. (Obviously, if the car is delivered in an unsafe condition, that is, with malfunctioning brakes or other safety equipment, it should be returned as soon as these deficiencies are discovered.) If you have done a good job of identifying the problems, and the dealer has repaired all of them, there may never again be need to return this car for repairs under the terms of the warranty.

The owner might wonder why the new car has so many problems. It often seems that the only one who really inspects the finished product is the buyer. The modern automobile is basically well designed, but there are many things that can go wrong. If everything is adjusted to function correctly, and then properly serviced, the vehicle should give good results for many years.

keeping the warranty in effect

It is very important that the owner of a new car comply with the terms of the warranty "to the letter." In most cases, compliance requires that the vehicle be serviced at specified intervals (in miles or months, whichever comes first). If the vehicle is not properly serviced, the warranty may automatically be voided. Another common warranty provision is that any repairs must be made with parts approved by the manufacturer. Automobile owners frequently misinterpret these statements to mean that all *servicing* must be performed at a dealership of the manufacturer. Unless specified, this is usually not the case, however, and the car may be serviced at any service station, or the owner may do the work himself. A written record must be kept of exactly *what* was done and *when* it was done; write down both the date and the odometer reading when servicing was performed.

Specific service requirements in terms of lubricants and other suppliers also must be met. If, for example, the engine of the new car suffers a major failure, the dealer may send a sample of the engine oil to a chemical testing laboratory to determine whether it met the specifications required under the terms of the warranty. Since engines are very expensive, there is obviously a lot of money at stake. If the testing lab reports that the engine oil did *not* meet the warranty requirements, the warranty will probably not be honored and the owner will have to pay for a new engine.

Necessary *repairs* that are covered by the warranty should always be performed at an authorized dealership. The parts that might be installed by a private garage may be of equal or superior quality to those that originally came with the car, but the repairs will be charged for and the warranty may be voided. If repairs are required, the vehicle can usually be driven or towed to a participating dealership and performed under the terms of the warranty.

The message here is clear: *Comply with the terms of the warranty*. They are spelled out in the owner's warranty manual. Don't expect any more than is written there—but don't settle for anything less.

dealer and manufacturer responsibility

Dealerships are usually private businesses having franchise arrangements with the manufacturer. Although the manufacturer builds and warrants the new car, the dealers must honor the warranties. While the owner buys a car manufactured by one organization he must rely on another one to handle his complaints and perform the needed repairs. A similar situation exists within the dealership. Owners often bring a new car back for repairs only to find that the salesman is no longer interested and simply refers the owner to the service department. Claims or promises made by the salesman are honored by the service department only to the extent they are outlined in writing in the warranty manual.

In many cases, the manufacturer pays a dealer less for performing repairs under a warranty than the dealer would receive from a customer for the same work on a car that is no longer in warranty. Since many shops have more business than they can handle comfortably will give priority to cars that are no longer under warranty. Dealers also must supply the manufacturer with considerable documentation of all warranty work and often encounter delays in receiving payment from the factory. In addition, dealers sometimes make repairs that they believe should be covered by the warranty, only to have the manufacturer disagree and refuse to pay for the work. The dealer then suffers the loss. Bear these factors in mind if you have difficulty with warranty adjustments.

None of these factors, of course, excuses the manufacturer from meeting the terms of his written warranty agreement with the buyer. Sometimes the automobile owner must go beyond the dealership and make contact directly with the manufacturer to obtain satisfactory service. Every manufacturer has regional representatives to handle owner complaints that cannot be resolved at the dealership level. These representatives may authorize needed repairs in situations where a dealership might be hesitant to perform them. Many automobile owners do not realize that these representatives exist, and dealers don't seem particularly enthusiastic about publicizing them. If enough complaints about a dealer have to be resolved by a "rep", the manufacturer may cancel the dealer's franchise.

The Hot-Line

Some manufacturers maintain a "hotline," a toll-free telephone number through which an owner having warranty problems can contact the manufacturer directly. A local rep is then assigned to contact the customer. The owner will be requested to take the vehicle to a nearby dealership and meet with the rep, who will personally examine it and make a judgment as to whether or not the needed repairs are covered by the warranty.

Most manufacturer's reps are very sympathetic to the position of the customer, and dealers are frequently overruled (or given authorization) regarding warranty repairs. If a dealer still refuses to cooperate after you have made a reasonable effort to get satisfaction, there should be no hesitation in contacting the manufacturer and requesting a meeting with a representative. When meeting with a dealer or a rep, always have all pieces of paper related to ownership, maintenance and repair of the vehicle available.

Toll-free "hotlines," like the warranty, are sales devices, and they come and go depending on their effectiveness as an aid in selling cars. In any case, the cost of a telephone call directly to the manufacturer or the inconvenience of writing a letter are small when compared with the cost of having major work done that should be covered by warranty. There are numerous special "factory modifications" that will be performed free, but only if the customer makes a specific complaint related to the needed modification.

Automotive Recalls

Since government pressure has forced manufacturers to recall vehicles that may have potential safety faults, nearly one out of every two vehicles manufactured has been called back. In some cases, the vehicles are recalled and major safety modifications are performed. Some of the recalls have seemed trivial, however, and critics have claimed that vehicles out of warranty have been re-called so that their owners could be sold additional repair work not related to the recall. In any case, do not disregard a registered letter or a telegram informing you of a defect in your car. Failure to take the car to a dealer for inspection could constitute a waiver of liability against the company. Should some failure occur in the future, you might not be able to sue the manufacturer for damages effectively.

Buying a used car

An astute buyer can save hundreds of dollars by buying a used car. Many serviceable used cars are available which original owners have traded or sold in order to change to a larger or smaller model or to get a new car. Many of these cars will provide miles of good reliable service. The purchase of a used car involves many more unknowns than the purchase of a new one. It is possible to locate a good used car, however, by carefully evaluating the condition of each prospect and by understanding dealer practices in regard to pricing and selling used automobiles. Long-term economic considerations of an older car are compared with those of newer automobiles in Chapter 16.

External Evaluation

There are many ways of determining whether an automobile has been abused. Some evidence is available from an inspection of the exterior of the car. If a car that is two or three years old has been repainted, ask why. The color may have been changed to suit the desires of the previous owner, or repainting might have been necessary to cover surface damage such as pitting caused by a sandstorm. In either case, the new paint does not mean that the car is not sound, however, the most common reason to repaint a car is to repair damage caused by collision or rust. If a paint job is poor, as evidenced by runs in the paint or overspray on the rubber around windows and over chrome trim, it is likely that the car has been repaired only to the extent necessary to "unload" it. Beware of cars with this appearance. Another cause for suspicion is a price that is below normal for the make, model, and age of the car. "Bargain cars" can be quite expensive in the long run.

Look the car over carefully for evidence of body and fender repairs. Sight down a smooth surface such as long side panels, doors, and along the roof line just above the doors. Waves, ripples, or flat spots are indications that the body has undergone repairs necessitated by a collision or severe rust conditions. You may detect evidence of sanding or file marks in the form of closely spaced, parallel lines similar to brush marks in paint. It is difficult for even a skilled body and fender man to completely eradicate evidence of his handiwork, particularly if large areas of the body have been damaged.

Pock marks, bubbles, or chipping of the chrome or other bright metal trim usually indicate bad body rust underneath the paint. Be extra suspicious if the car came from a coastal region where the salty atmosphere drastically exaggerates rust problems. In areas where ice and snow make road conditions hazardous, salt is often spread on the roads to improve traction. Salt damage from this source may be severe and may make an otherwise desirable car totally worthless. If you suspect rust damage, look at points that are not readily accessible or easily visible: rocker panels under the doors well back toward the chassis, metal pans under the grille or radiator, or roll-unders around the rear bumper. If these areas show evidence of serious rust, it is likely that the whole car body is in similar condition. Do not buy that car. Body repairs are very costly.

Checking the Mileage

The average car is driven 10,000 to 15,000 miles a year. Some people have jobs that require a great deal of driving, however, and it is not uncommon for them to drive 70,000 or even a 100,000 miles in a year. Most states have laws prohibiting the seller from turning back the odometer (mileage indicator). This practice used to be widespread, but in recent years the penalties have been made more severe. The guilty dealer often must not only pay a stiff fine but also may have his license revoked. Where the penalties are high and strictly enforced, the indicated mileage is likely to be accurate. In areas where penalties are light or the laws do not seem to be vigorously enforced, it is wise to suspect the mileage shown on the odometer.

interior evidence of wear

Although an unscrupulous individual may set the odometer back, most high mileage cars will have other visible evidence of use. For example, look at the foot pedals. If the rubber is badly worn, the car has been driven over 50,000 miles; on the other hand, new pedal pads may indicate replacement of old ones that were worn out. The finish on painted or plated knobs on dash controls, window cranks, and door handles may be worn through. Worn spots in the upholstery adjacent to these handles indicate heavy usage. Sagging seat springs, particularly in the driver's position, show that the seat has been occupied for long periods of time, which can only come with high mileage driving. Worn floor mats and seats are other giveaways, and new seat covers and mats are reason to be suspicious.

tires

Obvious indications, such as worn tires (including the spare), will provide additional evidence of the miles the car has traveled. If the spare is one of the original tires and the running wheels have tires from a different company or bearing a different tread, the original tires have probably been worn out and replaced. The average mileage for a set of original tires is about 20,000 miles. Thus, if the tires on the car seem to be replacements and are nearly worn out, assume that the car has gone at least 40,000 miles.

service records

When a car is serviced, many attendants and garage mechanics enter the odometer mileage on a label and stick it to the car, usually on the doorpost on the driver's side. A seller attempting to conceal a high mileage car will usually have the presence of mind to remove these stickers. They are sometimes overlooked, however, particularly if they were put in an unusual place such as inside the rear doors on the jamb or under the hood. Some equipment, such as fuel filters, oil filters, air filters, batteries, and thermostats, are sold with labels or spaces to record the mileage at the time of such service. Reasonable evidence of tampering should be sufficient justification to look elsewhere for a car.

the retired fleet car

Cars that have been used in taxi, police, or other fleet service can often be detected by looking for evidence of meter installations or two-way radio equipment. In taxis, the meter is often installed in the glove compartment so look for a missing, severely damaged, or new box. Since most fleet service vehicles are radio equipped, there is usually evidence of such installations in the form of extra holes drilled in the bottom lip of the dash. Examination of the roof and the trunk deck will often show evidence of installation of

"This one was owned by a little old lady who had it
towed by a horse to fight air pollution."

antennae or taxi or police signs. Be suspicious of a patch of new, unfaded paint over the area of the roof just above the front seat, in the middle of the roof, or near the hinges of the trunk. Dealers sometimes paint the whole top to conceal this type of body work, and the evidence may be difficult to spot.

Mechanical Evaluation

If a car has passed the visual inspection outlined above, take it to a competent mechanic not associated with the seller and ask him to check it out mechanically. Tell him you are thinking of buying the car, and be prepared to pay a reasonable fee for his services. Some mechanics will give the car a cursory onceover and not charge for it; such an inspection is worth just what you pay for it. If the inspection takes an hour, the charge should be the prevailing hourly rate for shop time. In some areas, there are diagnostic centers that have published rates for such service. Choose a center that does not have repair facilities but simply inspects and advises as to required repairs.

Remember, a used automobile cannot be expected to be in perfect condition. In some cases, the diagnostic examination will uncover faults in the car that the dealer was unaware of, and quite often he will agree to correct those faults before you buy. He should not increase his asking price as a result, however.

It should be emphasized that *most* automobile dealers, whether they are in new or used cars, are honest businessmen. They operate their businesses around sound legal practices, and attempt to provide the best of merchandise and service to their customers. As with all other businesses, they attempt to operate at a profit. Unfortunately, the automobile business—like any other business—has attracted its share of sharp operators who attempt to turn a quick dollar with little regard for the customer, and it pays to watch out for them.

Where to Look for a Good Used Car

the new car agency

The best place to look for a used car is at a dealership where new cars are sold, and only carefully selected used cars are on the lot. At such agencies, most of the used cars are trade-ins from new car sales. Many dealers will give the same guarantee or warranty on their used cars as they do on their new cars. The general practice among these dealers is to restore cars traded in to "nearly new" condition, in terms of both mechanical performance and appearance. Obviously, this work costs money, and such expenses will be reflected in the selling price. As a rule, however, it is much cheaper to buy a used car from a reliable dealer and pay the difference than to buy a doubtful machine from a private party or a shady used car dealer, with the inevitable high costs of labor to have the car repaired yourself.

the used car lot

There are many reputable used car dealers who are not directly associated with a new car dealership. These dealers buy their cars at wholesale prices from the new car agencies or at dealer auctions, and often provide the same type of maintenance support and warranty service as new car dealers. As a general rule, the car bought from such a dealer can be expected to have nearly the same quality as that obtained from the new car dealer. However, since this type of dealer gets second choice of cars after the new car dealer has made his selection, it stands to reason that the odds of finding that "perfect car" favor the new car agency.

the iron dealer

There are some used car dealers who are little more than way stations en route to the wrecking yard. They get used cars from any source they can. Sometimes they will actually take a car that has been sent to the wrecking yard to be junked. These dealers are often referred to an "iron dealers" because the cars they sell are little more than scrap iron. Fortunately, such operators are not hard to recognize. Their place of business is usually as shoddy as their merchandise, and there is rarely any sort of maintenance facility associated with the operation. The main attractions offered by such dealers are low prices and easy credit. The prices are low because the cars are not worth much, and financing is usually high interest and short term. Because they make their money more on the financing than on the car, they are really just finance companies with an inventory. Such dealers are to be avoided.

classified advertising

Answering a classified ad for a used car may lead to a bargain or to someone else's problem car. A car bought from an individual in this way must be subjected to the same close scrutiny as the car bought from the iron dealer. Obviously, the individual cannot offer the buyer any real warranty protection. He may glibly offer a warranty, but probably cannot be legally held to it. When you drive away from the curb, that used car—good, bad, or indifferent—is all yours.

Used cars offered through classified ads also are risky because many of them are cars that a dealer would not accept as a trade-in or at a price that was acceptable to the owner. In addition, the favored market for stolen cars is through classified ads. The attitude of some individuals with a used car to sell is that any subterfuge is acceptable to "unload the old heap." Many good cars are sold through classified ads, but the prospective purchaser must be particularly thorough in his evaluation of any automobile offered in this way.

Pricing a used car is a difficult job. Age is not an accurate criterion. Many old automobiles that have been well maintained and carefully driven are superior to newer cars that have been abused. The make and model do not always provide a good guide. A car that originally cost a great deal as a prestige car may have a used car value well below that of a car which sold new at a lower price. The prestige features and accessories that made the new car desirable for a particular buyer may pull the price down later because of the increased likelihood of high repair costs. *Condition* is the only measure of value that can be accurately applied to all types of used cars.

Because of the many variables involved in pricing a used automobile, the "trade" has established standardized pricing guides, commonly referred to as the *Blue Book.* These books are similar in content, if not in color, and provide pricing guidelines for dealers in all sections of the country. The National Automobile Dealers' Association prints guides of this type, sometimes are known as the "NADA Book," for a number of areas.

The type of information provided in such guides generally includes average retail, wholesale, and loan values for all types of motor vehicles, including imports and trucks, by year and model. An example is shown in Table 15-1. These prices are adjusted to include valuable accessories and extras that are not normally provided as standard equipment, and there are scales for adjusting prices according to mileage. The prices shown in the book are *average* prices for the cars as identified. These averages are derived from actual transactions in the region for which the book is valid, during the period just before the dates shown on the cover. The books are updated quarterly and sometimes bimonthly. As a rule, this book will list all popular makes and models over the previous seven years; the value of older cars is deemed to be so doubtful that each buyer or seller is expected to determine it for himself.

Note that the prices shown are average prices for average cars, so if the car you are dealing with is substantially better or worse

	Original Cost	Insurance Code (6)	Insurance Code (8)	Shipping Weight	Average Dollar Value Wholesale	Average Dollar Value Retail
ADD FOR: Low Mileage See Table "A"						
Sun Roof					50	65
Pwr Windows					25	35
Vinyl Top					50	65
Power Seat (Split)					25	35
Tilt Steering Wheel					25	35
AM-FM Stereo					25	35
Tape Stereo					50	65
Roof Rack (Wagons)					50	65
Cruise Control					50	65
DEDUCT FOR: Excess Mileage See Table "A"						
No Air Cond.					175	235
3 Speed Man. Trans					150	200
4 Speed Man. Trans					100	135
3 Speed & Overdrive					100	135
No Pwr Steering					100	135
6 Cylinder Engine					75	100

1971 CHEVROLET   All models equipped with
Automatic Transmission
Power Steering
Air Conditioning

Wheel Base 121.5", Tires F78 × 151B
Std Engine V8, 245 H.P., 350 C.I.D. Optional 6 cyl. 145 HP, 250 Cid

	Original Cost	Insurance Code (6)	Insurance Code (8)	Shipping Weight	Average Dollar Value Wholesale	Average Dollar Value Retail
V8 Biscayne - V.I.N. 15469 1(-) 1000 001 and up.						
15469 Sedan 4D-6	 3885	4	4	4000	1200	1660
V8 Bel Air - V.I.N. 15669 1(-) 1000 001 and up.						
15669 Sedan 4D-6	 3722	4	4	4000	1300	1785
V8 Impala - V.I.N. 16439 1(-) 1000 001 and up.						
16469 Sedan 4D-6	 4156	4	4	4018	1350	1850
16457 Sport Coupe 2D-5	 4173	4	4	4010	1500	2040
16447 Cust. Coupe 2D-5	 4239	–	4	4010	1535	2100
16439 Sport Sedan 4D-6	 4226	–	4	4080	1395	1910
16467 Convertible 2D-5	 4483	–	5	4190	1400	1920
V8 Caprice - V.I.N. 16639 1(-) 1000 001 and up.						
16647 Cust. Coupe 2D-6	 4493	–	5	4062	1670	2255
16639 Cust. Sedan 4D-6	 4545	–	5	4146	1600	2175
V8 Wagons - V.I.N. 15435 1(-) 1000 001 and up.						
15435 Brook. 4D-2S	4366	–	5	4598	1450	1980
15635 Towns. 40-2S	4430	–	5	4598	1490	2035
15645 Towns. 4D-3S	4544	–	5	4636	1600	2175
16435 Kings. 4D-2S	4550	–	5	4650	1600	2180
16445 Kings. 4D-3S	4664	–	5	4668	1695	2295
16635 Kings Est. 4D-2S	4816	–	5	4724	1700	2300
16645 Kings. Est. 4D-32	4930	–	5	4738	1800	2425

than average for its year, you can expect the actual price to be adjusted upward or downward, as appropriate.

Referring to Table 15-1, consider a 1968 **Kingswood Estate** station wagon that originally sold for $4,930. Assume that it is in average condition and has been driven 30,000 miles. The car is equipped with power windows and a roof rack; it does not have power steering. Under the page heading "Chevrolet" and the year in which the car was manufactured, the first item of note in Table 15-1 is the boldface statement "loan value is 80% of wholesale." The specific car is found by locating its body style, in this case a four door (4D), three seat (3S) wagon. The new car price is shown along with an insurance symbol used in determining insurance rates. Next are shown two figures in italics, $1,800 and $2,425. These are the average *wholesale* price and the average *retail* price, respectively, and apply to a car with all equipment considered standard on it. These figures are *increased* for extra equipment and *decreased* for the absence of standard equipment. The book indicates that $25 (wholesale) and $35 (retail) should be added for power windows and $50 and $65 for a roof rack.

Blue Book value adjustments based on mileage are shown in Table 15-2, which indicates that this vehicle with only 30,000 miles may be increased in valuation by $190. Table 15-3 shows Blue Book guidelines for acceptable mileage, by model year, and for determining standard versus optional equipment. Since power steering is considered standard on this car, the absence of that accessory requires that $100.00 be deducted from wholesale and $135.00 from retail (Table 15-1). The total Blue Book value of the car is, therefore:

		Wholesale	Retail
Basic Vehicle		$1800	$2425
Add:	For air	25	35
	For vinyl top	50	65
	For low mileage	190	190
Total		$2065	$2715
Subtract:			
	Conventional steering	100	135
Total Adjusted Value		$1965	$2580

If the car in this example were traded in on a newer one, the dealer could be expected to allow $1,572 for it. As a used car for

Table 15-2

Value Adjustment In Dollars Based On Mileage And Age

Mileage in Thousands	Age in Years						
	0	1	2	3	4	5	6
1							
2	*250*						
3	*225*		*MAXIMUM AMOUNT*				
4	*225*		*TO BE DEDUCTED 50%*				
5	*225*						
6	*200*		*OF THE WHOLESALE*				
7	*200*		*VALUE*				
8	*175*	*250*					
9	*175*	*225*					
10	*150*	*225*					
11	*150*	*225*					
12	*150*	*225*					
13	*125*	*200*					
14	*100*	*200*	*250*				
15	*100*	*200*	*225*				
16	*75*	*175*	*225*				
17	*50*	*175*	*225*				
18	*25*	*175*	*225*	*250*			
19	**0**	*175*	*225*	*225*			
20	**75**	*150*	*225*	*225*			
21	**100**	*150*	*200*	*225*	*250*		
22	**150**	*125*	*200*	*225*	*225*	*250*	
23	**175**	*125*	*175*	*225*	*225*	*225*	*250*
24	**225**	*125*	*175*	*200*	*225*	*225*	*225*
25	**250**	*100*	*175*	*200*	*225*	*225*	*225*
26	**275**	*100*	*175*	*200*	*225*	*225*	*225*
27	**300**	*100*	*150*	*200*	*225*	*225*	*225*
28	**325**	*75*	*150*	*200*	*200*	*225*	*225*
29	**350**	*75*	*145*	*190*	*190*	*220*	*220*
30	**375**	*50*	*125*	*175*	*190*	*190*	*190*
31	**400**	*50*	*125*	*175*	*190*	*190*	*190*
32	**425**	*25*	*125*	*175*	*175*	*190*	*190*
33	**450**	*0*	*125*	*175*	*175*	*190*	*190*

ADD figures in Italic type

DEDUCT figures in boldface type

Table 15-2 (continued)

Value Adjustment In Dollars Based On Mileage And Age

Mileage in Thousands	Age in Years						
	0	1	2	3	4	5	6
35	500	50	*100*	*150*	*175*	*175*	*200*
37	525	100	*75*	*150*	*175*	*175*	*175*
39	550	150	*50*	*125*	*150*	*175*	*175*
41	600	225	*25*	*100*	*125*	*150*	*150*
43	650	275	0	*100*	*125*	*150*	*150*
45	675	325	50	75	*125*	*125*	*150*
47	725	350	100	75	*100*	*125*	*125*
49	750	375	125	*50*	*100*	*125*	*125*
51	800	425	175	25	75	*100*	*100*
53	825	450	200	0	75	*100*	*100*
55	850	500	275	25	*50*	*75*	*100*
57	900	525	250	50	25	*50*	*75*
59	925	550	275	75	0	*50*	*50*
61	975	600	325	125	25	25	25
63	1000	625	350	150	50	0	25
65	1025	650	375	175	75	25	0
67	1050	675	400	200	100	25	25
69	1075	700	425	225	100	25	25
71	1125	725	450	250	125	50	50
73	1150	740	450	250	125	75	50
75	1175	775	475	275	150	75	50
77	1200	800	500	300	150	75	75
79		825	525	300	175	75	75
81		850	550	325	200	100	100
83		875	575	350	200	100	100
85			575	350	200	125	100
87			600	375	225	125	100
89			625	400	225	125	100
91				400	250	150	125
93				425	250	150	125
95					250	150	125
97					275	150	125
99						175	150

DEDUCT figures in boldface type

ADD figures in Italic type

Table 15-3
Guidelines Shown in Buyer's Books for Equipment

General Information:

Wholesale and retail prices included in this booklet are predicated on cars in good mechanical condition and appearance with mileages as indicated.

Current year models	20,000 miles
One year old models	34,000 miles
Two year old models	44,000 miles
Three year old models	55,000 miles
Four year old models	60,000 miles
Five year old models	65,000 miles
Six year old models	65,000 miles

Models of a given year with more or less mileage must be adjusted in price in accordance with the data of Table A.

1. Prices quoted on all U.S. automobiles include automatic transmission radio and heater.
2. Prices include air conditioning for all full size cars of the following makes: Buick, Cadillac, Chevrolet, Chrysler, Dodge, Ford, Thunderbird, Imperial, Lincoln, Mercury, Oldsmobile and Pontiac.
3. Prices for all U.S. cars, except compact cars and stationwagons, include power steering.
4. Prices on imported cars include only radio and heater.

Optional equipment listed under each model series warrants addition of value indicated to the base price. Similarly, indicated values should be deducted for equipment not provided, as explained above and as listed under each model series.

Insurance symbols are used for determining insurance premium rates.

---

for sale, its loan value, 80 percent of the wholesale value, is $1,965, and the purchaser wishing to buy this car must pay the difference, in cash, between the retail value and the loan value, or $1,008. (Many lending agencies will loan 100 percent of the car's wholesale value if the dealer is willing to accept "recourse," which means that he can repossess the car if the loan is defaulted and will make good the note.) He also could offer an older car in trade, but if it did not have a Blue Book value of at least $1,008, he would still have to pay some amount in cash. Either way, a balance of $1,572 remains, on the retail price, and it must be financed.

Economic considerations of automobile ownership

Owning an automobile is a very expensive proposition. Many, if not most, of the transportation needs of the average person could be better met by alternate means.

There are many reasons for automobile ownership,—prestige, a desire for luxury, the need to move from one place to another with relative speed, the ability to travel at any convenient time, and so on. These factors often assume a greater importance then economic considerations. One needs only to review automobile advertisements briefly to see how manufacturers appeal to the personal whims and habits of the buying public. In-depth analysis of some of these reasons and rationalizations is more appropriately left to psychologists. This chapter concentrates on the financial considerations of automobile *ownership*. (Leasing has no significant economic advantage over buying, except when automobile costs can be written off as a business expense. If in doubt, check with an accountant.)

Comparative Costs of Public and Private Transportation

Public transportation is almost always more economical than travel by car. Costs are changing rapidly but the average cost of travel by inter-city bus, for example, is about 8 cents a mile. Travel by train averages 10 cents a mile, and travel by airplane costs about the same. Studies done by various automobile clubs and federal agencies indicate the average cost of operating a full-sized American car varies between 15 and 25 cents a mile, depending in part on the area of the country in which the car is operated. The cost of operating a compact car is 10 to 15 cents a mile. Viewing the true cost of automobile transportation impassively in the cold hard light of financial reality, we can see that automobile transportation usually has to be justified on some basis other than economy.

A car owner's first reaction to learning the true operating cost per mile is one of disbelief, for the most obvious recurring cost, that of fuel, divided by the number of miles per gallon, indicates the cost to be only a few cents a mile. The other very large costs related to car ownership are often forgotten.

There are two types of automobile operating expenses: fixed costs and variable costs. *Fixed costs* are the costs of owning the vehicle, whether or not it is actually driven. These are costs that go on day after day, week after week, even if the car just sits in the driveway. *Variable costs* are those incurred only when the car is actually being driven; when the car is not being operated, these expenses are zero.

Let us examine the fixed and variable expenses of a full size new car driven 10,000 miles in its first year. Typical figures for this example are given in Table 16-1; they will vary slightly, of course, from car to car and in different parts of the country. Similar data for a compact car is given in Table 16-2.

The Full Size New Car

fixed costs

Depreciation. Depreciation is the silent thief. It is the loss in value due to aging. The only cars that escape the ravages of depreciation are the true antiques that have become collectors' items.

TABLE 16-1 First-year (10,000 MILES) Operating Costs of a New $5,000 Full-size Sedan					TABLE 16-2 First-year (10,000 MILES) Operating Costs of a New $3,000 Compact Sedan			
Fixed Costs		*Variable Costs*			*Fixed Costs*		*Variable Costs*	
Depreciation	$1,250	Gas and oil	$450		Depreciation	$600	Gas and oil	$225
Interest	500	Tires	100		Interest	300	Tune-ups	25
Insurance	200	Tune-ups	75		Insurance	200	Tires	75
License	75	Repairs	0		License	50	Repairs	0
	$2,025		$625			$1,150		$325

$$\begin{array}{l} \$2,025 \\ +625 \\ \hline \$2,650 \end{array} \quad \frac{\$2,650}{10,000 \text{ mi}} = 26\frac{1}{2} \text{ center per mile}$$

$$\begin{array}{l} \$1,150 \\ +325 \\ \hline \$1,475 \end{array} \quad \frac{\$1,475}{10,000 \text{ mi}} = 14\frac{3}{4} \text{ cents per mile}$$

Automobiles depreciate for several reasons: (1) As the car gets older and new models are introduced, our $4,000 car becomes less stylish; and (2) normal wear and tear increases the likelihood of costly repairs. The new car is the hardest hit by depreciation. The typical full-sized U.S. car will depreciate between 20 and 30 percent of its original cost in the first year. The example given in Table 16-1 assumes 25 percent first-year depreciation, or a loss of $1,250, typifying the often-heard expression that "It costs a thousand dollars to drive a new car off the showroom floor."

Interest. Interest expense is paid directly on a car loan (in the first year, a typical figure might be $700) or indirectly in the form of interest lost on money that might have been deposited in a savings account but instead was used to purchase the car outright (a typical figure might be $200). The figure of $500 was used in Table 16-1.

Insurance and License. Insurance is covered in detail in Chapter 17. For purposes of discussion, an annual cost of $200 is assumed for insurance coverage. License costs vary widely from state to state; here we assume an average figure of $75.

Summary. Before our new $5,000 car has even been driven, the fixed costs for the first year add up to $2,025. If we assume this car will be driven 10,000 miles during the year, these fixed costs alone will average 20¼ cents per mile ($2,025/10,000 mi = 20¼¢).

variable costs

Gas and Oil. Again referring to Table 16-1, we find that gas and oil for the $5,000 car driven 10,000 miles, including oil and oil filter changes performed at a service station, will cost approximately $450. The exact cost depends on the mileage the car achieves per gallon of gas, and on the price of gas and oil.

Tires, Tune-ups and Repairs. The original tires should be good for approximately 20,000 miles. Thus, they will be about half worn out at the end of the first year. Half the cost of a set of tires would be about $100. If steel-belted radials or other more expensive tires are used, the cost per set will be substantially higher, but they will wear longer and will cost somewhat less per mile. A tune-up, including plugs and points and other minor maintenance items not covered by warranty, may run around $75.

Repairs during the first year should be near zero, since the car will probably be under a warranty.

Summary. The variable costs outlined above add up to $625, or 6¼ cents per mile.

Total Annual Cost of the Full Size Car

The total cost of operating the $5,000 car for the first year is $2,650, or about 26½ cents per mile. Each figure will vary, depending on location and the condition of the economy at a given time, and these cost data should be adjusted to reflect local conditions. When the figures are all added up, however, the fact remains that owning a new car is a very expensive proposition.

The Compact Car

The cost of operating a new $3,000 compact car (Table 16-2) amounts to about 14¾ cents a mile, roughly half of the cost of the full-sized U.S. car. Note that the depreciation *rate* is slightly lower on a $3,000 compact car so the total depreciation dollars are less than half those of the $5000 full-sized car. Insurance expense is about the same, but this will vary in different regions, as will license fees. Interest and gas and oil costs are about half those of the larger car. Many compact cars require tune-ups more frequently than larger cars, so these costs are comparable on an annual basis. Tires last twice as long on a lightweight car as on a heavy car; tires for the compact car also cost only half as much. The cost per mile for tire wear on a compact is therefore only about a fourth that of a heavy car. All in all, when total fixed and variable costs for the two models are compared, we see that the new compact car can be operated for about half the cost of the new full-sized car.

Used Car Costs

Table 16-3 shows the operating costs during the fifth year of life of a used full-sized American car with a market or replacement value of $1,000. The car is assumed to have run 50,000 to 60,000 miles.

TABLE 16-3
Fifth-year (10,000 MILES) Operating Costs
of a Used Full-sized Sedan Worth $1,000
(Total Assumed Mileage: 50,000–60,000)

Fixed Costs		*Variable Costs*	
Depreciation	$200	*Repairs	$335
Insurance	100	Gas and oil	450
Interest	100	Tires	75
License	25	Tune-ups	50
	$425		$910

$$\begin{array}{l} \$425 \\ +910 \\ \hline \$1,335 \end{array} \quad \begin{array}{l} \$1,335 \\ \hline 10,000 \text{ mi} \end{array} \quad = 13.3 \text{ cents per mile}$$

*Brake overhaul	$75
Carburetor overhaul	50
Radiator repair	50
New muffler and tail pipe	50
Repair window mechanism	30
New battery	25
Starter repair	25
Front end alignment	20
Front wheel bearing	10
	$335

Note that the fixed costs are much lower than in either of the new car examples, while the variable costs are much higher. The total cost of operation of the used car comes to 13.3 cents per mile.

Comparing the $5,000 new car and the $1,000 used car, the two most significant differences in operating costs are in depreciation and repairs. The used car has already lost $3,000 in value due to depreciation, (assuming a new cost of $4,000) and its annual depreciation has dropped to only $200. This used car is worth only about 25 percent of its original price, and the annual expense for interest (or loss of interest on equity) is about a fifth of that associated with the new car. The used car, however, now requires fairly substantial repairs amounting to $335 per year. Table 16-3 includes a list of repairs that may be required during the fifth year. These are typical of what may be expected to keep a car of the specified age and mileage in good operating condition.

A Comparison of New and Used Car Operating Expenses

Figure 16-1 shows the relationship between annual depreciation and repair costs throughout the normal 10-year life of an automobile. The depreciation cost, as noted, is very high during the first few years. It tapers off quickly, dropping to almost zero at the end of ten years, when the car has almost no resale or trade-in value. Repair costs begin slowly, with no expense during the first (warranty) year, and increase gradually until about the sixth or seventh year when they may rise very quickly. At that point, repairs can become very expensive, because key components wear out. Failures of transmission and differentials, wheel bearings, air conditioning compressors, and even the engine are not uncommon, particularly in the cars that have not been well maintained. Once these expensive repairs have been made, the yearly repair cost drops back to a lower value until the body and frame rust out near the end of the car's life. The cost of required body repairs then exceeds the value of the car, and it is useful only for scrap.

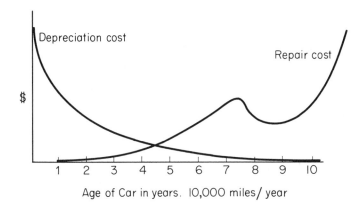

Fig. 16-1 Graph showing relationship between annual depreciation and repair costs during 10-year average life of automobile

The actual shapes of the curves in Fig. 16-1 depend on the specific vehicle and how well it is cared for. Since the two major costs of operation of the vehicle are depreciation (a fixed cost) and repairs (a variable cost), the sum of these two costs during any given year is a good indicator of the economy of operation of the vehicle. As shown in Fig. 16-1, this sum is at its lowest between years 3 and 6, indicating that a good used car that is two or three years old, if properly cared for, will provide economical transportation for a period of three or four years. It should suffer neither the high depreciation of its early years nor the high repair costs of its later years.

The car buyer interested in maximum economy will normally get the most for his money by buying a good, clean used car, two or three years old, and paying a little extra, if necessary, to get one that has been very well maintained.

Implications of Operating Cost Data and Other Factors

incremental costs

We have seen that fixed costs remain constant regardless of the number of miles a vehicle is driven, while variable costs are directly related to vehicle use. If the $5,000 new car was driven only one mile during the first year, the operating cost would be $2,025 per mile! Driven 10,000 miles, the same car costs about 26½ cents per mile to operate; if the mileage driven in the first year reaches 100,000, the cost drops toward 10 cents per mile.

The *cost per mile* decreases with higher yearly mileage; but it varies with the age of the vehicle. If the car is new, the fixed costs may be five times the amount of the variable costs, and the gas and oil expense will be small compared to the cost of just letting the car sit in the driveway. With an older car, however, the variable costs may be twice as high as the fixed costs, and it is not nearly as "costly" to just leave the car setting and not take an extra side trip. Thus, to drive a *new car* one additional (or incremental) mile over 10,000 may not cost the full 26½ cents but only about 6¼ cents per mile. The fixed costs will continue, whether or not

"Here's one in fine condition. It was owned by a man who couldn't afford to buy gas after making the monthly payments."

the car is driven additional miles. An extra side trip in the *used car* with its higher variable costs, however, will cost over 9 cents per incremental mile.

The subject of fixed costs and variable costs is extremely important to owners of trucks, taxicabs, airplanes, and ships, as well as factories and industrial equipment. Maximum economy of operation is achieved when a vehicle is run continuously so that the fixed costs appear small in comparison to the variable costs. This is why some airlines, for example, use their planes to carry passengers during the day and remove the seats to fly freight all night, then replace the seats to carry passengers the next day.

personal transportation requirements

Economy of operation is one of many factors to be considered in the purchase of an automobile. The prospective car buyer must evaluate his personal transportation requirements in terms of these factors and their relative importance.

The operating cost for our used car of Table 16-3 is only about half that of the new car. The reliability of the used car, however, may be significantly lower than that of the new one. A salesman whose income depends on his ability to be in certain locations at certain times cannot afford to have a car that is not highly reliable; he may well consider that reliability worth the extra cost per mile. A businessman may wish to have a car that promotes an image of prestige and success helpful to his business. As an additional consideration, both may be able to write off automobile costs on their income tax.

A commuter, on the other hand, may be willing to forego some prestige, luxury, styling, speed, reliability and convenience in favor of economy. He may drive only to work and back, using the car for perhaps a total of one hour per day. The other 23 hours it sits while the fixed costs of ownership go on. He may find that this type of transportation need is best met by a somewhat less reliable older car, taking public transportation when necessary.

The emotional appeals inherent in automobile advertising obscure the genuine transportation needs of individual car owners. The great American love-affair with the automobile clouds our thinking. An understanding of the basic points outlined in this chapter should at least help the automobile buyer evaluate the true cost of owning and operating a car. He can then decide whether to drive or take public transportation on the basis of factors other than "How much will it cost for gas?"

Accidents and insurance

Accidents do happen! One out of every two cars manufactured is in a serious accident sometime during its useful life. Since the average car's life is about 10 years, the "average" driver may expect to be in one serious accident every 20 years. Knowing this, you will want to consider carrying insurance against the financial loss that may result from an accident.

Many states have laws requiring that an owner either carry insurance, or prove that he has assets (in the hundreds of thousands of dollars) sufficient to pay for damages his car might cause. It is the car and its owner that are insured, not just the driver. The insurance covers the car, regardless of who drives it, provided the driver is properly licensed and has the owners consent. Each car must be separately insured. Insurance coverage does not follow a driver from one car to another.

The Insurance Tangle: Types of Coverage

Auto insurance is not as complicated as it is sometimes made to seem. When written in simple language, the provisions of an insurance policy can usually be understood. The insurance policy is divided into several distinct types of *coverage*, and while policies will vary from state to state in their degree of coverage and some details, the general philosophy behind each type of coverage is essentially the same. Insurance can be purchased with as few, or as many, types of coverage as the car owner desires.

liability insurance

Liability insurance is the most important type of coverage, and is the only coverage some states require by law. Liability insurance protects the car's owner against claims for damage to other persons or property caused by his car, regardless who is driving it.

Typical liability insurance coverage might protect the owner against claims of up to $100,000 for *personal injuries* caused to any one person, with a maximum of $300,000 to be paid in injury claims for one accident. In addition, it might pay up to $50,000 for damages to the *property* of others resulting from an accident. Insurance agents describe this liability coverage as "100, 300, and

50." An accident involving a bus in which passengers were injured and the bus was wrecked could easily result in damages in the hundreds of thousands of dollars. If the car or its driver was determined to be at fault, the insurance company would pay these damages up to the maximum figures stated in the liability part of the policy. In addition, since the insurance company is liable for legal judgments against the car's owner, the company pays the legal expenses necessary for defense in lawsuits that may result from an accident.

Juries are noted for awarding huge accident settlements for personal injuries, and accident judgment claims usually cannot be escaped by declaring bankruptcy or other means. Therefore it is wise to carry as much liability insurance as possible. The driver who cannot afford to buy much insurance should give liability insurance priority over all other types of coverage.

collision insurance

Collision insurance covers the cost of repairing the owner's *car* in the event of a collision. If the collision is *your* fault, *your* insurance company will pay to repair *your* car. If the other driver is judged to be at fault, *his* company will pay to fix your car. If the other driver does not have insurance or cannot pay to repair your car promptly, your company will pay your repair costs and may sue the other driver or his insurance company to get their money back. In either case, collision coverage protects and insures *your car* in the event of collision with another car or any other object.

Most collision insurance coverage has a "deductible" provision which requires that the owner pay the first $50, or $100, or $250 needed to repair the car. This provision relieves the insurance company of numerous small claims for chipped paint and small dents that commonly occur when cars are parked close together, as in parking lots. Owners may also drive more carefully if they know they will have to pay at least part of the repair bill.

The car owner can select the level of accident risk he wishes to take by selecting the "deductible" amount. The less risk he is willing to take (that is, the lower the deductible amount), the more he has to pay for collision coverage. By way of comparison, taxicab fleet owners typically carry "$1,000 deductible," to keep their collision insurance rates low. In effect, they insure themselves for the first $1,000 of damage, with an insurance company protecting them for all costs of repair over that. Owners of jet aircraft or ocean-going ships may carry a "million dollar deductible."

The *new car* owner probably will want to carry collision insurance. Collision insurance may be a waste of money, however, if the car is older and the owner if financially able to replace it if necessary. Let's examine a car with a replacement value of $600 and see what the owner would *really* stand to lose if his car was seriously damaged in an accident.

A damaged car is seldom a *total* loss. An auto junkyard may pay anywhere from 0 to 40 percent of the pre-accident value of the car, depending on the kind of car and which parts are salvageable. Older U.S.-made cars that were manufactured in large numbers and for which replacement parts are plentiful have very little value. Foreign sports cars and classics like the Edsel, Hudson, etc., may bring good prices. A wrecked Volkswagen, which can readily be turned into a "dune buggy" or other specialty vehicle is always in strong demand and brings a good scrap price. Of special interest to wrecking yards are undamaged low mileage engines and drive trains, undamaged front suspensions, and certain hard-to-find grill and trim items, which can be readily resold to garages or individuals who need these parts.

For the sake of discussion, assume that we have an older model $600 car that is seriously damaged, but is still worth $100 to a wrecking yard. If we had carried $100 deductible collision insurance, we would have to pay the first $100 if we were going to repair the car. If we chose not to carry collision coverage however, the car value of $600 minus the $100 scrap value minus the $100 deductible leaves a loss of only $400 instead of the full $600.

The insurance premium just for collision coverage on this vehicle might run $80 a year. The $80 is 1/5 the loss against which we are insuring ($400). In 5 years these $80 payments would equal $400, but the car is "due" for a serious accident only once every 20 years. If the car is in an accident, there may be a 50-50 chance that the other driver will be at fault, and *his liability insurance coverage* will pay for the damages (all $600 worth). So the financial wisdom of carrying collision coverage on our older model $600 car is of doubtful benefit.

A round figure may be used in deciding whether or not to carry collision insurance. If a car's replacement value is less than $1,000, the owner is often better off saving the collision insurance payments and putting the money into the bank—essentially carrying his own "collision insurance." Each owner must decide how much risk he wishes to take. A reliable insurance agent can provide guidance.

comprehensive insurance

Comprehensive insurance covers the *owner's vehicle* from damage caused by something *other than collision*. Examples are fire, theft, vandalism, glass breakage, and damages resulting directly from floods, earthquake, sandstorm, and the like. Comprehensive insurance is available on a full coverage or deductable basis. Since it is relatively inexpensive, and the cost of replacing a broken windshield is very high regardless of the age of the vehicle, it is usually wise to have comprehensive coverage. Comprehensive insurance covers the car for damages that are essentially beyond the owner's control. Read the fine print in the policy, however, for if you live in an area where for example, flooding, is common, flood damage coverage might be specifically excluded.

uninsured motorist insurance

Uninsured motorist coverage is frequently misunderstood. It does *not* normally cover damage to your car caused by another motorist who does not have liability insurance; such damages are covered by your collision insurance. Uninsured motorist coverage does provide the *personal liability* coverage that the other driver may not have, including personal injury expenses of you and your passengers. This type of coverage is very inexpensive. Some states require that all drivers who are licensed in that state carry liability insurance; in these states the need should be carefully weighed.

medical insurance

Medical payments insurance has little to do with car insurance as such, except that it pays small medical expenses that might be incurred by the driver and his passengers as a result of an automobile accident. Many individuals carry separate accident and hospitalization insurance, so the need for this type of insurance should be carefully weighed. Ordinary personal injury liability insurance does not normally cover the car's driver and passengers, but you may feel an obligation to pay their medical expenses in the event of an accident. Anyone who frequently carries passengers should consider medical payments coverage.

insurance riders

Insurance "riders" are special additions to a policy that change it in some way, usually by expanding its benefits. In some policies, for example, the comprehensive coverage does not extend to the theft of stereo tape decks, two-way radios, or other expensive automobile accessories that are particularly attractive to thieves. For an extra charge, a rider can be added to the policy to cover these or similar items.

Before taking a car into a foreign country, it is important to confirm that the automobile insurance policy is in effect in that country. If it is not, a "foreign travel rider" can be obtained. Often such coverage is free, but it must be requested well in advance of the trip. For travel in Mexico, it is very important to take out special short-term insurance from a *Mexican company*. This coverage is usually available through your regular insurance agent, and is always available at the Mexican border. It can be purchased for as short a time as one day. A "Mexican rider" to a regular policy (not the same as insurance from a Mexican company) will protect the driver's financial interests alright, but waiting in a Mexican jail for an accident case to be closed (regardless of who is at fault) can normally be avoided only by carrying regular Mexican insurance as well.

Other types of riders are available to meet special needs.

insurance rates

Insurance rates are based at least in part on the accident and claim histories of different categories of policyholders. The insured persons are grouped by sex, age, education, miles driven per year, and other characteristics. Individuals who have had many accidents may not be accepted for coverage at the usual rates for their group, and will be placed in a special high risk and high premium category. Premium rates for young men often run triple the rate for young women of the same age.

© Field Enterprises, Inc., 1972

"You must forgive my husband, officer . . . he has a
gift for turning a phrase!"

rules to remember

An auto accident and its aftermath can be very distressing and
complicated, however, the rules to follow immediately following
an accident are quite simple:

1. Don't panic. Whether the accident is minor or serious, it is
   important to keep cool and not let emotions rule. It takes a
   clear head to follow the rest of the rules.
2. Administer first aid as needed, but do not offer to pay the
   medical expenses for anyone.
3. Do not discuss the circumstances of the accident with anyone
   except the police and your insurance company. Do not let

anyone else listen to your discussion with the police. You have the right to tell the facts without engaging in a dialogue with the other driver or third parties. Give the police all the *facts* you can remember.

4. Do not admit to any guilt or negligence. Avoid such statements as "if only I had. . . ." State only the facts as you know them. Do not state any conclusions. These will be determined in the investigation.
5. Write down a complete identification of the other driver, including driver's license number, auto license plate number, name of his insurance company, and names of any passengers. Note in writing any obvious injuries and vehicle damages. Your insurance company is *much* more interested in the other party's personal injuries than in auto damage, as it is personal injuries that are the source of expensive lawsuits.
6. Look for witnesses. Write down their names, addresses, and telephone numbers. Without them, it might be just your word against the other driver's.
7. Don't sign anything.

After the injured are cared for, have your car towed (if it cannot be driven) into a storage lot. Contact your insurance company promptly and give them the information you have collected. Advise them of your preference in terms of repair location. If damage to the car is substantial, request that it be towed to a garage in your home town, as there will probably be some problems with it after it is repaired.

auto repairs

Review the insurance policy with your agent to determine the exact extent of your coverage. Having paid the insurance premiums, you have every right to expect that the car will be repaired to its pre-accident condition. It is the responsibility of the insurance company to supervise and pay for fixing the car. The company is not doing the auto owner any favors, but merely their job in taking care of the car.

Do not sign any papers at the garage before taking possession of the repaired car. Some garage operators will insist that before the owner even test drives the car he must sign a paper indicating his satisfaction with the repairs. If the garage will not allow sufficient test driving, or demands a signed release before giving up the car for a test ride, notify the insurance company and request that they act in your behalf. Insurance companies supply garages with a great deal of business and can easily apply pressure where the car owner cannot.

If any problems show up (as they usually do) *after* you have taken possession of the car, return it promptly and insist that they be rectified. Timidity is no virtue here, and any excuse the garage may offer for delays, such as other jobs in the shop, is not your concern. Again, let your insurance company fight for you, and if the local insurance agent will not do so, call the company head-quarters office.

The garage operator's usual technique for "cooling off" car owners who may not accept shoddy workmanship is to let the car sit for a week or two while "waiting for parts." This is known as the "fresh air and sunshine" method of auto repair. The owner becomes so impatient for the car that he often accepts it "as is," and the garage gets paid for work it did not complete. A delay of several days while the car is worked into the repair shop schedule may be expected. Once work has begun, however, a week to 10 days is sufficient time to repair any car that is repairable.

When the car is repaired and released from the shop, it is worth the small cost of having an auto diagnostic center examine and test it, looking for dangerous short cuts or shoddy work, and providing an estimate in writing of what is required to complete the work properly. Take this report to your insurance company and let them get back to the garage. Do not let yourself get caught in a "runaround" between the insurance company and the garage. It is you and the insurance company versus the garage—and don't let anyone (especially the insurance company) forget it.

medical expenses

If you suffered serious personal injuries and incurred large medical bills as a result of the accident, you may wish to retain an attorney. If so, the following facts should be kept in mind. The attorney will charge between one-quarter and one-half of what he can collect from the other driver or his insurance company. The amount collected for personal injuries varies widely, but a "ball-park" figure often used is "three times the amount of the medical bill." The attorney will get perhaps one-third of the gross settlement, that is, money received before any expenses are paid. You will get the remaining two-thirds, from which you must pay the medical bills, investigative and court expenses, "expert witness" fees, and any auto repair bills not covered by the insurance. These expenses may be small, but sometimes, they can add up to more than the total settlement, in which case you will actually have lost money by pursuing the case and "winning" in court. Weigh the figures carefully before turning down any reasonable offer that might be received from the opposing insurance company. It's pretty hard to "break even" after an accident, even by taking legal action. The only apparent winners are the attorneys.

No-Fault Insurance

Insurance figures show that less than 50% of the money paid in as premiums for auto insurance is returned to the policyholders (compared with 90% returned to policyholders for other types of insurance). The remainder goes for overhead, insurance company profit, agent commissions, and attorneys fees. In many accidents, both drivers are partly to blame, although the driver who triggered the accident is obviously much more at fault. Frequently, because of this concept of "contributory negligence," neither party collects anything despite an expensive legal battle.

It has been proposed that auto insurance coverage be written like most other insurance: that is, if a person has a loss, his insurance company pays him. This is the case with home insurance, fire insurance, and other property-loss policies.

Theoretically, "no-fault" insurance, as it is called, means that neither driver involved in an accident must be judged "at fault." This eliminates the lengthy trials, legal actions, and delays in settlement. No-fault insurance has been in operation in some provinces of Canada for years, and various forms of it are in effect now in some of the United States. It is being proposed in other states and on a nation-wide scale. Trial lawyers oppose the "no-fault" program because it eliminates a large part of their business, so, some proposals for no-fault insurance are watered-down in an attempt to please both the public and the trial lawyers. Few of the plans now in effect seem to offer much to the consumer/driver. The careful development of no-fault insurance may in years to come significantly reduce the insurance cost of car ownership.

Taking a trip

One reason frequently given for purchasing a car is the anticipated convenience, economy, and pleasure of taking a trip. Local and commute driving account for most auto mileage, and routine maintenance procedures usually assure satisfactory auto performance. For the occasional trip of more than a day or so, some special precautions and procedures are advisable to prevent breakdowns on the road and expensive servicing or repairs in unfamiliar towns along the way. It also is important to be aware of the common deceptions encountered at tourist-oriented gas stations and how to avoid them. Other factors considered in this chapter include the effects of varying driving conditions on vehicle performance and safety, and some general safety precautions that apply equally to long-distance and local driving.

Preparing the Car

Cars last longer and show much less wear when run steadily at full operating temperature and constant speed than when driven around town under stop-and-go conditions. However, a number of things can happen to a car that has performed well for months in local traffic when it is subjected to long periods of highway driving. Belts and hoses are exposed to continuous operation at high speed and high temperature. Tires that have spun slowly are now spinning fast, and out-of-balance conditions that were not noticeable at slower speeds become apparent. The engine may have a partially plugged cooling system and may overheat when forced to work harder. Oils and greases usually not subject to high pressure and temperature now are fully challenged. Poor front end alignment and shock absorbers and steering system wear show up at expressway speeds. In short, long-distance driving requires different things from a car than local driving does.

Before taking a trip, therefore, you should make a number of inspections and tests to minimize the possibility of breakdown on the road. A breakdown a hundred or a thousand miles from home is not at all the same as having an inoperable car sitting in the driveway at home.

Careful adherence to the detailed maintenance instructions and the weekly walkaround discussed in previous chapters will minimize the extra effort in preparing for a long trip. You may already have noticed, for example, that certain belts and hoses are developing small cracks and that one of the tires is starting to show its "wear bars." These conditions might not be critical for local driving, but now they must be corrected. Repair of a broken belt or burst radiator hose could cost 10 times more on the road than at home.

When the little maintenance items have been discovered, they should be corrected promptly—not the day before the trip. Minor repairs themselves can lead to problems. Consider the frustration of discovering—50 miles from home—that the new tire purchased for the trip is out-of-round or not properly balanced. It might be necessary to stop and have the problem corrected, perhaps wasting half a day in the process.

The car should be completely lubricated prior to departure. At home, this job is relatively inexpensive; on the road, it is much more expensive and time consuming. A complete check of all fluid levels should be made, and the battery terminals, tires, belts, and hoses inspected. Similarly, check headlights, taillights, turn signals, and wiper blades. These items all cost much less to service at home than at tourist-oriented service stations and garages along the way.

Finally, the car should be road tested. Run it on a highway for about half an hour at the normal driving speed to bring everything up to temperature and see what happens. If nothing abnormal happens, you can leave on the trip knowing that if something should go wrong later, it will not be because of inadequate preparation.

What to Take Along

If the car is serviced regularly and known to be properly cared for, about all that is needed on a trip are those very basic tools needed to keep the car going from town to town, where repairs can be made if needed. A minimum list might read as follows:

1. Red flares for night protection in case of breakdown
2. Spare tire and changing equipment
3. Hand cleaner towlettes and roll of paper towels
4. First aid kit
5. Medium-sized screwdriver
6. Medium-sized pair of pliers

7. Medium-sized hammer
8. Medium-sized adjustable wrench
9. Medium-sized vice grip wrench
10. Roll of adhesive or black tape
11. Several cans of oil
12. Battery jumper cables

Additional items can be added to the list, depending on your own ability and interest.

Service Facilities on the Road

The vacation or business trip is supposed to be for fun or business, and the last thing a traveler wants to be concerned with is the car. Visits to service stations should be only for the purpose of getting gas and perhaps a little oil and water. To better understand the potential perils that accompany long distance auto travel, you should know something about the nature and operation of the three different types of service stations you may do business with.

the neighborhood station

This is the local service station, situated away from the main thoroughfares, which depends almost entirely on neighborhood residents for its business. Like the other two types of stations, it usually is leased by an individual from a major oil company. These stations sell only a modest amount of gas (anything above 50,000 gallons a month is considered to be "high volume"), and nearly all the profit from gas sales goes to pay the rent, utilities, and general overhead expenses. The operator's salary and return on investment have to come from sales of TBAs (tires, batteries, and accessories) and from lube jobs, oil changes, repairs done in the "back room", rental of trailers and trucks, etc.

The neighborhood station may employ a mechanic who does not wait on the gas customers but installs TBAs sold by other employees and performs tune-ups, brake jobs, carburetor cleaning, alternator, starter, and water pump replacement, and other minor repair and maintenance functions. The mechanic usually receives a percentage of the total labor charges (typically about 50 percent) instead of a fixed salary plus part of the profit on the parts. He furnishes his own tools, while the service station operator supplies the workspace and expects to make a profit from the mechanic's services. Bear these facts in mind when service or repairs are suggested by a station employee.

The neighborhood station relies on repeat business. The operator must satisfy his customers consistently or he will lose them, and there is no other large source of customers because of the station's neighborhood location. At home, try to do most of your business at this type of station; become known there, and you can reasonably expect the operator and the employees to provide reliable and honest service.

the tourist station

At the opposite side of the spectrum is the tourist-oriented station, whose operator relies almost entirely on customers he will see only once. He has to make a profit on the spot, because there is no opportunity for good-will repeat business.

The tourist station usually is located on a major interstate highway or in a tourist vacation area, pumps large volumes of high priced gas, and often tries to "sell you the store." The operator stocks TBA in depth, knowing that vacationing customers will not wait for a new tire or battery to be delivered from the station's wholesale supplier. If the station is located in a tourist town, it may give local residents several cents per gallon off the tourist price for gas.

The tourist station may or may not have a bona fide mechanic in the back room. Some are staffed with one or more of what are called "50 percenters," special types of auto fraud artists that deserve careful attention. The "50 percenter" is a service station attendant who pumps gas and tries to sell drivers everything possible, even going so far as to damage a car to make purchases necessary. He is typically clean cut, a good talker, of honest face, and professes concern with the customer's car and its well being. He gets 50 percent of the profit on what he can sell at any price he can get. One of his simpler tricks is to push the oil dip stick only part way in when checking the oil level to make it appear low.

Now that he is under the hood he can really go to work. He may conceal a sharpened screwdriver in a rag. With this he can punch a hole in a radiator hose or cut a fan belt. While checking the battery water, he may drop in a few lead bb's, shorting out a cell or two and ruining the battery. Needless to say, the station stocks these items, and the price for them is sky high—whatever he thinks he can get. *He should not have been allowed to lift the hood in the first place.*

That same sharp tool can be used to poke a hole in a tire. While the driver is inspecting the leaking tire, the attendant can poke a hole in another one. This means that even with a good spare along, the victim cannot get out of the station without having at least one tire repaired and probably another one replaced with a new tire. Another trick involves a solution of soap and alcohol, which the attendant squirts on a tire where it will bubble and foam, giving the impression the tire has sprung a leak. Once he's got his customer buying tires, he may offer an apparently good price on four new tires. The driver may decide to replace them all, spending far in excess of what he would have spent after some shopping. There are no bargains on the expressway or in the tourist village.

The hapless tourist's car is now up on the lift having a tire repaired or replaced. The attendant has the opportunity to squirt oil on one or more of the shock absorbers. If a shock absorber leaks oil, it loses its effectiveness. The driver is told that the oil on the shock has come from inside it, and he is warned of the severe danger of faulty shocks. The "50 percenter" also may take a metal bar and pry around the front end steering rods and they will move dangerously. All sorts of "king pin" and "tie rod end" wear problems will be noted. The fact is, however, that when the weight is removed from the car, some play in the steering mechanism is normal. Service station attendants who are overly concerned with suspension and steering invariably have the special tools and parts on hand with which to make the "needed repairs" or know of a garage that does.

Tales of auto fraud have been the subject of complete books. The stories of deception along Route 66 in America's southwest are legendary. The Mojave Desert, which travelers must cross to get to Southern California, enhances the scare factor that is the basis for so many unnecessary sales. Several years ago massive state raids in the desert rounded up many fraudulent operators. One operator was reported to have made training films for new employees showing ways to cheat customers. The main route

"Is that the price you're asking, or is that your zip code?"

from New England to Florida has its own legends, as do all long desolate stretches of highway where gas station customers are "here now and gone in a few minutes."

This type of cheating does not occur only at the tourist station but is just more common there. The back room mechanic at any station must be supplied with enough business to make a living, and if business is slow, the gas pump attendants may "generate" business for the mechanic either as a favor or for part of the profits. This is not meant to imply that most or even many service station operators are dishonest. But when you pull into a strange station, you have no way of knowing who you are dealing with.

The best way to avoid difficulties at the tourist station is to *never, never* leave your car unattended while having it fueled. Never let an attendant open the hood. Never let an attendant check your tires. Be doubly careful if you are attended by two or more people as one may distract you while the other damages the car. If you do let the attendant check the oil, be right there on top of him, and don't let him touch anything else. If he starts pulling on the belts and suggests you start the engine so he can watch them, you can be pretty sure you are being set up as a sucker. While you have your back turned walking towards the driver's seat, he may slash a belt or hose—it only takes half a second.

The city station ranks somewhere in between the neighborhood station and the tourist station in mode of operation and significance to the driver. The operator depends largely on commuter traffic for fuel sales and on people who work in the area for maintenance and repair jobs on their cars while they are at work. He also has a more or less regular clientele of salesmen who work in the area. He may have fleet accounts, performing the maintenance and repair of all the cars and trucks owned by a nearby business or factory, and giving them a special price on fuel and repairs in return for most of their business.

The city station operator thus has a more or less regular clientele like the neighborhood station, but like the tourist station, he also has many customers who will never be seen again. Unlike the neighborhood station, a city station tends to have a high turnover of both station operators and attendants. This means that you might receive good service today, but not tomorrow.

Morning Inspection

Clearly, it is unwise to let tourist station attendants do more than put gas in the car. Therefore, the *driver* must assume responsibility for checking it each morning before starting the day's travel. Before starting the car, give it the typical weekly walkaround regularly performed at home. Check all the fluid levels yourself right there at the motel or at the campground, and check the tire air pressures and look for cuts or bulges. Make a note of those items that need attention. On a trip, the weekly walkaround becomes the daily walkaround.

Then proceed to a station for fuel, and personally add the radiator water needed, the air for the tires and any battery water that is required. By this time the service station attendant knows you are in command of the situation and will leave you alone. If oil is needed and you don't have extra cans along, ask the attendant to add a quart while you watch. Tell him everything else is okay, and that will be the end of it. At this point the car is ready for a full day's driving with stops for fuel only.

Repeat this brief procedure each morning of the trip, and barring mechanical breakdown, the car should need no other attention. Experience has shown that the chances of being defrauded are much lower first thing in the morning when you are alert and the station is barely open and not fully staffed, then later in the day when you are tired from driving.

If you should want to check something on the car while stopped for gas, complete the gas purchase, pull the car out of the gas pump lanes and over to a corner of the lot and make the check yourself. Follow the same procedure when using the restrooms or restaurant facilities. Again, do not leave the car unattended while it is being fueled or serviced.

In Case of Breakdown

A mechanical breakdown far from home carries with it a certain fear and confusion that is different from handling auto problems at home. A sense of deep loneliness and perhaps helplessness makes the striken driver a ready victim for the sharp operator. Assuming the breakdown is not just a flat tire, which you have learned to handle, but a mechanical failure, the first concern is to get the car to a place where the necessary repairs can be made. Perhaps the water pump has failed, causing the car to overheat, or the alternator is not operating properly.

If the car is still in warranty, make every effort to get it to a dealer who will honor the warranty. If the car is not in warranty and you are in a strange town, the dealer still is usually the best place for repairs. It may cost a bit more in the short run to have it repaired at a dealership, but a dealer is more likely to have the exact parts on hand, as well as mechanics experienced on your make of car. In addition, dealer repairs often are accompanied by a short warranty that may be honored by the factory. If the problem recurs again on the trip, another dealership of the same manufacturer could handle the repair, and while it might be necessary to pay cash both times, you at least would have some recourse to the manufacturer for a refund and a good chance of getting the work done right. This is certainly no guarantee of satisfaction, but it does improve the odds. The operator at an unknown private garage or service station may blithely tell the customer "bring it back if anything goes wrong, and we'll make it right," knowing full well the driver is not going to return the car a hundred miles to have the problem corrected.*

If the car cannot be driven, it will be necessary to get a road service truck or have a tow truck haul it in. Either alternative can be expensive. The charge is typically so much a mile plus so much an hour plus the cost of parts. By the time a road service truck makes several trips back and forth to town for parts the total bill may exceed the towing charge to reach a garage where all the parts are available. Frequently, the road service vehicle *is* a tow truck, so if the repairs cannot be made on the spot you can arrange for a tow without further delay.

A fair price for a tow truck plus driver is from one to two dollars a mile. This permits the truck owner to make a reasonable return on his truck, which may be used only a few hours a week but must always be available. It is helpful to check with your local insurance agent before the trip regarding current towing rates in the areas you plan to drive. A few states require that the operator provide a written estimate of the charges prior to the tow. Some states require that customers receive written estimates prior to having the repair work done. In any case, find out what it is going to cost to get hauled in before the truck hooks on.

Some tow truck operators, called "road runners," cruise freeways in cities and interstate highways looking for cars that have broken down. Their activities are often not regulated by law, and they can charge whatever the traffic will bear. These operators have been known to hook up to a car, pull it off the freeway to a nearby service station, then present the owner with a bill for several hundred dollars or more, refusing to let the car down from the hook until it is paid. The tow truck operator has a mechanics lien on the car for services rendered, and since there was no prior agreement as to how much would be charged, the owner has to pay it. While this practice has been outlawed in some counties and states, it still prevails in much of the country.

As a preventive measure against this type of consumer abuse, numerous drivers take out towing insurance along with their regular

* A private garage in your neighborhood may offer good work and at a lower price than a dealer's shop, but this is no time to experiment.

auto insurance. Other drivers join one of the several automobile clubs that offer free towing as one of their services. The largest of these is the Automobile Club of America (AAA).

Auto clubs will typically arrange with service stations across the country to provide free towing for their members in return for a guaranteed towing rate paid by the club on behalf of its members. The large volume of business assured to participating stations allows them better utilization of their tow trucks, and they can cut their rates accordingly. One precaution: If you belong to an auto club and call for a tow truck affiliated with that club, be sure the truck that tows in your car is the one you called and not just a "road-runner" who happens along and *says* he is responding to your call.

Effects of Different
Driving Conditions on
Vehicle Performance

In traveling across the country, you will encounter a wide variety of climatic and geographic conditions, some of which will affect the car. The most significant of these will probably be changes in elevation above sea level. Only when the elevation reaches a mile above sea level or greater is there a significant difference in the functioning of most cars. The air gets thinner at higher elevations, and there is less air to mix with the fuel to make a burnable mixture. This means the mixture is "too rich," having too much gas and not enough air, and the car will have noticeably less power. The driver who is only passing through the mountains and doesn't intend to stay long need do nothing except note that the car doesn't have as much power as usual and bear that in mind when passing other cars. If the car will be operated at higher elevations for some time, the carburetor mixture screw on some cars can be adjusted and then readjusted on returning to lower elevation. (See Chapter 5 for instructions.)

Another common effect of this "high altitude air starvation" is that the car is much harder to start, particularly when it is hot. The overrich mixture of gas and air does not burn as well and tends to flood the carburetor with gas. Do *not* pump the gas pedal; instead, push it all the way to the floor and hold it there while cranking the engine until it starts. If black smoke comes out of the exhaust pipe as the engine starts, the problem was just too much gas for the available air.

A common problem on hot days is called "vapor lock," the solution for which is discussed in Chapter 5.

Desert driving tends to magnify problems that occur from time to time under ordinary circumstances. Some service stations do a thriving business in "desert water bags" and other regalia. The desert heat does make car engines, bearings, and tires run hotter during the summer months, and the distances between towns and assistance are relatively long, but a well maintained car should have no problem. No special devices or gadgetry are needed, but carry extra drinking water, which can also be used for the radiator and overcoming vapor lock. The main highways are well patrolled. Because of the distances involved, however, costs of towing and repairs can be outrageous.

Driving Hazards and Safety Precautions

Some climate conditions also pose hazards, particularly for travelers who are unfamiliar with them. Drivers who live in areas where rain, ice, and snow are common are aware of these hazards and know how to drive with them. The driver from drier climates should exercise extreme caution when driving in these conditions. Chances are his windshield wiper blades, having dried out and cracked from his hot climate, will have to be replaced.

Similarly, the driver from the wetter areas should use extreme caution when driving in dry areas, like the desert. Desert sand storms can arise quickly, and within only five minutes, every window in the car, as well as the chrome and paint, can be ruined. Chipped, pitted, or scratched windshields are hazardous. Insurance companies recognize this hazard, and if there is comprehensive insurance on the car, they are usually very cooperative in replacing such a windshield and thereby perhaps preventing an expensive accident later.

Desert travelers listen to radio reports from desert radio stations, and if sand storms are occurring or are forecast, they don't travel. If you are caught in one, stop and tape newspaper over the outside of the windows on the side where the wind is blowing. The paint and chrome seem more durable than glass. The wind on the desert often runs in "channels," and driving a short distance will sometimes take you out of the storm area.

The driver from the wet country also should be careful of rain storms in the drier areas. Where rains occur infrequently, or during the first rains after the dry season, vehicle oil drippings built up on the highways mix with the rain, creating a very slippery surface. See Chapter 11 for additional information on snow tires and chains.

A frequent cause of accidents is the overloading of a car. It is very dangerous to load the rear window deck with items that could fly forward and strike the driver or passengers if the car is stopped quickly or struck by another vehicle. Similarly, small items cluttering the floor of either the front or back seats can work forward and become wedged under the brake pedal, so that when brakes are needed they are not available. Objects on the floor also have been known to apply pressure on the accelerator pedal. The overloading of a station wagon, particularly by distributing too much weight in the rear, can cause it to become unstable and very dangerous to drive.

Every once in a while, newspapers report an accident caused by an accelerator pedal that became stuck. This, of course, can be a serious problem, but the quickest way to overcome it is to simply turn off the ignition key. If there is more time, give the accelerator pedal a sharp kick, depress the clutch, or move the automatic transmission lever into neutral. An accelerator pedal that shows a tendency to stick should be serviced promptly to avoid a potentially serious accident.

If gas fumes are evident after the gas tank is filled, the problem is usually a faulty gas cap gasket. These gaskets dry out after several years, and the simplest solution is to purchase a new gas cap. Failure to do so can lead to spillage of gas and consequent fire, or the illness of the driver or passengers due to prolonged breathing of the fumes. Before buying a new gas cap, check to see that the service station attendant didn't simply get the gas cap on wrong.

A car that vibrates or shakes when driven above a certain speed is an accident waiting to happen. The problem will usually be found somewhere in the running gear, such as an out-of-balance or out-of-round tire, front end out of alignment, loose wheel, worn suspension system, etc.

If another driver flashes lights at you, this usually means (1) your headlights are not on, but should be; (2) one of your headlights is burned out; or (3) dim your lights. In some places, truck drivers warn each other of speed traps or communicate other information by flashing their lights.

It is becoming increasingly common to turn on the headlights as a safety precaution whenever the vehicle is operated, day or night, particularly on rural, two-lane highways. The lights make the car more conspicuous and thereby decrease the probability of a collision with another vehicle. Repeated tests have proven that this safety technique is highly effective. Some bus and truck lines require their drivers to leave the headlights on at all times when the vehicle is moving.

After the Trip

After the trip is over, the car should be given a complete inspection, similar to the one before the trip. It may be time again for a lube job. The tires may show wear patterns that were not there at the beginning of the trip, and tire rotation and readjustment of pressures may be in order. A wash and waxing is probably needed. If the trip was a long one, it may be time for another tune-up. Take care of the necessary service promptly, then continue the weekly walkarounds as usual.

New challengers:
stratified charge and Wankel engine

Since it won the competition with steam and electricity in the early 1900s, the internal combustion engine has had few challengers. It has enjoyed a position of "King of the Road" for more than sixty years. To meet new demands for better control of emissions, new designs for automobile engines have been explored. Two have progressed beyond the development stage and are currently used in commercial passenger cars. These are the *stratified charge engine*, which is only a slight departure from the conventional internal combustion engine, and the *Wankel engine*, a radical new adaptation of internal combustion principles.

The Stratified Charge Engine

The basic operation of the stratified charge engine is similar to the precombustion system used on diesel engines for many years. The concept of precombustion is explained later. The adaptation of this system to gasoline engines involved many modifications. The firm that perfected the stratified charge system, Honda of Japan, has 230 patents covering their engine.

head arrangement

All significant differences between the stratified charge and the internal combustion engine are in the head. The reciprocating parts, crankshaft, rods, pistons, and the associated bearings and rings, remain essentially the same as those of the internal combustion engine described in Chapter 2. The combustion process in the stratified charge engine, however, involves two fuel/air mixtures of different ratios. The use of two fuel mixtures required three major changes in the engine itself. The first is the addition of a third valve to each cylinder. Second, two carburetors are required, or a carburetor with two systems. Finally, a second combustion chamber is provided in a "cave" connected to the main combustion chamber by a port, or small opening. A cutaway view of the stratified charge engine is shown in Fig. 19-1.

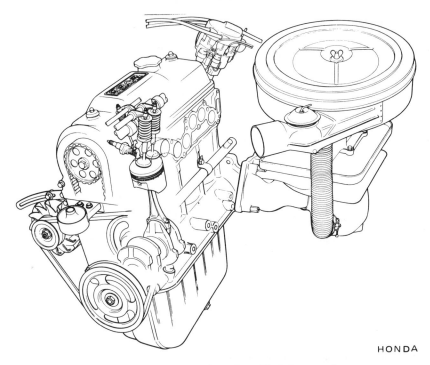

Fig. 19-1 Cutaway view of stratified charge engine

the combustion cycle

To visualize how the combustion cycle works on the stratified charge engine, review the six steps of Fig. 19-2.

1. As the piston goes down on the *intake stroke* fuel is drawn into both chambers, a rich mixture into the precombustion chamber and a lean mixture into the main cylinder. Both intake valves are open at the same time, and the carburetor must be able to deliver the two kinds of fuel mixture at the same time.

2. At the end of the intake stroke, some of the rich mixture may attempt to mix with the lean mixture, but as both intake valves close and the piston starts up on the *compression stroke*, the two mixtures undergo compression, each in its own chamber.

3. As the piston begins to go back down after reaching top dead center, the spark plug ignites the rich mixture in the precombustion chamber. The mixture explodes and would cause a "ping" if it were in a conventional cylinder. In this case, however,

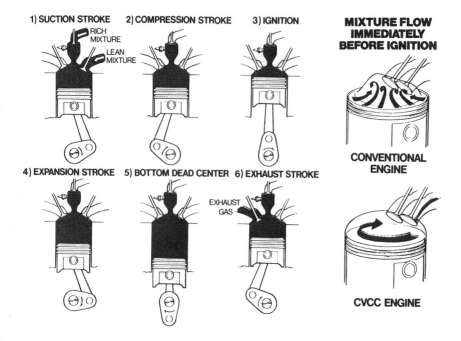

Fig. 19-2 The six steps of the combustion cycle in the stratified charge engine

the explosive jet "sprays" fire into the lean mixture through the port connecting the two chambers. The general distribution of fire throughout the main cylinder causes the fuel to burn more thoroughly than it would if ignition occurred at a single point as it does with a single spark plug in the conventional engine.

4. As the burning gases expand, just as with the conventional engine, the piston is forced downward and power is delivered to the crankshaft. The fuel continues to burn long after all useful power has been taken from the burning charge. This means that more fuel will be consumed in the cylinder and there will be less unburned hydrocarbon in the exhaust to cause pollution. This process has been compared to the "afterburning" in jet airplane engines in which some fuel is burned after the normal burning in the chamber inside the engine. Afterburning is used in aircraft to provide more power and is used at take-off and in flight wherever extra power might be demanded.

5. After the piston passes bottom dead center and begins its upward stroke, the fuel mixture continues to burn as the exhaust valve opens.

6. With the exhaust valve open, the still burning mixture is forced out the exhaust valve port into the exhaust manifold where the last of the hydrocarbons are consumed before the exhaust leaves the vehicle. This engine is naturally low in output of pollutants and because of that feature has gained wide interest.

efficiency

The stratified charge engine uses about 20 percent more fuel than equivalent engines of other types. However, because this new engine does not weigh as much as other engines developing the same power, ideally it should give better gasoline mileage than its more conventional competitors. Under normal driving conditions, this engine can give nearly pollution-free performance and achieve about the same gas mileage as a conventional engine equipped with antipollution devices. Figure 19-1 shows the Honda stratified charge engine, which the manufacturer calls the Compound Vortex Controlled Combustion (CVCC) engine.

The Wankel Engine

The Wankel engine has been in use for a longer time than the stratified charge engine and therefore has a wider range of uses. Dr. Felix Wankel conceived the operating principles of his engine in 1926 and devoted nearly forty years to its development. The culmination of this effort was the first use of the Wankel engine in the NSU Spyder in 1965.

The Wankel engine is a radical departure from conventional internal combustion arrangements. It does not reciprocate. It has no conventional pistons and no crankshaft. The rotor is connected directly to the output shaft. The operation is actually rotary; that is, the working parts of the engine rotate in a circle instead of moving up and down. Intake, ignition, power, and exhaust, "strokes" occur as the rotor spins around the circle. This is made possible by the triangular shape of the rotor and the combustion chamber in which it rotates. The method of gearing the rotor to the shaft eccentrically, or off center, enables the four-stroke action to occur while the actual motion of the engine's moving parts is in a smooth, circular pattern. This operation makes the Wankel

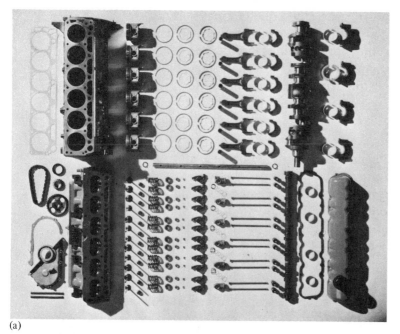

(a)

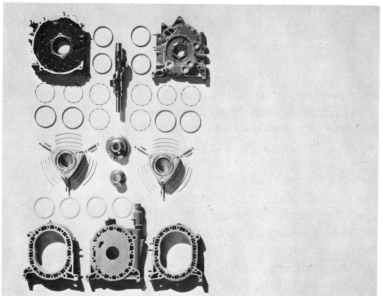

(b)

Fig. 19-3 (a) A comparison of the OF parts used in the normal
internal combustion engine (b) and those used in the Mazda version
of the Wankel

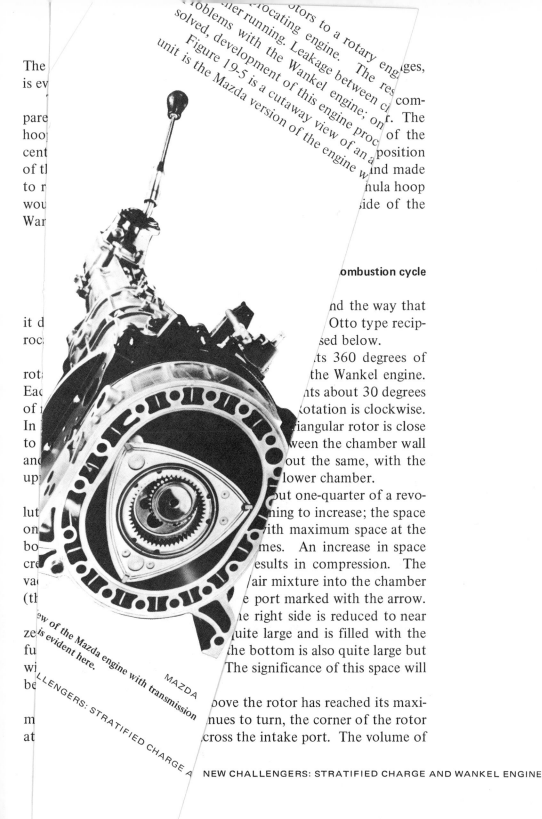

The
is ev

pare
hoo
cent
of th
to r
wou
War

com-
r. The
of the
position
and made
hula hoop
side of the

ombustion cycle

it d — nd the way that
roc — Otto type recip-
— sed below.

rot — ts 360 degrees of
Ea — the Wankel engine.
of — ts about 30 degrees
In — Rotation is clockwise.
to — riangular rotor is close
and — ween the chamber wall
up — out the same, with the
— lower chamber.

lut — ut one-quarter of a revo-
on — ning to increase; the space
bo — with maximum space at the
cre — mes. An increase in space
va — esults in compression. The
(th — air mixture into the chamber
— e port marked with the arrow.
ze — he right side is reduced to near
fu — quite large and is filled with the
wi — the bottom is also quite large but
be — The significance of this space will

m — bove the rotor has reached its maxi-
at — nues to turn, the corner of the rotor
— cross the intake port. The volume of

ew of the Mazda engine ... is evident here. MAZDA ...with transmission

otors to a rotary engines,
roblems with the ... running engine. The res... com-
solved, development of the Wankel engine; on... r. The
Figure 19-5 is a cutaway view of an a... position
unit is the Mazda version of the engine w...

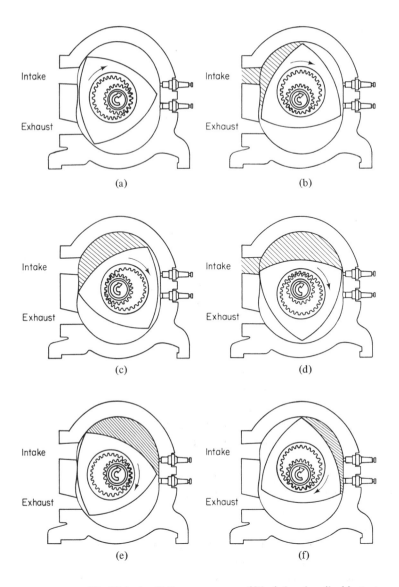

Fig. 19-6 (a - 1) Power sequence of Wankel as described in text

the other two chambers does not mean much at this time since this is the first revolution of the rotor and there is no fuel in those spaces and ignition has not occurred.

In Fig. 19-6e, continued rotation of the triangular rotor results in a rotor position and volumes similar to those of the first picture.

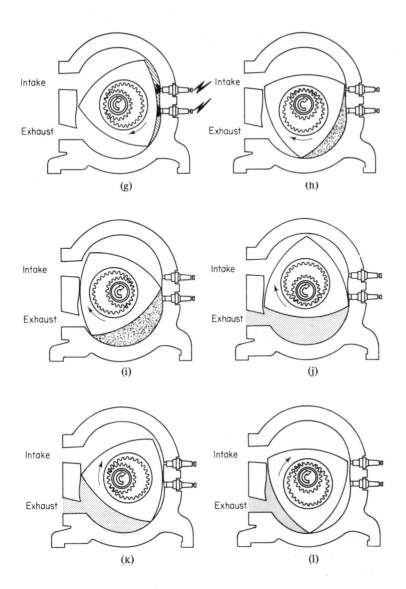

(g)   (h)

(i)   (j)

(k)   (l)

Now, however, the upper chamber is filled with the fuel/air mixture, and the intake port is completely sealed off because the "corner" of the triangular rotor has moved past the intake port. The fuel/air mixture is trapped in the upper chamber.

In Fig. 19-6f, the rotor position and volumes are similar to those in 19-6b, except that the space on the right is decreasing and the fuel/air mixture is being compressed.

In Fig. 19-6g, the fuel/air mixture trapped against the right face of the rotor under maximum compression and is ignited by the dual spark plugs (for positive ignition and cleaner burning) located in the right-hand wall of the chamber. The rotor has passed the "top dead center" point, and expanding gases pushing against its face force the rotor to continue to turn. As the gases expand, the volume that contains them increases. Up to this point, the rotor had to be turned by external means, for example, by the starter motor. As soon as ignition occurs, the rotor will be forced to turn by expansion of the burning gases and the engine will turn under its own power.

In Fig. 19-6h, the rotor is moving under the pressure of the gases and the volume at the lower right-hand side is increasing in size. At the same time, the upper chamber, having taken in a new charge of fuel/air mixture, is beginning to decrease in volume.

In Fig. 19-6i, the expanding gases have forced the rotor farther around so that once again the intake port is sealed off. While expansion in the lower chamber continues, compression begins in the upper chamber.

In Fig. 19-6j, the rotor has moved around far enough to open the exhaust port at the lower left. The burned gases in the lower chamber escape through this port and out the exhaust system, while the mixture in the upper right-hand corner is further compressed. A new charge of fuel/air mixture is being drawn into the chamber at the upper left as a result of the vacuum developing there.

In Fig. 19-6k, the second fuel/air charge is fully compressed against the right-hand side of the chamber, most of the burned gases have escaped from the lower left-hand chamber, reducing the pressure in that chamber to near atmospheric, while vacuum in the upper left-hand chamber continues to draw in fuel and air.

In Fig. 19-6l, the compressed charge on the right-hand side is ignited by the spark plugs, expanding gases force the rotor to continue turning, and the cycle repeats.

The Wankel engine thus duplicates the intake, compression, ignition/power, and exhaust strokes of the conventional engine. The entire cycle is rotary rather than reciprocating and therefore is much more smooth. Moreover, since operation of the three faces of the rotor is continuous, intake compression and exhaust emission take place simultaneously in their separate chambers. Two rotor Wankel engines as used by Mazda thus can generate power equivalent to that of a normal six-cylinder engine of equal displacement.

efficiency

The Wankel engine produces nearly twice the horsepower of the ordinary piston engine of equal size. Unlike the stratified charge engine, it does not inherently improve pollution characteristics. It does, however, have the distinct advantage that its small size permits addition of smog control apparatus without crowding the engine compartment or excessively increasing weight. Much of the emission control apparatus in use on reciprocating engines has a bad effect on engine valves. This is due largely to increased heat in the region of the valves resulting from continued burning of the gases after opening of the exhaust valves. The Wankel engine, having no valves, is not affected by this problem.

These various advantages in engine operation make it relatively easy to keep the exhaust emissions from the Wankel engine within the limits prescribed by law. The most widely used system for cleaning the exhaust of a typical Wankel engine, this one made by Mazda, is the *thermal reactor* (Fig. 19-7). This system, like the

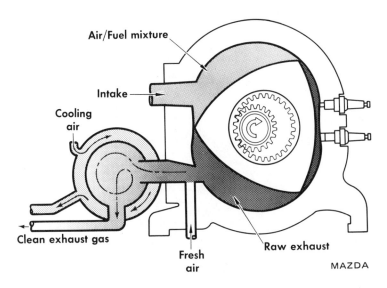

Fig. 19-7 Illustration of the thermal reactor attached to the rotary engine to reduce the output of smog producing pollutants

process used in the stratified charge engine, consumes unburned hydrocarbons before the exhaust is released to the atmosphere.

Between the Wankel and the stratified charge engines, it seems that a new era in automotive power systems is beginning. Just as the reciprocating internal combustion engine replaced the steam and electric cars of yesteryear, it in turn may well be replaced by newer systems.

The car
of the future

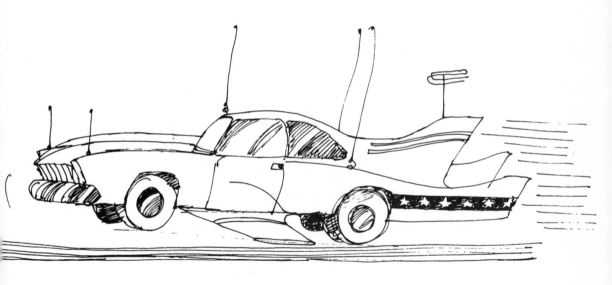

When the automobile was in its infancy around the turn of the century, there was a lot of experimentation under way. This new-fangled invention, the automobile, captured the imagination of people as nothing has ever done before or since. In those early years, the car buyer was offered a choice of electric-, steam-, or gasoline-powered cars with engines operating on a variety of principles. For 25 years, the competition between these methods of automotive power was fierce. One manufacturer offered the same body with a choice of gasoline or electric drive, while still continuing a very lucrative business in horse-drawn buggies.

As time wore on, the gasoline-powered car pulled ahead of the competition until the mid to late twenties when all serious efforts to manufacture steam and electric cars came to a halt. The gasoline engine operating on the Otto cycle with its reciprocating parts had won the race, and its position was secure for the next 30 years. During this period, there were sporadic attempts to revive the steam and electric cars but with scant success. One manufacturer of a luxury class electric car managed to stay in business into the early 1940s, but the field was limited mainly to specialized vehicles such as golf carts, warehouse trucks, and vehicles that had to operate in dangerous environments such as mines and chemcial plants.

The last of the commercial steam-powered cars manufactured in America was the Doble (Fig. 20-1). This fine automobile, which embodied all of the best features of those that had gone before (the Stanley, the White, the Locomobile, and others) was excellent in both performance and appearance. Had it come into being 20 years earlier, the internal combustion engine might not have been so quick to take over.

In spite of the clear advantages of the gasoline engine, it has never had the field entirely to itself. There have always been efforts to keep alive other principles of automobile propulsion. Up to the end of World War II, maintenance garages were able to show a profit by keeping these "orphan" cars running for their owners. The operators of such garages were more often than not experimenting with new and better ways to keep their charges on the road. There was a surge of interest during World War II when gasoline rationing brought an increasing number of the old steam or electric cars onto the highways. Old Stanley Steamer engines were even installed in some modern cars as a means of beating the gasoline rationing while maintaining an appearance of luxury.

Fig. 20-1 The world-famous Doble steam car, regarded by many as the ultimate in steam-powered automobiles (1930)

For a few years after World War II, interest in these forms of transportation faded. The public found the new cars coming off the assembly lines entirely to their satisfaction. These new, sleek cars had a particular appeal, especially after four years in which no automobiles were produced for public use. Most of the cars then on the road were worn out, and people were tired of making do. Of course, the few older steamers and electrics that were still around were the first to go.

Air Pollution Brings New Motivation

When it became apparent that the largest source of air pollution was the exhaust of the gasoline engine, automobile manufacturers throughout the world revived long-abandoned experiments in new forms of power. To simply do away with cars was unthinkable. The car had long since ceased to be a luxury or a rich man's plaything. A car was essential to the life style of nearly everyone. The whole range of industry and commerce depended on the mobility provided by the modern automobile. The logical approach was to develop an alternative power plant to replace the noxious internal combustion engine.

Attempts to provide alternatives to the automobile itself have met with little success. Such ideas as buses, street cars, rapid transit systems, and expansion of railroad passenger service are all under study and in operation in some areas. These concepts do little to relieve the problem, however, because people simply will not give up the convenience of the automobile, which enables them to go anywhere at any time and, within practical and legal limits, at any speed. It would seem that the true solution to the problem lies in automobiles with power plants that do not poison the air.

Turbine Cars

Perhaps the earliest serious attempt to replace the internal combustion engine was Chrysler's turbine-powered car. Although this car still needed gasoline or kerosene as fuel, pollution was reduced to absolute minimum because the fuel was burned outside the engine (external combustion) as opposed to internal combustion. Pollution from such an engine is no greater than burning the same amount of fuel in a fireplace or barbecue. Its operation (Fig. 20-2) is similar to the engine used on turboprop aircraft.

For a number of reasons, the turbine engine has not made any serious inroads into the automobile industry. One problem is the difficulty of providing transmissions to reduce the inherent high speed of the engine to speeds suitable for road vehicles. A turbine-powered car failed to complete the Indianapolis 500 mile race a few years ago because of the failure of gears in the speed reduction transmission.

Turbine-powered cars have been permanently disqualified from the Indianapolis 500 mile race as a result of another operational problem. The high temperature exhaust that is emitted from the large exhaust ducts is evident in the phantom view of the Chrysler engine in Fig. 20-2. This condition poses a hazard for closely following traffic, whether on the highway or the racetrack. The highly pitched whine given off by this engine as a result of the high gear ratio is still another annoyance.

These problems have limited the application of turbine power to heavy trucks and railway engines that operate in places where

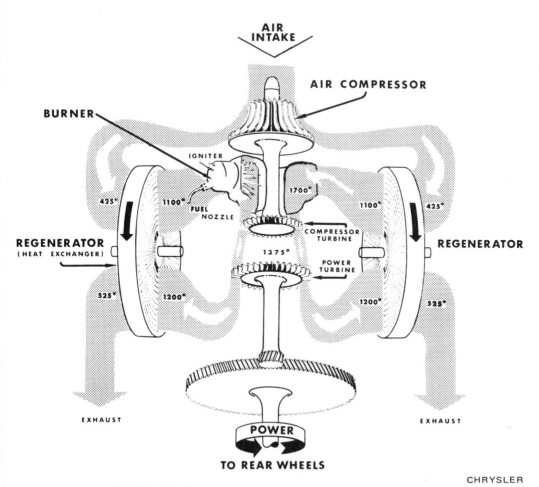

AIR
INTAKE

AIR COMPRESSOR

BURNER

IGNITER

425°   1100°   1700°   1100°   425°

FUEL
NOZZLE

COMPRESSOR
TURBINE

REGENERATOR
(HEAT EXCHANGER)

1375°

POWER
TURBINE

REGENERATOR

525°   1200°   1200°   525°

EXHAUST   EXHAUST

POWER

TO REAR WHEELS

CHRYSLER

Fig. 20-2 The Chrysler turbine powered system

the problems can be tolerated. Development of the turbine power plant continues, however, and it is possible that your next car could be turbine powered with an engine that has been purged of these problems.

Diesel Cars

Diesel engines are being used in increasing numbers of passenger cars. The diesel does not contribute significantly to smog-producing air pollutants, although its exhaust does have an offensive odor.

The diesel principle is technically known as *compression ignition internal combustion*. All the reciprocating parts are essentially the same as for the gasoline engine. The diesel, however, has neither spark plugs nor carburetor. Fuel is injected into the combustion chamber at just the right time by means of a *fuel injector*, a device similar to a squirt gun. Air is drawn into the chamber through a conventional intake valve. Sometimes a *blower*, or *compressor*, is used to force sufficient air into the chamber to support combustion. The diesel engine is a very high compression engine, therefore, the heat caused by compression is also quite high. When the piston comes up on the compression stroke, the compressed air mixture becomes so hot that when fuel is injected it bursts into flame. Some idea of how this heat is developed may be obtained by feeling the walls of a tire pump as it is being used; the heat developed is the heat of compression.

One advantage of a diesel system is that the fuel need not be so highly refined as gasoline. A product similar to kerosene or stove oil, called diesel fuel, is used, and is usually less expensive than gasoline. The efficiency of the diesel engine is greater than that of the gasoline engine. The overall efficiency of the gasoline engine from fuel to wheels is about 25 percent, whereas the diesel engine achieves around 35 percent efficiency.

The two major deficiencies of the diesel engine that have hindered its acceptance for the family car are its noise and its weight. Because of the high compression required, the engine must be made more rugged and, therefore, must be heavier. Further, because compression ignition causes a condition similar to "ping" in the gasoline engine, the diesel engine has a characteristic "rattling" sound when it is running, particularly at idle speed. These problems are not objectionable on large trucks and other heavy equipment, so the diesel engine finds its greatest application on those vehicles.

In spite of the drawbacks of the diesel engine, a number of manufacturers in Europe and Japan are using it in passenger cars. The most common example in the United States is the German-made Mercedes, which has been in use on American roads for several years. Diesel-powered autos are popular as taxicabs because of their low cost of operation. Sometimes an operator will equip an American sedan for taxi service with a diesel engine. The Checker Motor Company, an American firm, manufactures cars specifically intended for use as taxis and provides a diesel engine as a direct factory option.

As lightweight alloys with the necessary strength become available, and assuming that the noise problems can be overcome, the diesel-powered car, with its advantages in pollution control, could well become the car of the future.

The Steam Car

Automobile enthusiasts have been fascinated by steam cars ever since the Stanley brothers made their "Steamer" famous as the most reliable, quiet, and, notably, the fastest car on the road. In 1906, Fred Marriot drove a Stanley steam car with a 30 hp engine at a speed of 127 mph. As noted, the Doble steam car was the last of the line, and it went out of production in the early 1930s.

As with other alternatives to internal combustion engines, the steam car has been given renewed attention in recent years by the urgent need to reduce smog. One steam-driven system purporting to be a break-through in steam technology was reported to be under consideration by General Motors in the early 1970s. Although extensive tests were carried out in passenger carrying buses in major cities, no great success was achieved, and the project was abandoned (Fig. 20-3*a*, *b*).

A new system of steam power holds considerable promise as a useful application of the steam engine to automotive use. This is the Minto "Steamless Steam Car." This is a modern adaptation of the expansion process that made the steam engine possible. In this system, a refrigerant called "Freon" is used, instead of vaporized water, to form steam. The process is somewhat like the operation of a refrigerator in reverse. The refrigerant, which is the same substance used in a kitchen refrigerator, is heated so that it expands. The force of expansion pushes against pistons similar to those in the conventional internal combustion engine. The exhaust stroke of the piston pushes the spent gas into a condenser where the Freon is condensed then pumped back to the heater where it is reheated, expanded, and used again to push against the pistons.

This unique system is completely enclosed, and there is no exhaust from the engine itself. The burner that provides the heat

**Fig. 20-3 General Motors steam car, showing a steam engine
mounted in a stylish body (Experimental 1974)**

is an open flame, much like a plumber's blow-torch, which burns
kerosene, butane, or other low-cost, low-polluting fuels. In the
early 1970s, a practical example of this engine as a means of automotive power was demonstrated (Fig. 20-4). It could well be that
the car of the future will have under the hood a Minto steamless
steam engine.

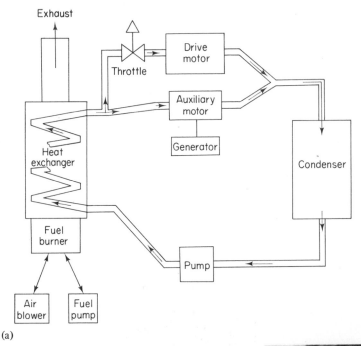

(a)

(b)

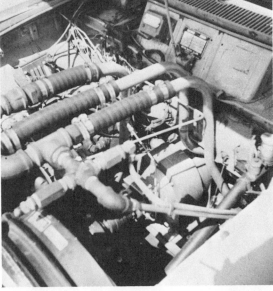

(c)

KINETICS

Fig. 20-4   A new steam car development, the Minto "steamless"
steam car (a) schematic diagram (b) truck
(c) view under the hood

357

The "in car" of the early 1900s was an electric. Electric cars were developed before their gasoline counterparts and were noted for quiet operation. The absence of objectionable odors of gasoline, oil, and exhaust made the electric car the favorite of women and many men as well. Because of the electric cars' ability to operate in cold weather, when internal combustion engines froze or refused to start, they were widely used as taxicabs in many cities, notably New York and Chicago. (Fig. 20-5)

The reason for the demise of this popular car was the lack of batteries that could produce sufficient power to compete with other types of engines. There was never any question of reliability. One electric truck first placed in service in Philadelphia in 1913 was not taken out of service until 1955, after nearly 40 years of continuous use. It was taken off the road simply because it was too slow to keep up with traffic. The reason for the passing of all

MOTOR VEHICLE MANUFACTURERS ASSOCIATION

Fig. 20-5 Example of an early electric vehicle

electric cars was the same: A suitable source of electrical power was not, and is not yet, available to enable an electric vehicle to compete with the modern gasoline-powered car.

There are a few electric vehicles in use, but they are slow vehicles, such as trucks for delivering milk and bread and mail trucks. Modern electric vehicles also include shopping and golf carts. Virtually all are powered by lead acid batteries which proved too weak to compete some 40 years ago and are used now in gasoline cars to turn the starter.

Nearly all of the electric vehicle companies that make industrial equipment as well as various battery companies have continued experiments with electric cars. The results of these experiments still indicate that performance cannot substantially exceed that of the 1900 electric models. This situation is likely to continue until a new form of electrical storage can be found (Fig. 20-6).

the electric car

One promising experiment was carried out by the Electric Fuel Propulsion Company a few years ago. A conventional automobile, stripped of its engine, was provided with an electric motor and a set of batteries. The battery pack consisted of a large, lead-acid battery and a smaller, nickel-cadmium battery. These two battery systems worked together to provide power with the nickel cadmium unit coming into play only when passing or climbing hills. This car was driven at freeway speeds above 50 miles per hour over a distance of more than 600 miles, the round trip between Chicago and Detroit.

This project was more than a car, however; it was a system (Fig. 20-7). Five recharging stations were established at selected motel/diners approximately evenly spaced along the route traveled by the vehicle. A recharge was needed at each station and at the destination, for a total of 11 charges for the round trip. With an average charging time of one hour and twenty minutes, this mode of travel was fairly leisurely. The car weighed 5,500 lb., about twice the weight of the original car from which it was made, and about the same weight as three Volkswagen "beetles." The price tag on this electric vehicle, $10,000 at a time when a conventional gasoline car of equal proportions could be bought for about $3,000, points up another disadvantage of the modern electric car.

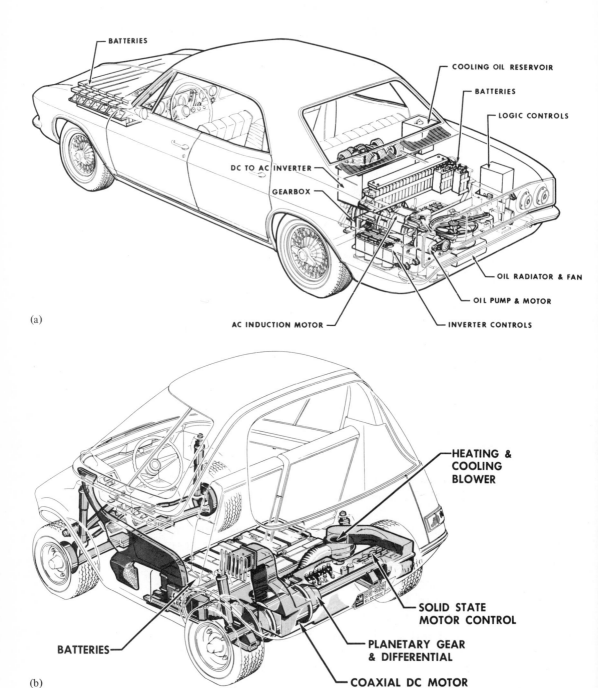

Fig. 20-6 (a) Battery powered electric automobile (b) Battery powered "shopper"

GM

the worlds first electric car expressway

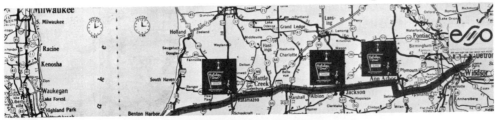

(a)

(b)

(c)

EFP HORNET

Fig. 20-7   The Electric Fuel Propulsion electric car, and the
highway charging stations to support it

361

Lead-Acid Battery. At present, there is only one battery even marginally suited to vehicle propulsion that can be bought "off the shelf;" is the lead-acid battery, which exhibits virtually no technical improvement since 1900.

Silver Cells. One battery manufacturer has proposed the use of silver cells (a lightweight battery system) as power for the electric car, but since each car would require nearly $3,000 in silver, there seems little likelihood of many such cars being put into common use.

Fuel Cells. Fuel cells hold the greatest promise as an adequate source of electrical power for the automobile. A fuel cell is a device that converts a fuel, such as natural gas or alcohol, directly into electrical power (Fig. 20-8). Devices of this nature have been used

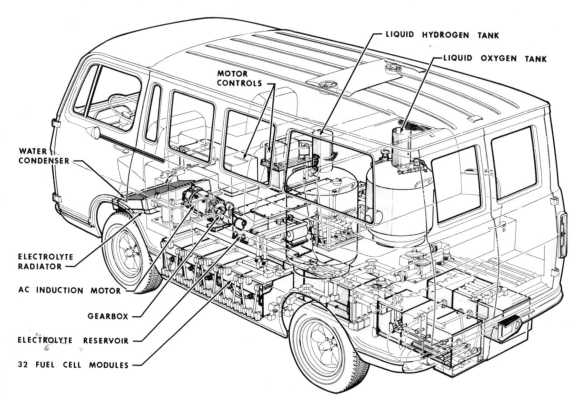

Fig. 20-8 An example of an experimental electric car powered by fuel cells.

GM

experimentally, but their cost is prohibitive and in some cases the hazardous reactants used render them unsafe for highway use.

The most famous application of this power source is in the vehicle operated on the moon by the astronauts. Its cost, including space environmental systems, was up in the millions of dollars and obviously out of reach for the average car buyer. It is possible that continued investigation will lead in the near future to the development of a fuel cell that will be capable of providing sufficient power for vehicles, use nontoxic fuels and produce no harmful pollutants.

Electronic Systems

A number of significant developments in electronics are bringing greater safety and reliability, as well as convenience and comfort to the automobile. These include both instrumentation and automatic controls for safety purposes.

digital speedometer

The conventional pointer and scale type of speedometer still used is little different from the first speedometer installed in a car. The new *digital speedometer* consists of a framed area on the dash, perhaps even at the lower edge of the windshield, with small but clearly visible numerals that light up to indicate how fast the car is going. The numerals can be made to change color when a pre-set speed limit is exceeded. Since the only numbers showing are those indicating the speed of the car, there is little likelihood that a driver could misread the speedometer.

Fuel level, oil pressure, charging rate, and engine temperature could be indicated similarly by digital instruments.

radar

The use of radar systems in the car has been proposed for a long time, and some have actually undergone testing. One such system is radar-controlled braking, in which the radar would detect any object ahead that was either stopped or not moving as fast as the radar-equipped vehicle. On detecting such an object—whether a bridge, fallen tree, or slow-moving traffic—the radar system would apply the brakes and either slow the car or bring it to a complete stop as necessary. Such a system could do its job even though the driver might be incapacitated. A variation of this concept connects the radar control to the steering system so that the radar would steer the car away from a head-on collision with a car going the wrong way. This system could be operated by the radar signal or headlights of the oncoming car.

voice warning systems

Voice warning systems have been proposed (and actually tested) that would play a pre-recorded warning of a developing dangerous condition. For example, a driver could be warned of the approaching failure of the engine lubrication system so that he could stop the car before any permanent damage was done. It could also warn an inattentive driver that he is exceeding the speed limit.

other measures

Preventive measures that can help save lives and prevent property damage may show up on new cars in the very near future. One such device, very simple by electronic standards, prevents the car from being started if the brakes are inoperative. This same device can stop the engine if a dangerous condition develops, such as too much exhaust gas in the passenger compartment or inadequate oil pressure.

Highway Design

Along with new developments in the automobile itself, many new approaches in highway design have been proposed, tested, and in some cases installed. The highway system has developed to a degree of sophistication undreamed of a few years ago. The modern freeway is a far cry from the pair of ruts that passed for a highway when your grandmother first took the wheel.

roadways

Roads used to be made flat until it was found that cars rounding corners at high speeds often went out of control and rolled over. This problem led to "banked" turns, which could be safely negotiated at higher speeds. On modern roads, the slant of the road is carefully calculated to keep the car upright as it goes around the turn at the posted speed limit.

Road shoulders are being constructed to provide braking action so that a car that leaves the road can be safely slowed and brought to a stop without doing serious damage to car or passengers. Signposts are being designed that will shear off on impact if struck by a car out of control. Bridge abutments are being padded and engineered so that cars striking them will be slowed and caused to veer off in a safe direction rather than being thrown back into the lane of traffic where a major accident is almost sure to occur.

road signs

Another motoring problem of bygone days has been overcome by means of lighted road signs. No longer must the motorist in strange territory pore over his maps and slow down to read poorly displayed road signs. The modern highway provides advance notice of lane change requirements, road conditions, stop lights, signs, and cross traffic well in advance and by means of electronically controlled, illuminated signs. New developments in this area include radio transmissions to warn motorists of dangerous conditions or of traffic ahead. These devices are designed to be heard whether or not the car radio is turned on.

the total highway system

Total highway systems have been proposed that place the car under control of a computer, which automatically directs changes of speed, lane, and route, or causes the car to stop and go depending on the safest approach available in traffic conditions at the time.

One such system is based on the use of a punched card which can be inserted in a card reader in the car. The card would be printed and punched with the necessary data to inform the computer of the desired destination, route, and time of arrival. Data from the card would be sent to the computer by means of radio signals. The computer would work out the best way for the car to make the trip and direct it over the chosen route, monitoring its progress by radar or by signals picked up on cables buried in the highway.

There would be no need for stoplights, because the computer would direct traffic safely through intersections simply by controlling the speed of all approaching vehicles. North- and southbound traffic would be alternated with east- and westbound traffic through an intersection on a first-come, first-served basis. This steady flow of traffic would almost assuredly ease the problem of stop-and-go traffic jams that now bottleneck the freeways.

In the event of an accident on the freeway, the computer would reroute traffic around the problem area and, at the same time, direct emergency vehicles to the scene. When the car left the automated freeway, the driver would take over and operate the car through the neighborhood streets or in the downtown area in the normal way.

The Car of the Future

What will the car of the future be like? If it embodies all these new developments, you might find yourself sitting back enjoying the scenery, watching TV, playing bridge, or even reading a good book, while the computer directs your vehicle along the automated freeway by the most expeditious route to your destination. You will be riding in air-conditioned comfort in your personalized, form-fitting seat. You will be able to relax, safe in the knowledge that even in the event of an accident there are no sharp protrustions or hard surfaces in the car that might cause bodily harm.

Even if you should run off the road or into a lane of oncoming traffic, the automatic system will steer you clear of oncoming cars or other obstacles. If you should strike a signpost, it will break away or bend, allowing you to continue unharmed. Through it all, forces will be at work that will bring the car to a safe halt. Automatic systems will notify emergency stations and help will be on the way before the car actually stops.

Such an accident is highly unlikely with the automated system suggested here, and you could expect to speed along toward your destination in near absolute safety under the guidance of the computer. Your speed will always be optimum for the condition of the road and the traffic. You will travel in quiet comfort as the electric motor runs silently, powered by a non-polluting fuel cell operating on a plentiful, nonhazardous fuel. If you want to drive the car yourself, just for old time's sake, you need only signal the computer—it will steer you off the freeway by the nearest, safe exit, and you can take the wheel yourself—just for the sheer fun of it.

To gain some idea of what driving might be like in the future, turn to the next page. There is one manufacturer's design—from the driver's seat—of one of these cars of the future.

Appendix A

Powerflow Diagrams

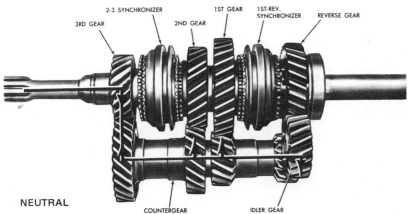

2-3 SYNCHRONIZER
3RD GEAR
2ND GEAR
1ST GEAR
1ST-REV. SYNCHRONIZER
REVERSE GEAR

NEUTRAL

COUNTERGEAR
IDLER GEAR

A Power flow from the input shaft at left, through the transmission in *NEUTRAL*. No power is delivered to the output shaft on the right because the counter-gear and idler-gear turn freely. (Synchronizers not engaged)

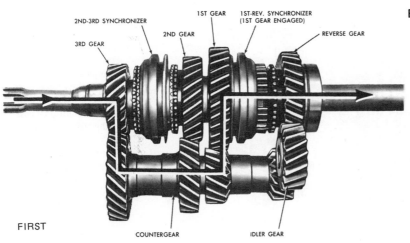

2ND-3RD SYNCHRONIZER
3RD GEAR
2ND GEAR
1ST GEAR
1ST-REV. SYNCHRONIZER (1ST GEAR ENGAGED)
REVERSE GEAR

FIRST

COUNTERGEAR
IDLER GEAR

B Power flow from the input shaft at left, through the transmission in *FIRST GEAR*. Power is passed through the first gear ratio because the 1st-Reverse synchronizer is engaged with the first gear, so the output shaft turns at a speed determined by the *first gear ratio.*

371

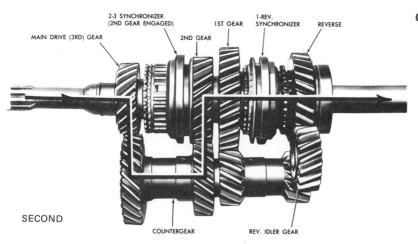

SECOND

MAIN DRIVE (3RD) GEAR — 2-3 SYNCHRONIZER (2ND GEAR ENGAGED) — 2ND GEAR — 1ST GEAR — 1-REV. SYNCHRONIZER — REVERSE — COUNTERGEAR — REV. IDLER GEAR

C Power flow from the input shaft at left, through the transmission in *SECOND GEAR.* Power is passed through the second gear ratio because the 2nd-3rd synchronizer is engaged with the second gear so the output shaft turns at a speed determined by the *second gear ratio.*

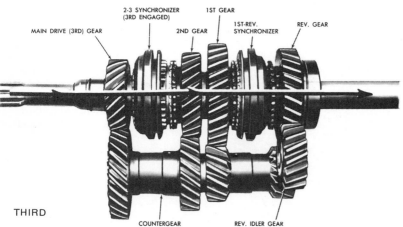

THIRD

MAIN DRIVE (3RD) GEAR — 2-3 SYNCHRONIZER (3RD ENGAGED) — 1ST GEAR — 2ND GEAR — 1ST-REV. SYNCHRONIZER — REV. GEAR — COUNTERGEAR — REV. IDLER GEAR

D Power flow from the input shaft at left, through the transmission in *THIRD* or *HIGH GEAR.* Power is passed directly through the transmission from the input shaft to the output shaft because with the 2nd-3rd synchronizer engaged with the 3rd gear, the output shaft turns at the same speed as the input shaft. The counter gear and reverse idler gears turn freely.

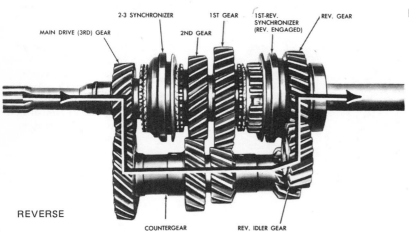

REVERSE

MAIN DRIVE (3RD) GEAR — 2-3 SYNCHRONIZER — 1ST GEAR — 2ND GEAR — 1ST-REV. SYNCHRONIZER (REV. ENGAGED) — REV. GEAR — COUNTERGEAR — REV. IDLER GEAR

E Power flow from the input shaft at left, through the transmission in *REVERSE.* Power is passed through the counter shaft and reverse idler to the reverse gear. The reverse idler constitutes an additional gear in the train and causes the output shaft to turn in the opposite direction to that of the input shaft. The 1st-Reverse synchronizer is engaged with the reverse gear.

Appendix B

Tire Size Identification and Equivalents

83 Series Sizes	Metric Radial Sizes	78 Series Sizes	70 Series Sizes	60 Series Sizes
520-10	145-10	—	—	—
520-12	145-12	—	—	—
550-12	145-12	—	—	—
550-12	155-12	—	—	—
560-12	155-12	—	—	—
600-12	155-12	—	—	—
520-13	145-13	—	—	—
550-13	145-13	—	—	—
560-13	155-13	A78-13	A70-13	A60-13
615-13	155-13	A78-13	A70-13	A60-13
560-13	165-13	A78-13	A70-13	A60-13
600-13	165-13	A78-13	A70-13	A60-13
645-13	165-13	B78-13	B70-13	B60-13
640-13	175-13	B78-13	B70-13	B60-13
650-13	175-13	C78-13	C70-13	C60-13
700-13	185-13	D78-13	D70-13	D60-13
725-13	185-13	E78-13	E70-13	E60-13
560-14	155-14	A78-14	A70-14	A60-14
615-14	155-14	A78-14	A70-14	A60-14
590-14	165-14	A78-14	A70-14	A60-14
600-14	165-14	A78-14	A70-14	A60-14
645-14	175-14	B78-14	B70-14	B60-14
695-14	175-14	C78-14	C70-14	C60-14
735-14	185-14	E78-14	E70-14	F60-14
775-14	195-14	F78-14	F70-14	F60-14
825-14	205-14	G78-14	G70-14	G60-14
855-14	215-14	H78-14	H70-14	H60-14
885-14	225-14	J78-14	J70-14	J60-14
560-15	155-15	A78-15	A70-15	A60-15
590-15	165-15	B78-15	B70-15	B60-15
600-15	165-15	B78-15	B70-15	B60-15
735-15	185-15	E78-15	E70-15	E60-15
775-15	195-15	F78-15	F70-15	F60-15
825-15	205-15	G78-15	G70-15	G60-15
855-15	215-15	H78-15	H70-15	H60-15
900-15	225-15	J78-15	J70-15	J60-15
915-15	235-15	L78-15	L70-15	L60-15

Appendix C

Troubleshooting Checklists

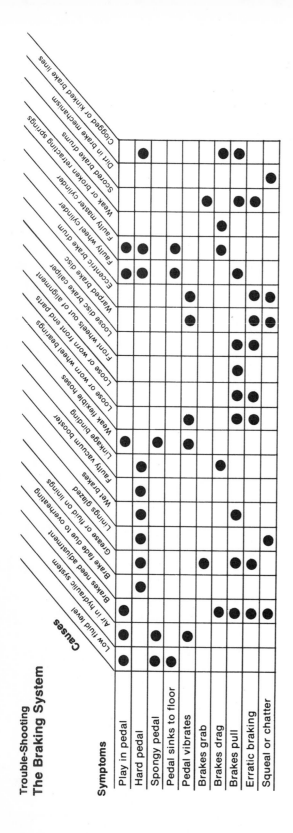

Trouble-Shooting
The Braking System

The columns (causes), listed left to right, are:

1. Low fluid level
2. Air in hydraulic system
3. Brakes need adjustment
4. Brake fade due to overheating
5. Grease or fluid on linings
6. Linings glazed
7. Wet brakes
8. Faulty vacuum booster
9. Linkage binding
10. Weak flexible hoses
11. Loose or worn wheel bearings
12. Front wheels out of alignment
13. Loose or worn front end parts
14. Loose disc brake caliper
15. Warped brake disc
16. Eccentric brake drum
17. Faulty wheel cylinder
18. Weak or broken retracting springs
19. Scored brake drums
20. Dirt in brake mechanism
21. Clogged or kinked brake lines

Symptoms (rows):

Symptom	1	2	3	4	5	6	7	8	9	10	11	12	13	14	15	16	17	18	19	20	21
Play in pedal	•	•							•									•			
Hard pedal								•										•		•	
Spongy pedal	•	•																			
Pedal sinks to floor	•																	•			
Pedal vibrates															•	•	•				
Brakes grab			•							•									•		
Brakes drag								•													
Brakes pull			•		•					•	•	•		•			•		•	•	
Erratic braking	•		•							•	•	•		•					•	•	
Squeal or chatter	•					•								•	•						•

Trouble-Shooting
The Cooling System

The columns (causes), listed left to right, are:

1. Low coolant level
2. Cooling system clogged
3. Loose or broken fan belt
4. Thermostat stuck closed
5. Thermostat stuck open
6. Debris on radiator
7. Faulty water pump
8. Collapsed water hose
9. Leaking cyl. head gasket
10. Late ignition timing
11. Heater core clogged
12. Faulty temperature control
13. Low refrigerant charge
14. Loose or broken drive belt
15. Faulty compressor clutch
16. Debris on condenser

Symptoms (rows):

Symptom	1	2	3	4	5	6	7	8	9	10	11	12	13	14	15	16
Engine overheats	•	•	•	•		•	•	•	•	•						
Engine warms up slowly					•											
Insufficient heat	•				•						•					
Insufficient air conditioning												•	•	•	•	•
No air conditioning												•	•		•	•

376

Trouble-Shooting
The Electrical System

Symptoms	Battery discharged	Loose or broken cables	Faulty starter or solenoid	Faulty ignition switch	Faulty neutral switch	Faulty distributor points	Spark plugs fouled	Improper spark plug gap	Faulty coil	Faulty condenser	Damaged dist. cap or rotor	Damaged ignition cables	Incorrect spark timing	Alternator belt slipping	Faulty voltage regulator	Low regulator setting	Faulty alternator	Battery worn out
Starter won't operate	●	●	●	●	●													
Starter turns, engine won't start						●	●		●	●	●	●	●					
Engine stalls						●	●		●	●								
Engine misfires						●	●	●	●	●		●						
Engine cuts out at high speed						●	●	●	●	●								
Engine knocks, or 'pings'											●		●					
Engine lacks power						●	●		●	●	●		●					
Engine idles roughly						●	●		●									
Battery frequently discharged														●	●	●	●	●
Alternator does not charge														●	●		●	

Trouble-Shooting
The Engine

Symptoms	Burned or worn valves	Worn piston rings	Worn valve guides	Oil leaks	Faulty valve lifters	Valves need adjustment	Valve sticking	Valve spring broken	Broken timing gear or chain	Broken distributor drive	Broken engine mounts	Damaged main bearing	Damaged connecting rod bearing	Worn piston pins
Engine lacks power	●	●												
Poor fuel mileage	●	●												
Excessive oil use		●	●											
Fumes from engine		●		●										
Light clicking noise					●	●								
Rough operation					●	●	●							
Engine won't run							●	●	●	●				
Engine shakes											●			
Heavy thudding												●		
Sharp metallic knock													●	●

Causes

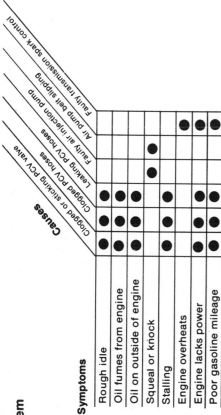

Symptoms

- Rough idle
- Oil fumes from engine
- Oil on outside of engine
- Squeal or knock
- Stalling
- Engine overheats
- Engine lacks power
- Poor gasoline mileage

Causes (diagonal labels):
- Faulty transmission spark control
- Air pump belt slipping
- Air injection pump
- Faulty air injection pump
- Leaking PCV hoses
- Clogged PCV hoses
- Clogged or sticking PCV valve

Causes

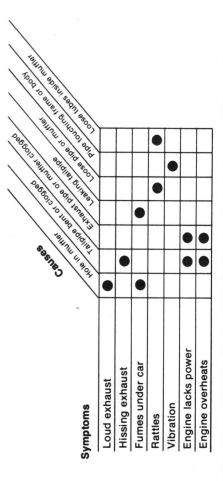

Symptoms

- Loud exhaust
- Hissing exhaust
- Fumes under car
- Rattles
- Vibration
- Engine lacks power
- Engine overheats

Causes (diagonal labels):
- Loose tubes inside muffler
- Pipe touching frame or body
- Loose pipe or muffler
- Leaking tailpipe
- Exhaust pipe or muffler clogged
- Tailpipe bent or clogged
- Hole in muffler

Causes

Symptoms	Faulty automatic choke	Low fuel pump pressure	Faulty carburetor adjustment	Fuel line hot — vapor lock	Dirt or water in fuel	Clogged fuel filter	Dirty carburetor	Clogged air cleaner	Faulty accelerating pump	Binding accelerator linkage	High fuel pump pressure	Sticking needle valve
Hard starting when cold	●											
Hard starting when hot		●										
Engine stalls	●		●		●	●						
Smoky exhaust	●				●	●			●	●		
Poor gasoline mileage	●				●	●			●	●		
Engine 'starves' at high speed			●	●	●							
Rough idle	●		●		●			●	●	●		
Engine stumbles on acceleration			●		●		●					
Flooded carburetor	●		●			●			●	●		
Engine backfires			●	●								

Causes

Symptoms	Battery discharged	Bulb burned out	Faulty wiring	Fuse blown	Faulty flasher unit	Faulty wiper motor	Faulty wiper linkage	Fluid low in reservoir	Tubing disconnected	Clogged nozzle	Faulty washer pump	Faulty stop light switch	Short circuit in wiring
Lights very dim	●												
One light doesn't work		●	●										
Turn signals flash on only one side		●	●										
Turn signals do not flash		●	●	●									
Windshield wipers don't work			●			●							
Windshield wipers don't park						●	●						
Windshield washers don't work								●	●	●	●		
Stop lights don't work		●	●									●	
Stop lights stay on		●	●									●	
Headlights flash on and off													●

The Steering and Suspension System

Causes (left to right):
Low or uneven tire pressure · Steering linkage dry · Front end out of alignment · Suspension arms damaged · Ball joints binding · Sagging springs · Power steering belt slipping · Power steering fluid low · Loose front wheel bearings · Worn ball joints · Loose steering linkage · Maladjusted steering gear · Worn shock absorbers · Wheels and tires out of balance

Symptoms	Low or uneven tire pressure	Steering linkage dry	Front end out of alignment	Suspension arms damaged	Ball joints binding	Sagging springs	Power steering belt slipping	Power steering fluid low	Loose front wheel bearings	Worn ball joints	Loose steering linkage	Maladjusted steering gear	Worn shock absorbers	Wheels and tires out of balance
Hard steering	●	●			●		●	●						
Car pulls to one side	●		●							●				
Car wanders from side to side			●						●	●	●	●		
Uneven tire wear	●		●						●				●	
Front wheel shimmy									●	●	●			●
High-speed vibration													●	●
Car not level				●		●								
Heavy thumps on rough roads				●		●							●	
Play or looseness in steering										●	●	●		
Rattle in steering gear											●	●		
Thump from front end					●					●				

The Transmission and Drive Line System

Causes (left to right):
Clutch needs adjustment · Clutch disc worn · Transmission low on lubricant · Incorrect grade of lubricant · Shift linkage out of adjustment · Low fluid level · Bands need adjustment · Control valve sticking · Throttle linkage needs adjustment · Leaking seals or gaskets · Worn universal joints · Unbalanced tires · Unbalanced driveshaft · Worn rear axle gears · Worn rear axle bearings · Tire noise

Symptoms	Clutch needs adjustment	Clutch disc worn	Transmission low on lubricant	Incorrect grade of lubricant	Shift linkage out of adjustment	Low fluid level	Bands need adjustment	Control valve sticking	Throttle linkage needs adjustment	Leaking seals or gaskets	Worn universal joints	Unbalanced tires	Unbalanced driveshaft	Worn rear axle gears	Worn rear axle bearings	Tire noise
Clutch slips	●	●														
Hard shifting	●	●	●	●	●											
Gears clash	●	●	●	●	●											
Automatic transmission slips						●	●									
Automatic doesn't shift properly						●	●	●								
Transmission low on fluid										●						
Rough engagement of Drive or Reverse									●							
Heavy 'clunk' at low speed											●					
Vibration at high speed												●	●			
Whine from rear end														●	●	●

Index